Contents

Editorial: Working-Class Studies

Let us imagine what it would be like if the history and culture of working-class people were at the center of educational practices. What would students learn? What would they carry with them from elementary school to high school and college, and then into their jobs and community organizations? Surely they would know the long history of class warfare in the United States, what some historians call "the other civil war." They would see the stubborn power of capital in relationship to labor from the beginnings of the Industrial Revolution to the growth of Trans-National Corporations. They would have a sense of workers' culture—oral traditions, songs, literary expression, murals, sculpture, and photography. They would understand that culture is created by individuals within social contexts and that they themselves could produce it as well as consume it. They would be engaged in their communities, collecting oral history, participating in study groups.

Confronted by the complexity of working-class experience, students would develop an intellectual elasticity and a tolerance for difference. Conscious of the many intersections of class and ethnicity and gender and race, working-class studies would cultivate a capacity for mutual vision. Isolated issues would be seen in relational terms. Instead of being pitted against each other in competition for scarce jobs, they would be insisting on a workers' democracy. If capitalism still existed, they would be politically engaged in demands for full employment, a shorter work day (four hours seems about right), more vacation time (the U.S. currently has the least amount of vacation time for its industrial workers of any developed country). They would learn early in their lives that the "pursuit of happiness" should take precedence over the "protection of property." They would be subjects—not objects or things. They would insist that technology should be in service to humanity—not the other way around.

I write this brief utopia on the first day of 1995. It's a small indulgence to celebrate the end of 1994, a particularly mean-spirited year. I write from Rochester, New York, where on a daily basis the newspaper reports last night's shooting, this month's corporate downsizing, and the latest statistics on class polarities—according to today's newspaper, for example, one-third of all children in Rochester now live below the poverty line.

I view this special issue of the *Women's Studies Quarterly* as emerging out of the reality of this present to prepare the ground for the important work of building and sustaining working-class studies. I include "sustaining" because even though we are at the beginning of creating officially sanctioned programs of study, working-class studies rests on old cultural practices of self-education and group study, union organizing, summer schools for workers, and cultural expression. What is new is the emergence of this field in an academic context in solidarity with women's, African-American, ethnic, and labor studies. Our understanding of class identity is incomplete without the interplay of these other identities, but these other subjectivities cannot be properly studied without a class dimension.

The writers of this special issue on working-class studies span three generations. They are from different geographic and cultural places. Whether they speak with an intimate personal voice or a more distanced public (and academic) voice, they are all engaged in the process of witnessing. Each writer demonstrates a sense of connection to others across time, and a desire—even a responsibility—to use this occasion to provide a space where the silenced many may be heard and seen. In other words, whether the form is a poem, a syllabus, an oral history, or a theoretical essay, the connecting tissue is a collective class consciousness and a solidarity with working people.

We begin with personal voices. Rooted in the writing voice of Wilma Elizabeth McDaniel are the internal migrations of American workers looking for work, and of the desire for culture and beauty, bread and roses. Lisa Orr and Kristin Kovacic speak of the labor of their parents, of factory closings, of corporate and university downsizing, of betrayed expectations and promises. Barbara Horn and Joann Quiñones pay homage to the work of mothers and grandmothers, to production and reproduction. In her feisty lyrics and music, Pat Wynne sings for the invisible many, those who work their way through school or have to pawn their possessions for food.

What distinguishes working-class cultural studies from canonical histories and literatures is the emphasis on a collective sensibility. Often this involves the interplay of three narrative voices: the personal

"I," the referential "they," and the collective "we." One of the interesting paradoxes of working-class writing (especially women's writing) is that although it relies heavily on autobiography as a genre, its subject is rarely isolated or romanticized individualism. Rather, its *raison d'être* is to recall the fragile filaments and necessary bonds of human relationships, as well as to critique those economic and societal forces that blunt or block human development. This is evident in Maida Springer Kemp's oral history, in Jo Sinclair's *The Seasons,* and in the stories of the Bryn Mawr Summer School women workers. Even when the narrative is located in the recesses of the individual psyche and the writer (Jo Sinclair or Cy-Thea Sand) is fighting depression and despair, the emerging narrative—and the confidence to write it—comes out of, as Florence Howe shows, *working* class consciousness into the text.

Another important dimension of studying working-class culture is the double, even multiple, work of cultural production. It is important to recognize *how* working-class stories and subjectivities enter bourgeois institutions and become part of a larger intellectual conversation. Often it falls on the will and more privileged circumstances of the next generation, those from working-class families who acquired educations, to see that the experiences of the majority of the people are not forgotten. This is evident in the work of oral historians and publishers, but also in the careful scholarship of bibliographers like Cheryl Cline and in the labor of creating space for working-class texts and history in the classroom that we see reflected in the work of Linda Strom and Laura Hapke.

What is crucial to retrieving and producing working-class culture is the reciprocal and dialogic dimension of the process. We are generationally interdependent: the past is given voice in our work, but our work would not exist without this class history. It is a conversation of multiple voices across time. Working-class histories, stories, and images are not *taken* to be sold in the marketplace of ideas, but rather *claimed* as a valuable inheritance. The poets who write about the Triangle fire of March 25, 1911, have poetic voice because of the power of the tragic story. We have the stunning photographs of working people in this volume because of Marilyn Anderson's sense of kinship with her subjects; these are pictures given, not stolen.

Finally, the suspicion with which many practitioners of working-class studies regard theory is justified if theory is no more than an abstract, albeit playfully linguistic, reduction of reality. Purposeful theory and criticism are not divorced from the physicality of working-class lived experience. Working-class cultural theorists recognize the protean nature of working-class texts and how they cannot and should not be dominated, corralled, or mastered by the bullying voice of theory. We now have a developing theoretical practice addressing the body of working-class literature and history in print. Carole Anne Taylor's study of *The Maimie Papers* asks, appropriately, "how the world of writing relates to lived experience and why it matters." The "habitat" of working-class writing is further explored in Roxanne Rimstead's pioneering work on "Anti-theory" and the subjectivities of marginal women. Lisa Orr offers a moving and insightful reading of the cultural inheritance of Tillie Olsen's *Yonnondio*, and Julie Stein provides an important overview of working-class poetry and a necessary intervention into the gendered world of "industrial music." Constance Coiner's concluding essay offers a "pragmatic" model for reading working-class texts. Her essay is a map of the U.S. working-class literary landscape, essential cartography for any future study of working-class literary expression.

I have always felt that if working-class culture became merely an object of study, and not a means of struggle, then it would lose purpose. Let us hope that in a small way this issue of the *Women's Studies Quarterly* will advance our resolve to continue the struggle of earlier generations for economic justice for us all.

—Janet Zandy

Janet Zandy is the editor of Calling Home: Working-Class Women's Writings *(Rutgers University Press, 1990) and* Liberating Memory: Our Work and Our Working-Class Consciousness *(Rutgers University Press, 1995). She is an Assistant Professor of Language and Literature at Rochester Institute of Technology, Rochester, New York, and is an active proponent of working-class studies.*

In Memoriam

Ruth Seid (Jo Sinclair)

1913-1995

Cherished Author

School Clothes

Wilma Elizabeth McDaniel

Summer was Oklahoma hot and humid. Maybe it was a little worse than average.

People working in the fields had to carry extra jugs of water and knock off work at the height of midday heat. One fellow had to be carried out of the field.

Red-faced, with galled armpits, all agreed, "This here has been a scorcher."

Chickens responded miserably to the heat. They drooped around in yards and pens searching for a spot of shade, sometimes gasping with open mouths.

Mrs. McCarver was careful to keep fresh water in the pen for her chickens. It got almost scalding hot during the day.

She said, "That is the least that I can do. It is no wonder the poor things are not laying eggs."

She met her crippled neighbor, Orveta Walker, at the mailbox on the road the next day.

She mentioned the chickens' poor laying record during the heat and added, "I don't try to save enough eggs to fry. I keep all of them for baking. With my big family, I bake cookies or cake or some kind of dessert every day."

Orveta was painfully thin and pale and wore a sack dress of print whose pattern was almost faded to extinction.

She said, in a voice that matched her appearance, "I don't bake nothing except one-egg cakes. I'm saving them to buy school clothes for Anice. I have managed to save four eggs each day."

She added, with quiet determination, "I aim to start my girl off to school decent. None of them old faded hand-me-down dresses. They are always too long or too short. Some of the buttons are off, and you never can match 'em. The braid is all frayed out. No, indeed—I aim to start her in a spanking-new dress."

She worked toward her goal faithfully all summer. Each Saturday she caught a ride to town with the mailman and sold her week's collection of eggs.

She limped home, always saying happily, "I am proud to have a one-way ride. It sure beats walking both ways."

Two weeks before school began Mrs. McCarver invited Orveta to go with her to town. Everyone crowded into the McCarver's Model T sedan. Orveta had to hold Anice on her lap to make room, and seven-year-old Wanda McCarver scrunched down on the floorboard at her mother's feet.

They jolted excitedly over the rough roads to the small town of Depew, turned right at the railroad and up the slight hill to the one main street.

Mr. McCarver turned the group loose in front of Harrington-Pettigrew's Mercantile and said good-humoredly, "We leave for home at one-thirty in this car, unless someone wants to walk."

Mrs. McCarver and Orveta hurried inside the Mercantile with Wanda and Anice at their heels. The women parted, and Mrs. McCarver went back into the hardware department.

Orveta went straight to the dry goods department and stopped at the big barrel that held countless remnants. Wanda had followed her with great interest and stood beside the barrel, but Anice went exploring the aisles and recesses of the store on her own.

Orveta began methodically to lift out the many odds and ends of cloth. She examined each piece carefully and laid it on a counter, so that she would not lose time handling the same piece twice. Once she straightened up and sighed deeply, then bent over the barrel and began to dig out the remnants again.

Wanda was sorting through the remnants on the counter and thinking that there were only drab pieces of brown and navy blue and calico prints of black and white. Nothing there for girls her age.

The stack on the counter grew high with the depressing remnants. Finally, Orveta brought up a sausage-like roll of purple-and-white striped gingham. It had a piece of paper pinned to it.

Orveta stood holding the roll in her hand, staring at it in unbelief. She said, "Wanda, I cain't believe it. There is one yard and a half in this remnant, and it is marked *Ten Cents* in big letters. Plenty to make Anice a dress and bloomers."

She looked around and asked, "Where did Anice go? Probably a-gabbing with someone in the store."

Wanda said, "There she is over in the shoe department sitting in a chair like she was a customer." Orveta said, "What did I tell you? That child don't meet no strangers. It worries me sometimes." She took her precious find to a clerk and paid for it with two nickels tied up in a knotted handkerchief.

Wanda stood beside her, savoring the magic smell of bolts of cloth on the shelves. Orveta said, "This will work up fast. I have got a pattern that the preacher's wife give to me. When I get home I'll clear the table and get started on this before night."

She added, "Lord have mercy! Look over there at Anice. She is having that clerk try shoes on her just like she was gonna buy some. Will, she is gonna be disappointed there, if she thinks I can buy her new shoes. But she will have a nice dress and bloomers."

Mr. McCarver was a man of his word. At one-thirty sharp he started the Model T, and everyone scrambled to crowd in again.

The women's purchases filled the nostrils of the occupants with some of the magic aromas from back at the Mercantile.

As the car jolted over the worst of the road, Mrs. McCarver opened a sack and gave each child a stick of striped candy, saying, "I don't think this will spoil your supper." Wanda looked closely at her stick of candy. It was white with delicate purple stripes. From her floorboard seat she said, "Mama, this candy is exactly like Anice's new dress is going to be."

Anice spoke up from her mother's lap. "My candy is yellow striped." Little Hal, the McCarver's youngest, said "I think I got me a black stripe. I don't like it."

"Boy, you don't know what is good!" Mr. McCarver said heartily. "That is a licorice stripe. You pass that up here to me and ask your mother to give you another color." Little Hal reached his candy over to his older brother Kosh, sitting in front. "Here, you give this to Papa."

Wanda plagued her mother with her perennial question. "Mama, may I stop at Anice's house and play awhile? Please."

Mrs. McCarver said somewhat sternly. "You had better ask Orveta first. I don't want you to wear your welcome out."

Pleadingly, Wanda asked Orveta, "Do you mind if I stop and play with Anice awhile?" Orveta laughed heartily. It sounded almost robust, coming from her thin throat. She said, "No, I don't care one bit. Anice needs company to help her learn the ways of the world."

"Alright, Wanda," said Mrs. McCarver. "You start down the road by five o'clock."

Mr. McCarver pulled up the hill and stopped in front of Orveta's shotgun house. She got out slowly with her precious purchase. Anice and Wanda stumbled out after her. Orveta stood beside the car and spoke slowly. "I am sure obliged to you folks for taking us into town with you, like we was kinfolks. You know I don't have nobody of my own in this place except Anice."

The McCarvers said, almost simultaneously, "It is our pleasure to help a neighbor." The Model T gave a lurch and drove on down the Shamrock Road toward the McCarver's sharecroppers house.

Anice and Wanda immediately decided to go seining for minnows at the rock bottom sink below the barn. The water would be high from the last rain. They grabbed an old colander and some fruit jars and rushed off through the grove of blackjacks that ended sharply in a clearing around the sink.

Orveta swung into action immediately. She cleared the table of the spoon holder and sugar bowl and pepper sauce bottle and laid out the candy-striped cloth. Pinning the pattern to the cloth, she cut out the dress, quickly, expertly, losing no time. Within a few minutes she was sitting at the treadle sewing machine, whizzing the garments together.

When Anice and Wanda returned, sunburned and tired, they found Orveta already smocking the dress with purple embroidery thread. The girls sat and cooled off with the doors open, drinking cold buttermilk.

Wanda, in particular, watched Orveta's nimble fingers adorning the dress with the embroidery so popular just now. She finished the dress and hung it on a line above her ironing board, where it fluttered ever so slightly in a breeze wafting in through the front door.

Wanda said, "Look Alice! Your dress is just like that purple striped candy. It looks so good you want to eat some of it."

Anice barely looked up. Gulping down the remainder of her buttermilk, she said, "Boy, howdy, we caught us a tub of minnows." Orveta stood and looked at the dress. She picked up the small matching bloomers from the ironing board. "I will give these a good pressing, along with the dress, when I heat up the sadirons. It is time to start a fire and fix supper, anyway."

Wanda knew that Orveta did not have a clock and was too poor to buy one. "Don't you think it is about time for me to start home? Are the shadows about right?"

Orveta answered, "Yes, it is just about five o'clock, the time your mother told you to start home." Adding, aloud to herself, it appeared to Wanda, "There. Nobody can say that I didn't make an effort to start my girl off to school decent. People will know that I care about her schooling and the way I raise her up."

Abruptly, she changed the subject. "I have let myself run out of water. I'll have to go to the well before I cook supper."

As Wanda left the yard, she saw Orveta limping toward the well, which seemed an unreasonable distance from the house. She carried a large bucket. Wanda felt sorry for Orveta. That bucket was really too heavy for a crippled woman. Orveta had a hard row to hoe. She had heard her parents say so, many times. But she had really worked and managed to buy cloth and make Anice a beautiful dress.

Wanda thought about that dress as she walked slowly home down the dusty road. It seemed to her that Anice had a very special dress, different from any she had ever had herself, or ever would have.

She reasoned that her parents were sharecrop poor, but she had a *father*. He had not died when she was a baby, as Anice's father had.

A father could get credit all year until the crops were harvested, buy, groceries, liniment, lanterns, tools.

His wife could go into Harrington-Pettigrew's Mercantile and buy a whole bolt of gingham and muslin to make clothes for her family.

Yes, the purple striped–candy dress was one to be remembered always.

The picture of it was implanted in her mind for all time as she opened the gate and entered her own safe yard.

Go See Jack London

Wilma Elizabeth McDaniel

This incident was so critical to me, I found myself writing about it fifty years later. Nothing has changed except a bit of poetic license with Rosa's name. It was actually plain Rose.

My childhood friend and schoolmate Windy Tolliuer shared all of my interests except one. She did not care for literature and never read anything for pleasure except the Sunday funny papers when they were circulated in the neighborhood. She was crazy about "Little Orphan Annie" and the "Toonerville Trolley" section. That represented *all* her literary choices.

This difference in our tastes didn't seem too vital until the summer of 1927. That was the year that our hound-dog, hard-scrabble community had a writer move in among us—Rosa Paolita. Actually, she was an artist also, painted in oils and watercolor. Someone reported to my family, "That woman is a female Zane Grey. She writes like a man, and they say she has a copy of every book Jack London ever wrote."

The words caused a cold prickling sensation up and down my spine. I had to see that woman! It might not be easy. Her tarpapered shack sat well off the road. I recalled from a previous tenant, that the clothesline was in back of the house, and even a rough plank table for summer eating.

I couldn't saunter along the road and pretend to be studying ants or picking daisies and watch her eating or hanging up her wash. I began to have dreams of flying about her house invisibly and seeing her working at an easel under the host oak trees.

I attempted to convey some of my feelings to Windy on her way to the minnow pool. I said, "Windy, I am going to see a writer and artist who has all Jack London's books."

Before I could ask her to go with me, she slapped a mosquito on her leg, and answered acidly, "Go see Jack London, I don't care," and marched out of the yard toward the minnow pool where we usually fished together. I didn't attempt to follow her.

Anyway, Mama called me to wash the fruit jars for canning little yellow tomato preserves. It was a bumper crop for them. I don't think there has been or ever will be such a crop again, and Mama tried not to lose a single tomato. I ardently wished the vines would dry up before I had to wash another tub of fruit jars.

It was after lunch before Mama finished screwing the lids on the last hot sticky jar. She was carefully wiping each with a wet dishcloth, when Mister Barkus knocked at the door.

He said, "No Ma'am, I can't come in. My wife and I took our new writer neighbor Mrs. Paolita to the doctor yesterday. She fell across an old cultivator and broke her left arm. I thought you neighbor women ought to know about it. You will probably want to cook something and take it to her."

Mama was already taking off her apron as he left the porch. She said "My, I'm glad that I baked bread yesterday," adding, "and hid a few cinnamon buns." She smoothed her hair at the mirror above the washstand and instructed me further, "Get the wicker basket and put in two pints of tomato preserves and get our bonnets from the porch. It's hot."

It seemed like ages, but we were actually on the dusty road toward Rosa's house within ten minutes after Mister Barkus told us of her broken arm. I was still in shock at the way things were working out. Almost like what people called an answer to prayer. I hoped I hadn't been responsible for Rosa's broken arm, wanting so much to see her.

Mama walked fast carrying the basket, the tail of her bonnet flapping against her shoulders. I followed a step behind with the cinnamon buns, my thought entirely on Rosa. Usually, I would talk to Mama as we walked but now was silent.

She spoke, "Look, a snake has just crawled across the road. He was a big one, too."

I did think of something to say, "Mama, how far is it to Rosa's house?"

She answered, "It is three-quarters of a mile from our mailbox to the corner where we turn into her lane." She continued, "Look how thick the nightshades are growing there along the draw. They are so delicate, I can hardly believe they are as poisonous as people say they are."

I voiced another thought. "Mama, what do you think a writer and an artist woman is like? Won't she be different from people like us?" I walked faster to be beside her when she answered.

"She won't be any different from us. She broke her arm. She is just human. She needs neighbors. You wait and see, she will be delighted to have a visit."

We reached the quarter-mile corner, and Mama paused beneath a big mulberry tree. She set her basket down and told me, "Let's blow a minute before we start on down the lane." She even took off her bonnet and fanned herself.

My eyes were glued on the tarpapered shack at the end of the lane. I stood poised with the floursack bag of cinnamon buns held tightly by a knot in the sack. Suddenly, I saw a woman emerge from the front door of the shack. She wore a white dress and had some kind of queer black contraption around her neck. She took a few steps, stopped, held some part of the contraption up to her eyes, and looked down the road toward us.

I said with absolute conviction, "Mama, that's her, Rosa Paolita."

Mama agreed mildly, "I imagine it is." She put her bonnet on, picked up the basket, and we entered the lane.

The woman in white studied us a few seconds more then did what still seems to me, after fifty-some-odd years, a most remarkable thing. She broke into a run down the lane toward us. It seems all the more remarkable because her left arm was in a cast. She kept a steady pace in the center of the lane. It was the first time I ever saw the word *graceful* in action: smooth, deliberate motions. Nothing shook or wobbled on the tall lean frame. As she approached, I burst out, "Mama, her hair is on fire," and stood stock still in the lane. Mama stopped also.

The woman was before us. She swept her good arm around Mama and kissed her warmly on the cheek. She said "That strange bird in the mulberry tree was a good omen that something precious would happen to me today. I have searched for him with my binoculars, but he has disappeared." She turned and kissed me on the cheek under my loose bonnet, saying, "I see you have your treasure with you, a daughter."

Mama flushed slightly and said, "She is a bookworm and crazy about Jack London's stories, and she has been dying to meet you, and half-scared to, at the same time."

The woman's large green eyes pierced my soul. She said, "Take off your bonnet." I complied, and she asked a prophetic question, "You write poems sometimes, don't you?"

I nodded, unable to swallow a lump in my throat and speak.

Mama spoke for me, "She writes all her spare time, on the back of envelopes, grocery lists, any paper she can get her hands on."

The woman said "I knew it." She put her right hand on my shoulder and said, "This is actually your artistic odyssey," then she laughed like silver bells tinkling, and said, "Let's go have some tea in my tarpapered castle." She led the way down the lane.

All the fear and doubt and pain left me. I knew what writers and artists were like.

Wilma Elizabeth McDaniel *was born in 1918 in Creek Nation, Oklahoma, the fourth child in a sharecropper's family of eight children. McDaniel, with her family, she made the dustbowl trek to the San Joaquin Valley of California in 1936. Reluctant to give interviews, she writes, "Did a lot of hard, thankless, practically payless work, always a poet and a storyteller, have written twelve books of poetry, four books of stories, one novella, one play." Her first book of poetry was published in 1973.* Her books include: A Primer for Buford (1990), Sister Vayda's Song (1982), A Girl from Buttonwillow (1990), Tollbridge (1980), A Prince Albert Wind, *and* Vito and Zona (1993).

Stories from a Working-Class Childhood

Lisa Orr

Utica, New York, is a tiny upstate city, a milltown that boomed in the nineteenth century. For a while it was second only to New York City in population. By my parents' births the mills were closed, and growth was stalled, but a man, at least, could still expect to earn a living in the factories that punctuated the neighborhoods on the west side. By the time I was growing up, in the 1970s and early 1980s, the living was sketchy. Layoffs were cyclical, like the summer heatwaves; few could expect to be on the same job the next year. When the layoffs struck my father haunted the unemployment office then drank cup after cup of coffee at the kitchen table. He was forced to be grateful for minimum-wage jobs, working for $3.35 an hour. My mother scrambled to get out of such work, teaching her fingers to recall high school typing lessons on a mechanical typewriter from the swap shop. As I was finishing high school, she secured a secretarial job at a small local college—a sure jump in status as far as we were concerned—where she taught herself computers and got library privileges for her two daughters.

I read as much as I could, because in real life I was surrounded by stories that were never softened. The library's offerings were consoling next to my grandmother's story of my Great-Uncle Paul, who was hit on the head by something that fell off a two-story-high punch press and spent his few remaining years in bed, swinging a cane violently at whatever moved near him. The factory where he had worked was a block down our street; walking to the public pool in the summer, my sister and I would peer in the windows. It was dark and loud, with oil pooled dangerously on the floors and sooty-faced men with bandannas tied around their foreheads working machines that could crush a human being. In the neighborhood they called it the finger factory, because pieces of countless people had been lost there. My grandfather worked there during World War II; my father worked there for a time while I was in high school, until the morning the workers showed up to find the doors locked and plastered with bankruptcy notices. It was the middle of the week. No one outside of management had known what was coming. A man my father knew, a coworker, had just gotten married. On the strength of his and his new wife's income they had bought a modest little house. Forgivably, he had bragged a bit at work; who else, after all, owned their own home? The morning the facotry doors were locked against him, this man went back to his new house, climbed to the roof, and jumped off.

I viewed the scholarship I received to a university fifty miles away as an escape route. There I was surrounded by people from one-family homes with garages and wide lawns. They had no horrible stories to tell, or, if they did, middle-class strictures taught them to keep them to themselves. They didn't know how others lived, and I, at that point, could not tell them. After college I ran to the prettiest place I could think of: San Diego, as white and clean as a child's dream of heaven, where I could miss my hometown without watching its decline.

What I had yet to learn was what writer Tillie Olsen instinctively knew—that the divided self must acknowledge both halves of itself. In other words, I knew too many stories to ever forget. Even as I journeyed away from the site of my childhood, even as I moved toward the middle class, part of me would never leave the working class. Olsen never romanticizes that working-class self. She speaks of it as damaged but, at the same time, shows its value as a source of connection between people. This is a link one cannot choose to ignore. Living in my homogeneous, suburban San Diego neighborhood, I found myself drawn to any reminder of my former life. Instinctively, I sought out others who had seen what I had seen: the young man, how, along with his father and brothers, had fished aluminum cans out of dumpsters for the sake of the deposits; the young woman, scarcely any older than I, who worked two jobs to support both her unemployed parents. Like aging veterans, we told one another our stories over and over.

Eventually, I returned to Upstate New York, but as a graduate stu-dent, a position oddly reflective of my internal divisions. Going to graduate school is, obviously, rarely an option for young working-class women. Graduate students are notoriously "poor," yet I still make more per hour than my mother ever has. As a teaching assistant, I have some advantages: health insurance, a steady income, a pleasant apart-ment. No longer is the incentive to escape so pressing. At the very point when I have the time and the means to articulate what it is to be working-class, I am living like a member of the middle class. This is my way of keeping a flimsy wall of resistance between myself and these stories, so that what is destructive in them will not destroy me. It gives me a space to live that self that Olsen so clearly shows crushed to brief corners of time for most of the working class. When I was a light assembly worker, operating a heatseal machine, I had hours to think while my hands worked on automatic. But somehow the work deadened my mind in the same way that the hot die, where it touched, transformed my skin to brown paper. When my shift ended I was fit for nothing but escapism. To sit down then and write about working-class life was to continue the deadening.

To be able to journey back into that world by choice, by memory, is something entirely different. I can continue to work out, slowly, painstakingly, how the part of me which has survived can tell the story of uncles who died before I was born and the woman who worked at the next machine over, of the dirty brick factories, and the bars surrounding them, of small industrial cities that are dying even as I speak of them.

Lisa Orr *is a Ph.D. candidate in English at the University of California, Los Angeles.*

"Proud to Work for the University"

Kristin Kovacic

In June 1958 Bogdan Kovacic, my father, emigrated from Zagreb, Yugoslavia, to Pittsburgh, Pennsylvania. As he likes to tell the story, he had a quarter in his pocket as the train rolled into Penn Station, and he used that to buy some crackers, hedging his bets against his next meal. He was twenty-six years old and spoke little English. He had left behind family, all of his good friends, his teammates from the professional handball team he played for. He was alone, he figured, and about to see the world.

This is part of the myth of my family, a story familiar to many Pittsburghers with immigrant roots. I am, I'm afraid, about to tell you a very old story.

Jobs, in 1958, were plentiful in Pittsburgh. Cousin Francie got him in at the plate factory. He hauled plates, dropping them now and then and making a big crash. He went to English classes at night, penciled neat meaningless sentences in a grammar book I have here—"Only a few friends are bidden to come," and, with emphasis, "You are never too old to learn." He signed his new American name, Andrew, over and over in the margins. He learned the questions he'd soon have to answer: "Are you a Bolshevik, anarchist, communist, or polygamist?" "What does Thanksgiving Day mean?" He met my mother, practiced his new words.

Trained as an electrician in Zagreb, he looked for work in his field. A friend told him he could get him in at the mill, and he went to have a look: the heat, the smoke, the filth over everything. He said no thanks; he'd have to work in hell soon enough. He found a job as an electrician at West Penn Hospital, good clean work. He was promoted to foreman. He bought a Chevy, sky blue.

Then we were born: my brother Andy, my sister Lara, and I. This, apparently, changed everything. He started night school again, and, with an electrical degree from Allegheny Technical Institute, he landed a job at Carnegie Mellon University (CMU) in 1969—two years before Richard Cyert assumed the presidency of the university. I remember the

"Proud to Work for the University" originally appeared in the September 1990 issue of FOCUS, the faculty/staff newspaper of Carnegie Mellon University.

day Dad started, the new uniform my mother pressed off, and the first time the promise was made to us: you will get an education there. At that time, all Carnegie Mellon University employees were promised full undergraduate tuition for their children who were accepted there. That day, too, was the first time the challenge was set down: you will have to do well enough in school to be accepted. I was six, my brother seven, my sister was learning to crawl. It was a challenge we took very seriously; it was, we figured, our shot at seeing the world.

In those days we were required, on the first day of school, to say our names and what our fathers did for a living. One by one the kids would recite their names and then, simply, "J&L" or "Homestead," or "Duquesne Works." I would wait my turn, and then somewhat haughtily announce, "My dad is an electrician at Carnegie Mellon University. I'm going to college there, free." I told people even when they didn't ask me.

Carnegie Mellon became our identity, the greatest part of our family myth. While the men in the mills, our neighbors, were making much more money than Dad, locked into contracts in the glory days of steel, he, at least, had *invested*, had guaranteed our futures. We got Carnegie Mellon sweatshirts, tee-shirts, and notebooks for our birthdays. We cheered the buggys at carnival. When Dad worked weekends, we'd sometimes visit him on campus and ride in his little electric car, surveying what we knew would someday be ours—our library, our gymnasium, our student union. At night, passing by, we saw the beacon light in Hamerschlag Hall which Dad had installed. "That's my light," he'd say, and there it was, beckoning.

We also participated, through him, in Carnegie Mellon's road to academic glory. My dad didn't work at a factory, he worked for the university—among artists, engineers, and scientists. I didn't, for most of my early lifetime, see any fundamental difference between what my father and a professor of electrical engineering did for a living. They both worked for the university.

My father worked on experiments with monkeys and with robots. He helped harness energy from still water, bringing the physicist home for dinner after their hard day's work. Dad's work allowed Kathleen Mulcahy, the glass artist, to safely power her magnificent kiln. When he brought home the beautiful vase she made for him, my mother set it on the television set in the living room, eventually decorating the whole room around it—such colors we had never thought of bringing together. If my father was never going to see the world, Carnegie Mellon brought it closer to him and, by consequence, to us.

He was there when the computers arrived, the machines that would launch Carnegie Mellon's international star. I remember sitting at the dinner table while Dad told us about the computers, how, when we got to college, there would be a computer for every student; how we'd find a book in the library just by pushing a button; how there might not *be* any more books in the library, the computer taking over every aspect of our education. I remember being somewhat skeptical—this was long before *computer* was a household word, much less a household item. But, finally, I believed. Dad had the plans; he knew what was coming. He was the man who powered those glorious machines, who would later coordinate the installation of the "Andrew" computer network.

In 1981 I arrived and began my Carnegie Mellon education. On my first day of my first class—a core curriculum sociology course—we read about the concept of class in American society. We learned how to identify the working class from the middle class; there were just a few simple rules. The working class, my textbook said, works with its hands or, in the case of women, does clerical work like typing or filing. I did a little figuring. My mother is a secretary. My father is an electrician. His hands can get very dirty when he works, and he is scrupulous about washing them. He always carries Band-Aids in his wallet, ready for the daily cuts he gets at work, usually on his hands.

You can identify the working class, my textbook said, by the arrangement of their homes. The working class keeps its television set in the living room, for example, while the middle class keeps it in another place, like a den. I thought about our living room, Kathleen Mulcahy's vase crowning the television like a jewel. I thought, for the very first time, that I was working-class. It was a genuine surprise.

I'm told that Andrew Carnegie founded Carnegie Institute of Technology for the education of the working classes of Pittsburgh. Long before I arrived, that mission had been abandoned as unprestigious and, more to the point, unprofitable. My classmates were from out of town, the daughters and sons of doctors, entrepreneurs, foreign financiers. Many of them rarely saw their parents, much less ran into them in Baker Hall, fixing a switch box. I learned the difference between an electrician and an electrical engineer. None of that bothered me; it surprised me, opening my picture of the world, and where I fit into it, much wider. Likewise, much about my life surprised my friends, whom I would bring home with me on holidays and weekends, introducing them to a genuine working-class home, television set and all. During my years in school my parents responded generously to CMU's requests for giving from parents, believing, in a way that other parents could not, that the money was going to the university's collective pot, whose assets were essentially our own. They also, I think, enjoyed the letters that came to the house afterwards: "Dear Mr. and Mrs. Kovacic, thank you for your generous gift."

In May 1985 I graduated, valedictorian of my college. I was selected to deliver the student commencement address, and on that day, under the big tent, a number of our family dreams came together. My father was sitting, suit and tie, in the audience. My sister, who had just been accepted for admission in the fall, sat next to him, checking out *her* campus. My brother, who, after receiving his associates' degree in forestry from Penn State University, was hired by CMU as a gardener—following my father's path—stood on the edge of the tent in his uniform. His boss had given him special permission to attend; normally the gardeners have to stay in their shop during the ceremonies. I dedicated the speech to my father, and I used my remarks to remind my classmates about the wonder, the absolute fortune, that we were going to do our work in life with questions, theories, problems, and poems—not with our backs, not with our bleeding hands. "Very well done," President Cyert said, shaking my hand on the dais. He told the audience that he was pleased to see the daughter of a staff member be so successful at the university.

When I think about that day now, the memory is very sweet, but I am also reminded that certain dread wheels were already in motion. The university, at the time of my graduation, was about to divide the workers' union (SEIU Local 29), selling off the janitors to a management firm (ABM) and cutting them off from Carnegie Mellon benefits, including tuition benefits. Those people, many of whom were Dad's friends, no longer worked for the university. Shortly after my graduation the administration dropped *university* from its official name, suggesting that it was more like a corporation than an institution of higher education, more like a factory than a school.

Contract battles for Dad's union became increasingly difficult to win. The administration, which for years claimed that its pay scale could never compete with the steel industry's, took advantage of the labor climate in the wake of steel's collapse to demand concessions. The administration hired outside firms to "consult" on the efficiency of the physical plant. There were layoffs. One of those firms became the manager of Carnegie Mellon's building and maintenance operations, introducing suspicion among the physical plant workers—in spite of the administration's written assurances—that there would be further layoffs and that what had happened to the janitors might eventually happen to them.

In May 1990 my sister graduated with high honors, and we gathered again under the tent, to celebrate again the fulfillment of Dad's

promise. President Cyert, saying his last farewells, recalled the achieve-
ments of his twenty-one years in office, the remarkable rise of Pittsburgh's Carnegie Tech to the global institution called Carnegie Mellon.
My father, in the audience, could look back on those very same years,
knowing that he had had a hand in all of it and that he had, in spite of
all of the hard, physical work, made a very good investment in a
growing institution. A steel mill might close, rust, and be razed to a
clear toxic field, like the J&L South Side works he passed every day on
his way to Oakland. But the university would always be there.

My sister and I were on our way. My brother was doing well in his job.
Dad had three years until he could retire, and he was already planning. He would play more tennis (he is still, at sixty, a remarkable
athlete). He and my mother would travel, back to Yugoslavia, where his
family still lives, and to the other parts of the world they hadn't gotten
around to seeing.

In June, after the tent had come down and the campus emptied out,
the faculty and students returning to the cities that they come from,
Dad reported to work, punched his clock. He was told not to work but
to go directly through a door that closed behind him and seventeen
other people, including two-thirds of all of the university's electri-
cians, who were about to lose their jobs. They were told, for the first
time, that there was a budget crisis that would require layoffs. They
were told to turn in their keys and to be off the campus grounds by 10
A.M. They saw university police as they emerged, dazed by the blind-
sided blow. "Like criminals," my mother told me, through tears, over
the phone. She didn't think about the cost, the financial straits this
would place them in. She thought about betrayal. "They treated him
like a criminal, after all those years."

My father harbored no illusions about Carnegie Mellon's benevolence. He had seen, over the years, the university's antagonism toward
its union. But in 1969 he had signed what he thought was a lifetime
contract—he would give them a lifetime of hard labor; they would
educate his children and allow him to retire, not comfortably, but in
peace. It was not an extravagant plan.

Unfortunately for him, the Carnegie Mellon that let him go was not
the university that had hired him, or perhaps, sadly, it was. How could
he have known that the master plan of the global university, like that of
a global corporation, included the abandonment of its responsibility
to the blue-collar workers in its community, not to mention its utter
disregard for their intelligence and pride? At the same moment that
my father and sixteen other skilled construction and maintenance
workers were shown, by an armed guard, the door, the administration

announced the acceptance of a five million dollar gift from Paul Mellon toward new campus construction. Who, these men and women were forced to wonder, would be doing it? Who would design, construct, wire, and maintain the growth for which, as Dr. Cyert so elegantly phrased it for the reporters, "Carnegie Mellon's appetite continues to grow the larger [it] gets?" The arithmetic is tragically easy to do, even without a Carnegie Mellon education—why support loyal, lifetime employees when you can buy contracted work for less? At the same moment that my father faced the prospect of finding, at sixty, a new job, President Cyert eased into his retirement. The administration, as reported by the *Pittsburgh Post-Gazette*, was then finalizing plans to purchase a $1.9 million Sewickley estate for its new president, his wife, and their six horses.

"The emerging global company is divorced from where it produces its goods," Robert B. Reich, lecturer in public policy at the Harvard University Kennedy School of Government [now Secretary of Labor], told the *New York Times*. "It has no heart, and it has no soul. It is a financial enterprise designed to maximize profits. Many of the people who inhabit it may be fine, upstanding human beings, but the organization has its own merciless logic."

It was just this merciless logic, I have to believe, that caused my father to lose his job. Carnegie Mellon is a thriving, growing institution. It is not facing a budgetary crisis; it is facing a moral one—whether to cultivate the community of a university or the elite positioning of a corporation. My family felt, with great pride, a part of an educational community, until, without ceremony, Carnegie Mellon abandoned its role in it. Now, like too many other working-class families in Pittsburgh, we're left with the caution that it was foolish to have believed.

So now my father, writing in the workbook he received at his "transition" seminar, dutifully answers their questions. What do you feel is your greatest accomplishment? "My greatest accomplishment," he writes in the clipped, impossible language he has never learned to love, "is my family." What was most satisfying about your previous employment? "I was very proud," he says, carefully calling up the past tense, "to work for the university."

Kristin Kovacic *is a free-lance writer and editor in Pittsburgh. Her fiction and essays have appeared in* Cimarron Review, Kansas Quarterly, Carolina Quarterly, River Styx, Gulf Stream, *and other magazines. She recently completed work on the "Woman to Woman on Lifetime" television poetry project.*

Ruth in August

Barbara Horn

Ruth, my mother, was born 4 August, 1914. Whether it was her favorite month or not, August, as I remember, distilled her strongest, most compelling traits. That was when she harvested the bulk of her flower and vegetable gardens; when she saw that abundance, in some sense, never is enough.

Like most well-tended, pampered children, I took my mother for granted, little noticing the details of *her* life, except as they pleased or fretted me. But when Ruth was in her mid-forties and I in my early teens, I watched her, really watched her, and saw the tension August brings.

Almost daily she filled containers with vibrant cockscombs and dahlias; pale cosmos and sweet peas; bright zinnias, nasturtium, and gladioli. In August our house was a veritable garden, "too heavy with flowers," my father mildly complained. If he pulled open his dresser drawer too vigorously, a vase burdened with old-fashioned roses, ever Dad's favorite fragrance, threatened to topple into his socks. Bouquets spilled from piano top, end tables, kitchen counter, sink. They even softened the ugly metal surfaces of heating stoves. In opening our cool, dark pantry—where hundreds of jars of her home-canned produce rested—I might find clenched bunches of dandelions and marigolds, spots glowing like neon, which Mother had stuck, willy-nilly, in last year's empty jelly glasses. And when she attended a local function— such as a lodge meeting, fund-raiser, or Saturday night dance—Ruth took along containers of showy flowers "to decorate," as she called it. Every Sunday in August she rose early to pick and arrange elaborate sprays, which dad helped her carry to our nearby Methodist church. The aroma of Ruth's stately arrangements seeped, like incense, through the sanctuary to the belfry, and met worshipers at the door. As our accompanist pounded out the staccato strains to "Love Lifted Me" and we fifty members of the congregation responded in loud voice, vases of Ruth's offerings, which crowded altar rail and organ top, shook gently, startling some and soothing other bloodshot Sabbath eyes.

The weighty ripeness of her vegetable gardens gathered even more of Ruth's attention than did her flowers. She had plowed and planted, weeded and hoed, and now the labor of spring and summer brought rewards as certain, as inescapable, as the sun's glare. Near twilight on August evenings, when rural Missouri air began to cool and dew, as slick as oil, settled on lawn and field, Ruth carried arm loads of her harvest directly to our large, square kitchen. Soon bowls of sliced tomatoes, bell peppers, and muskmelons jeweled our supper table.

While my father, two brothers, and I waited hungrily, she neatly husked corn, making a quick zipping sound like the sudden tear of a garment. The effort caused Ruth's upper arms to jiggle, stretching— for the umpteenth time that day—the capsleeves of her flowered housedress. She then immersed a dozen roasting ears in a deep pan of boiling water. In exactly ten minutes Mother fished out the corn, shaking off its excess liquid, and then onto a heavy platter she piled the feast, pyramid fashion, centering it proudly on the table. As soon as we could comfortably handle them, we gobbled up the roasting ears—all the while watching, through the steam, for Mother's next batch.

When corn on the cob, always our favorite garden crop, was at its sweetest, we had little else for lunch and supper. Slathered with butter or margarine and rolled in salt and pepper, a half-dozen pieces per child satisfied. This was meal enough. I would look at my plump brothers, their chins shiny with butter and streaked with milky corn juice, and wonder if I presented as comically worshipful, as well-fed a sight, as they. Mother might also serve new potatoes simmered with snap beans or thin rounds of crookneck squash, dipped in egg and cornmeal batter and then fried to a succulent crispness—dishes that she and my father savored—but it always was the corn that left us kids exulting.

At least twice a week during the summer our family ate poultry that Ruth and my father tended at the edge of our property. Mother had assisted during the chicks' incubation, helped feed and water the growing flock, and participated in caponizing them. But she alone slaughtered our poultry. I often watched as she performed single-handedly—right in the chicken yard—all of the messy butchering. We had no plumbing system, so Mom heated pails of water at our kitchen stove and then carried them out the back door, past flower and vegetable gardens, berry patches, and grape arbor, and, finally, through a gate into the fenced poultry yard. Mindful not to splash the scalding liquid, I sometimes helped her haul the steamy buckets and position her paraphernalia near a well from which we drew fresh, cold water. Our two dogs, sensing a slaying, usually followed us, and the ever ravenous flock—expecting mashed grain, vegetable parings, or chicken innards—crowded nearby, pecking at one another and vying for a spot near Mother.

Ruth grabbed a chicken by its legs and put its head under a broom handle, which she then stepped on; by yanking the animal up, she beheaded it—as quick as a squirt. Then the bird ran wildly, drunk with death. Working rapidly, Ruth sent several headless birds, flapping their wings and swooping jerkily, into what looked to me like a headlong, hapless effort to fly, an attempt to leave this earth. I could not help but draw closer to the circling action. Trickling blood, a chicken would lie still—finally dead, I would think. But then it might struggle up and flop again, its body fiercely beating the ground. After throwing a finally motionless chicken into steaming water, which made removal of its feathers an easy chore, almost like detaching blanched skin from a tomato, Ruth then disemboweled it. During a half-hour she could dress six fowls. All the time she called softly to the dogs, shooed chickens out of the way, and reminded me to pump water so she could rinse the flaccid carcasses.

To me the butcher yard was bedlam—yelping dogs, cannibalistic chickens, headless animals careening at all angles, feathers floating in steamy, blood-clotted water. Sometimes I would gag and feel my stomach pitch. Sometimes I was dazed. My eyes—never adjusting to but unable to withdraw from the appalling sight—would blur in sadness, fascination, fear. But, as far as I could tell, Ruth never reeled from the stench of scalded feathers, warm blood, gritty gizzard. Nor did the sight of headless chickens, thrashing and zigzagging in their final, desperate dance, make her squirm or shudder.

She worked calmly, efficiently, wasting none of the carnage. Mother threw slippery entrails to the stampeding, hungry flock; chicken feet at our slobbering mongrels, who immediately cracked open this gristly treat; and cloudy butcher water, a tepid fertilizer, over the fence right onto the strawberry patch.

Because Mother was so seamless in her movements and even capable, while dressing poultry, of humming a popular song, I wondered what had been crossing her mind. As she separated out the squiggly livers and tiny triangular hearts—giblets that would flavor bread stuffing and gravy—did she contemplate what bulbs to transplant, come autumn? What chores to do next? What her husband was accomplishing today in his rows of wheat, corn, soybeans, and barley? Why, year after year, farming was an increasingly unreliable way to support a family? What to fix for supper?

Yes, more than likely she thought of food. While she herself found a thick onion sandwich and a plate of salted white radishes satisfying, she always fixed large, hot suppers for the family. Ruth's specialties included skillet fried chicken and milk gravy, boiled hen with homemade noodles, fowl smothered in cream sauce, and oven-roasted, stuffed capons—the latter smaller than tom turkeys but, because they were castrated, almost as full-breasted and much more tender and tasty. Each summer Mother raised, in addition to two hundred fryers, over a hundred capons, which she sold as holiday fare to a fancy-poultry shipper. But she always saved a few prize birds for us to eat before fall ended. During butchering was she figuring, then, what price this year's capons might bring? How that sum would help buy groceries?

I always hoped she was planning to bake pies and cakes. Even during her most harried August days of gathering and culling, of sterilizing and canning and preserving, of killing and eviscerating and frying, Mom made glorious desserts—fresh blackberry cobbler with lattice crust, just-picked peaches and whipped cream, caramel pie glazed with meringue, and, my favorite, a towering angel food cake encased in butterscotch frosting. She used exactly eleven egg whites, from hens nesting in our poultry house, for this delicacy. Working a hand rotary beater so furiously that the kitchen table shook, Ruth spent a half-hour producing this stiff, chalk-white concoction, held up only by air. Slow baking transformed the batter into a spectacular nine-inch-high cake. After she iced it I scraped the bowl of its creamy, burnt-sugar frosting, whose mellifluous name, butterscotch, merely when I pronounced it, filled my mouth with warm, smooth flavor. Some community women, Mother's peers, occasionally hired Ruth to make her celebrated angel food cake for an anniversary or birthday party. If I helped deliver it, I asked to carry this dessert and then navigated cautiously, as if I were walking on eggs.

When I think now of Mother I see her, laden with pitchers and platters and pans, bowls and vases and tubs, stepping quickly in the warm, sticky clutter of our spacious kitchen. Because we had no dining room, we took all our meals in this large, clamorous space, where she did much of her work. Countless times I watched mother stride from counter to sink to refrigerator to stove and, finally, to large rectangular table—miles of steps a day. Dad had glued red and black rubber tiles to the wooden table, making its top, which then resembled a floor, unattractive but easy to clean. Like most rural women's workplaces in the 1940s and '50s, Ruth's was not a well-designed, modern kitchen. Mother owned few labor-saving devices, and, because the house lacked plumbing, she frequently carried in buckets of water from the well just outside her kitchen door. Mom even emptied the cumbersome, twenty-gallon slop pails when my brothers neglected this chore. And always, even in heat-choked August, Ruth boiled tubs of water for cleaning chickens, dishes, and clothes.

I sometimes helped her do laundry, which routinely took a full day. Then piles of sorted clothes covered the linoleum kitchen floor, stuttering Ruth's usual brisk stride, as she maneuvered around them and rushed back and forth into a small side room, where she had set up the electric washer and tubs for rinsing, bluing, and starching. Wash day was the only time Mother wore pants. She had ordered a Montgomery Ward's pair of jeans, "for the large woman," and the stiff denim, though serviceable, made her stomach and chest more prominent than when she had on soft, faded housedresses. Elbows deep in suds, Mother used a mop stick to shepherd clothes through the wringer. I was in charge of the second-rinse water and also helped hang clothes to dry. When clothesline ran out she told me to fasten old towels and rags to the chicken yard fence. There, at our property's edge, near the fruit trees and ancient elm, my hands wrinkled from hours in warm water and sore from lifting and stretching, I thought of running away—all the while listening for Ruth's call from the kitchen. "Come in, Doll, and we'll rest a while," I hoped she would say.

Mother's seemingly constant motion was most evident when her family sat down to eat. Although we children helped with table clearing and dish drying, at the beginning of meals Ruth waited nonstop on us, hastily replenishing empty bowls and glasses. In the middle of the meal, however, if things were moving smoothly, she finally sat next to Dad and then visibly enjoyed her supper. She might laugh, nudge him, tell an amusing anecdote—like how, in pulling a particularly ornery stinkweed that afternoon, she fell backward, landing in a row of equally stinky turnips. "My padding saved me," she quipped. "And I didn't even hurt the turnips—much." At meals Ruth savored everything, even the lowly cabbage and the oddly named plants we kids abhorred, such as gooseberries, parsnips, and rhubarb. Truth to tell, she overate at every meal.

All of us had the hearty appetites of laborers: my father and brothers, who worked long hours in the fields and then faced heavy chores at home; mother and I, who plowed and weeded gardens, did laundry, and scrubbed floors. We ate, Dad said, like old-time threshers. None of us stopped at one serving of anything we relished. We were what Ruth called "pleasingly plump"; she herself was the most overweight. An ample size eighteen, Mother breathed heavily when she lugged buckets of chicken feed, stooped to pull weeds, or carried a dozen ears of corn to the table. At least, unlike the rest of us, she drank no sugary sodas or juices. Instead, Ruth loved coffee and took it piping hot and black; a cup of it, even during August's most sweltering days, was always near her plate. As I watched Mother gulp the stimulant, I

thought of someone hoarding an elixir. Her craving showed that mere
determination to stay alert and keep working was not always adequate,
even for Ruth.

In the trying heat of our midwestern August Ruth's gait grew heav-
ier, her face more florid. Even my adolescent eyes could see that hot
weather, constant toil, and too much food had left her overweary. I was
not surprised, then, that my vigorous mother, at meal's end, plopped
into our kitchen rocker, which faced a window overlooking the vegetable garden. Once seated she sighed deeply. I saw the strain and—
something that perplexed me—the worry and longing in her face.
Cooling herself with a cheap, lightly scented fan—some promotional
giveaway, undoubtedly, from a local funeral home—Mother seemed to
fold up like a half-blown morning glory. Perhaps dazed by the acrid
smell of spices, for it was high summer and she had pickled cucum-
bers, peppers, and peaches; perhaps weary to the bone from gathering
and sorting, cooking and canning, filling jars with the sticky, blood-
red essence of tomato, raspberry, damson, and cherry; perhaps lulled
by the wind in her favorite elm out by the chicken yard or the whir of a
fast, westbound evening train, Mother rocked and rested. For hours
she had labored, and, after eating quickly and far too heavily, she
suddenly lost energy.

But just before dark on some of these burdensome August days Ruth
rose to gather a bushel or two of her best beefsteak tomatoes. As firm
and large as my father's fists, these heavy, smooth globes were sweet
enough to eat—as you would first-picked apples—right at the moment
of harvest. After a shake of their vines ripe fruit dropped softly into
Mother's stained, calloused hands. I would run along the side yard,
cool dew at my feet, and watch her, a figure bending in the twilight.
Quickly, she scooped tomatoes into half-bushel baskets. "Mother, look
at my somersault," I might plead, but she moved on, not noticing me. At
those moments she was unreachable, refusing to answer or tend to
either children or husband. On such August evenings I slowly began
to realize that Ruth harvested in a mysterious, single-minded way;
that she was mesmerized by the smell and feel, the shape and promise,
of tomato.

By this point in the summer Ruth had canned one hundred quarts
of the crop, a year's supply, so Dad loaded the half-bushels into our
Chevy, and we drove seven miles to the closest city, where a liquor store
owner bought whatever "extra" produce Mother offered. There, in
that town of two thousand five hundred, she sold tomatoes for only two
dollars a bushel—even then, an embarrassingly small sum. But it
nonetheless supplemented Dad's income. A small farmer in peril, my

father could not keep a family of five solvent on field crops alone, despite good years, when corn yielded one hundred bushels an acre. In addition, then, to farming eighty acres, Dad took odd jobs in our town of two hundred twenty people. He was, by turns and sometimes all at once, Methodist church janitor, electric meter reader, seed corn agent, country school bus driver, and member of a railroad repair gang. Still, we bought almost everything on credit and needed more income.

Certainly, Mother's economic contribution was substantial—as the house, garden, and field work of rural women always has been—how ever difficult its dollar value is to calculate. Although defined as "farmer's wife," and thus officially "not gainfully employed," the more she raised and preserved, the less we had to purchase. The more she sold, even on a small scale, the less we worried about school clothes.

Some local women supplied cream, butter, and eggs to faithful customers who frequented their farms. Others occasionally bartered surplus products at one of the nearby grocery stores. But none, to my knowledge, actually delivered garden produce, as Mother did, to the customer. Her initiative, under other circumstances, could have led to a promising business. Untold thousands of farm women have sustained families with just such earnings. But that, for the most part, was decades earlier than the 1950s. Running a truck farm or fresh produce stand would not have been feasible for her, anyway—distant as Ruth was from any sizable town or well-traveled highway. Besides, most local people either had their own gardens and poultry, orchards and livestock, or else they shopped at the new attractions, large supermarkets. Mother was several years too late to truck products to Hannibal, twenty miles east on Highway 36; too late, as well, to ship eggs and capons by rail to Chicago. And, certainly, neither of the two Mom and Pop groceries in our Missouri village would have tried to sell Ruth's butterscotch pies and angel food cakes.

During the time we children became teenagers and wanted new, more durable textbooks, sports equipment, and school wardrobes, Mother and Dad experienced the crisis of American small farmers. Their soil could no longer provide.

The summer I was thirteen and Ruth forty-four I entered a consolidated high school in the town where mother peddled tomatoes. The day school started she began her first salaried job. It was across town from my school. Both of us had freshman nerves; starting work held just as many uncertainties for her as graduating from eighth grade did for me. I had left a four-room country school with poorly trained but attentive teachers and no plumbing or gymnasium. Ruth had left the farm. The kitchen. The garden. While adapting to a comparatively large, modern building, with its bells, lockers, girls' rest room, and demanding teachers, I sometimes would pause to imagine Mother, several blocks away, learning a factory job among fifty women, all of them dressed in similar uniforms.

I remember well the new outfit Mom helped me sew for my first day of high school: a pink gingham shirt, trimmed with white lace, which matched my pink corduroy tight skirt. "You look real streamlined, Doll," she said, when I tried on the set. I wore a variation of saddle oxfords, called rock 'n' roll shoes, tied with pink laces. And Ruth's attire for her equally important starting day? I was up at 6:30 and saw her leave the house to catch a ride with a neighboring coworker. Carrying a sack lunch of onion sandwiches and hard-boiled eggs, Mother moved soundlessly, as if walking on marshmallows. She had on white oxfords with thick rubber soles, sturdy shoes in which she could stand for eight hours. Her ample body, which I always saw as soft yet strong, looked strange—stark, distant, uncomfortable. She wore a white, loose-fitting nylon uniform, like that of a nurse or waitress. Her salt-and-pepper hair she had recently dyed black, and it was held flat by an almost invisible hair net. Mother smiled nervously. "Have a good time in school, Doll, and behave," she reminded me with a hug. Her bright red lipstick only made the white largeness of her figure more remote. Government regulations required that those working in a poultry factory wear such sanitized uniforms.

Ruth's job at Henderson's Produce Company was to grade eggs and eviscerate turkeys. Among other products the plant turned out powdered eggs (for cake mixes) and premium poultry at holiday time. Although the work paid only minimum wage and was seasonal and despite the fact that Henderson's often laid off employees, Ruth had embraced the chance for paid labor, possibly as much as thirty weeks a year—enough to sustain her household.

No longer able to trim flower beds and gather vegetables as extensively as she once did, Mother asked the rest of us to help out more in the gardens. I learned that first autumn to dig potatoes, dry cockscomb, and cook lima beans. We kids even found part-time jobs; mine included selling greeting cards door to door and clerking at a small grocery.

Ruth tended her plants in the early evenings and on Saturdays, but, as September wore on, she found little time to fill vases with asters, gladioli, and zinnias—little energy to bring in arm loads of just-picked vegetables. Often she arrived home from the factory later than the school bus deposited my older brother and me on our town's main street. Dad's field work at a hiatus until soybean and corn harvest, he met the bus and drove us the rest of the way home.

We all gravitated to the kitchen, now a quiet, uncluttered room. As soon as Mother arrived, she would join us and drop wearily into the rocker. Often she told stories about other workers or complained of federal meat inspectors, and then she tackled supper. More and more, a boxed macaroni dinner or tuna noodle casserole squelched our expectations of Mom's home cooking: her fried chicken, beef stew, succotash, biscuits, and freshly made pies.

One late fall day when Dad met the bus he was angry, mumbling about how Mother too often chatted with a coworker instead of "coming right home, where she belonged." As we sat in the kitchen, Dad's mood grew darker. Where was Ruth? Where was supper? As soon as Mother entered the kitchen, an hour after our regular mealtime, saying that she had been talking to a sewing machine salesman at a coworker's place, my father's fury peaked. Calling her a "black-haired runaround," he struck his wife, not with hard fists on her face but, instead, kicking at her—blows that glanced off mother's legs and scuffed her white oxfords. Ruth folded up, crumpling softly to the floor. Dazed, I could neither run to her nor approach Dad. I saw Ruth look up, not in pain or anger but in recognition. Less startled than we kids were by Dad's behavior, she understood his raw jealousy. And then Ruth got up and said, "I'll start supper."

Barbara Horn, *who grew up in rural Missouri, is a member of the faculty at the New School for Social Research and a Professor of English at Nassau Community College of the State University of New York, where she coordinates a Women's Studies Project. She has published in* Iowa Woman, Calyx, Belles Lettres, Esprit, Potpourri, *and* Nassau Review; *her research interests include images of rural and of aging women in American literature.*

Death Mask

Joann Quiñones

Three of your eight daughters flock around you
like fates, trying to comb your hair
so that the gray tufts won't seem so bare
on a bare, bare skull.
But you just don't care anymore about
how your hair looks,
or if your nails have been cut,
or if your eyes seem empty and stare.
A man loved you for your black hair
and married you for lively eyes,
but it dies, it dies.
And now your body is spread
like a Venus of some lost tribe. You hear
the murmur of your praying fates, calling
dead mothers to give you strength.
But you know Mary is a bad choice.
She never suffered,
had labor pains, laid in
a bed to wait for her flesh to decay.
You only know Eve,
and her punishment.
And this is the word of God.
And this is his last judgment.
And after you spewed eleven children
your flesh gives way.
Because there are only three things
a woman could be:
Mujer, Madre, Muerta
And Eve felt it in her ribs.
And Eve learned the base words.
And like Eve you shit in your bed
because leaning on your haunches

This poem was written before the death of my grandmother, Margarita Vargas, in April
1992.

begging for someone to wipe you is too much.
Your pubic hair is dry and scattered
like the tattered dying roots of a tree.
And this is where original sin starts,
with a man taking a bite, like a serpent,
your children being spit out like apple seeds.
And this is all that is left in life,
Not even to die, but to rot with old age.
And you fade as life fades, until
death do you part by part.

Joann Quiñones *is a senior at Rutgers University. She hopes to attend graduate school for a Ph.D. degree in English.*

The Pawnbroker's Window

Pat Wynne

I grew up in the 1940s in the Bronx. I was lucky. My father had a job. He worked as a clerk in the post office. It was a government job. That meant security, a pension, and vacation pay. I don't think it meant health benefits back then because I was always taken to the local city hospital for my health care.

But my parents always told me about the Depression. They had been married back then. My father graduated from law school and passed the bar in 1934. He'd worked his way through college in the post office, and after he graduated he couldn't find a job better than the one he had flipping letters into slots. He stayed in the post office, never accepting a promotion, because he was a shy man who had strong political convictions. He believed that it was wrong to be a foreman or a supervisor.

Still, he felt that he was lucky, because there were many who were not employed during the Depression.

Now we again are living in a time when many are unemployed, living on the streets, laid off, feeling desperate—drinking and using drugs to try to forget their demoralization.

The pawnbroker's window becomes a symbol for me of these times. I had a roommate whose family had always lived on the edge. She remembered the many times when her mother and grandmother had to pawn things from the house in order to buy food at the end of the month. The thought of people getting bargains because of other people's misfortune enraged her.

Note: *"The Pawnbroker's Window" and "Praise the Waitresses" are lyrics set to music also written by Pat Wynne.—Ed.*

The Pawnbroker's Window

1.   High School rings—wedding rings
       Gold and silver everythings
       Extensions of people's lives
       I couldn't buy them if I tried.
       Pocket watches, wristwatch too
       Pins and chains and dreams that died

CHORUS: We're only two paychecks away from the pawnbroker's window.

2.   Here's his guitar, his sax and flute
       Her trumpet with that special mute
       No music with no instrument
       How many tunes lost and silent?
       A synthesizer—keyboard too
       Play It Again, Sam—this swan song's for you

CHORUS: We're only two paychecks away from the pawnbroker's window.

BRIDGE: We're living in desperate times, Jack!
         Don't borrow what you can't pay back
         Don't look down on those who've sunk so low
         We're only two paychecks from that devil's window.

3.   Here's a bargain, buy a few
       No questions asked, they're good as new
       A bottle of milk, some kids to feed
       Maybe it fed a junkie's need.
       Save a dollar, two, or three
       Next one could be you or me.

CHORUS: We're only two paychecks away from the pawnbroker's window—the pawnbroker's window.

Praise the Waitresses

Pat Wynne

Living in the Bronx in the 1940s and 50s, in a two-room walk-in apartment, sharing my bedroom with Mom, while Dad slept in the living room / dining room/kitchen, was making me crazy. Both parents were nervous and high-strung. I guess having a child was constantly demanding on Dad's salary—he was a postal clerk. I needed music lessons, school clothes, books, everything.

At Music and Art High School in New York City, I was given a small scholarship—supposedly for books and clothing. (My mother insisted on putting it in the bank, and I continued to wear hand-me-downs, anyway.) This money was given to me because I excelled in music, and I guess I looked a little shabby.

I told the dean that I needed to get away from home. She helped me to qualify for a State Teacher's College up in New Paltz. My folks didn't think that they could afford it. I was only sixteen and, therefore, too young to go away. Eventually, the dean convinced them, and I went away to school.

In order to afford a few extras I tried to work as a waitress in the college dining hall. It was so hard I thought I would die. I later switched to the Administrative Offices and did clerical work.

So many people have had to work in order to put themselves through school. They've had to stay up half the night studying in order to keep up. In the song "Praise the Waitresses" besides appreciating these hard-working women, I wanted also to salute those many people who have to work in order to do other things, such as go to school.

This song is dedicated to the Hotel and Restaurant Workers who went on strike with Local 2 in 1984.

Praise the Waitresses

CHORUS: Praise for the waitresses. Praise for the maids.

VERSE:

1.   When I was a little girl, little girl,
I always wanted to be,
One of those pretty waitresses who always smiled at me.
How could I know how hard it was.
She always hid it well.
'Cause she always smiled and joked with me.
She hid her private hell.

CHORUS

2.   But when I went away to school,
I had to work at a trade
I finally got my dream come true,
A waitress I became.

     But the trays they just about wore me down
With eight to ten plates all in a row,
I tried, but soon I saw the glamour fade
They let me go, I was too slow.

CHORUS

3.   The jobs that women often hold, often hold,
Like waitresses and maids
Are thankless and submissive jobs
And mostly underpaid.

     So, when you're out in some hotel
Or in some chic cafe
Remember the tip is part of her pay
Our society likes it that way
If they unionized, it might not happen that way.

CHORUS

Pat Wynne *is a writer, musician, voice teacher, and performer. She belongs to the Freedom Song Network, a group of singers which keeps the labor song tradition alive in the San Francisco Bay Area. She performs a one-woman show called* We Were There, *and is currently creating a performance piece out of a memoir entitled* Days of a Red Diaper Daughter, *which appears in Janet Zandy's anthology* Liberating Memory *(Rutgers University Press, 1995).*

We Did Change Some Attitudes: Maida Springer-Kemp and the International Ladies' Garment Workers Union

Edited by Brigid O'Farrell and Joyce L. Kornbluh

In 1955, Maida Springer, a forty-five-year-old factory worker and union activist from the garment district of New York City, was one of the first African-American women to travel to Africa on behalf of the AFL-CIO. An international labor pioneer, she has worked for fifty years with trade union leaders from many countries, including Kenya, Nigeria, Tanzania, Ghana, and South Africa, establishing education and training programs and acting as a critical link between the labor leaders on both continents.

Interwoven with her work in Africa are activities in the International Ladies' Garment Workers Union, which she describes as "one of the most exciting unions in the world." After joining Local 22 of the ILGWU during the Depression, she became very active on several committees. Several years later, she became a local union education director, and one of the union's first African-American business agents. In 1945, she was chosen by the American Federation of Labor (AFL) to represent them on a good-will mission to England for the Office of War Information. It was there that she first met some of the emerging young African leaders and became committed to their need for training, education, and independence. That same year she was named one of the Women of the Year by the National Council of Negro Women.

In the 1960s, Maida became an international representative for the AFL-CIO International Affairs Department and then worked with the affiliated African-American Labor Center and the Asian-American Free Labor Institute. She also worked as a general organizer for the ILGWU in the South and as Mid-West director of the A. Philip Randolph Institute, and served as vice-president of the National Council of Negro

Brigid O'Farrell and Joyce Kornbluh, *Rocking the Boat: Women Activists in the Labor Movement*, copyright © 1995 by Brigid O'Farrell and Joyce Kornbluh. To be published in the Fall/Winter of 1995/96 by Rutgers University Press.

Women. Increasingly, she focused on the needs of women trade union-ists in the United States, as well as in Africa, Indonesia, and Turkey.

While recognizing problems of racism and sexism within unions, Maida continues to see the labor movement as a major force for improving the lives of working women and men. Today, she lives in Pittsburgh near her son and his family. She continues to travel to Africa, and her home remains a meeting place for visitors from around the world.[1]

Shool and Community

During the 1920s, the Harlem Renaissance symbolized a strong African-American culture in New York City, including music and literature, as well as intellectual and civil rights movements. Maida Stewart grew up in this atmosphere with her mother, Adina Stewart. Maida was born in the Republic of Panama in 1910. Her father had come from the West Indies to work on the Panama Canal; her mother was born in Panama. After her younger sister died at age three, they emigrated to New York, arriving at Ellis Island in August 1917. They lived at first with relatives in Harlem, and then her parents separated. Maida says little about her father, but describes Adina as intelligent, vivacious, and "always young." Her mother worked first as a domestic and then as a cook and beautician, eventually opening her own beauty shop. Family and church played important roles in Maida's youth, but she was also strongly influenced by the African-American leaders of that time. Her mother was a follower of Marcus Garvey (1887–1940), founder of the Universal Negro Improvement Association. Maida attended high school at Bordentown Manual Training and Industrial School for Colored Youth, a private boarding school in New Jersey, where she heard speakers like W. E. B. Du Bois (1868–1963), a leading intellectual and one of the founders of the NAACP, and Paul Robeson (1898–1976), a great actor and civil rights activist.

The first school I ever went to was in the United States. But I could read and write when I came here. The public schools in New York City—that was something else! I was enrolled in St. Mark's, the Catho-lic school near our home. Then I went to a black boarding school in New Jersey. This was a black industrial school for boys and girls. They had football and tennis and all of these things, but it was an industrial school. It wasn't a "hoyty-toyty" school. They attempted to set a stan-dard. They gave you the best that they could offer.

The teachers were excellent men and women who had very superior education. Miss Grant taught English literature. She spent the summer

in Europe, and every September she came back and opened up a whole
new world. Poetry had meaning. Medieval architecture had meaning.
Rome, Switzerland, Africa—all had meaning. One of the professors
there was William H. Hastie, later Judge Hastie. He taught me science.
My history professor was a Harvard graduate. His father had been a
janitor at Harvard. And seeing him stand there and talk about the *ex
post facto* law. . . . These were great awakenings. To see Paul Robeson
standing on the platform in our Assembly at the school. He was then at
Rutgers. He was great. These were the images I had. Dr. Du Bois
talking over our heads because he was always the elegant aristocrat and
giving you a world view. These were the role models of men and
women of intellect and men and women who talked about what a
social system should be.

In terms of identity, the Garvey Movement was another great influence on my life. We came to the United States at the point that Garvey,
the burly black Jamaican, was really at the top of the mark. My mother,
of course, immediately joined the Universal Negro Improvement Association. I listened to men and women of the day passionately speaking
a language that most black Americans were not speaking. These were
passionate men and women, envisioned Americans, West Indians, and
a few Latins, and they were talking about a society in which men and
women, regardless of color or race, should share. There should be a
caring, and then . . . the challenges: don't buy where you can't work,
develop your own industry, develop your own initiative in the community, own buildings. We were one of the early stockholders in the Terry
Holding Association, which was a building society.

My mother marched as a Black Cross Nurse in the Garvey Movement,
and she had this child by the hand. I went to the meetings because
there were no babysitters. We were not sophisticated enough for that in
those days—so wherever she went, I went. And so I listened to all of
this. In our home, people from our part of the world, from the
Caribbean Islands—many of them congregated in our house. My
mother was a marvelous cook and a joyous woman, so there was always
a coterie of people, and there was singing, and there was talking, and
beyond that, a realization of a role we had to play in this society.

It didn't matter whether on Monday morning you were scrubbing
floors or were a porter some place, or whether you were doing the
most menial job. This was all the society would permit to be open to
you. Many doctors and lawyers in that early period were people who
had worked at menial jobs, and worked on the shifts in order to
continue their studies. It was only a very small percentage of black
Americans whose families could support a fine education.

Factory Work

Like the lives of most young women of her day, Maida's life was dramatically affected by the Great Depression. While in high school, she got a job in a garment factory, one of the few places hiring young black women, where she learned to use a pinking machine, "to cut the jagged edges on the garments." After graduation, in 1927, she worked as a receptionist until she married Owen Springer, a West Indian from Barbados. Their son, Eric, was born in 1929. Owen had a good job in a dental equipment firm and expected his wife to stay at home, but when the Depression started, he had to take a large cut in salary and Maida went back to work in a garment factory.

In 1932, I went to work in a garment shop, first as a hand sewer and later as a power machine operator. In those days I had a lot of family in-laws. My sister-in-law lived on one floor and she had seven children. I lived on the top floor. I never had a babysitter, never needed one. When I moved away from 142nd Street, if Owen and I were going out some place, one of the older girls came and spent the night. That was the family.

The industry was in a chaotic condition. The union was very weak. People came in very early in the morning, didn't have their lunch hour, and all sorts of things. If the manufacturer of the garment thought something was wrong with it, you fixed it for nothing. Oh, it's hard to describe.

I kept threatening that I was going to the union. The cutter and I became very friendly. It was unusual in those days to see a Negro man a cutter, but he was excellent, and since they paid him next to nothing, and it was non-union, he was able to hold the job. Most shops were non-union shops. But I knew something about unions. I had heard A. Philip Randolph speak in Harlem and had some positive views about unions. I joined the Dressmakers' Union, Local 22, of the International Ladies' Garment Workers Union (ILGWU) in May 1933. I went in and told them what was happening at work because it was just getting under my skin. The fee to join the union was $2.50 and dues were $0.35 a month.

Union Activism

The unions in New York's garment industry were largely dominated by European immigrants with strong ties to socialist and communist organizations. Communist influence started to decline in the ILGWU beginning in 1926, with a disastrous five-month strike led by the communist trade unionists. In 1933, the National Industrial Recovery

Act first gave workers the right to organize unions. Under the leadership of David Dubinsky, elected president of the union in 1932, the
ILGWU's New York Joint Dress Board called a general strike. On 16
August 1933, 60,000 workers, mostly women, marched to the strike
halls in New York, New Jersey, and Connecticut. The strike was brief,
but the union won increased wages and better working conditions,
and union membership rose from 50,000 in 1933 to 200,000 in 1934.
The number of Black women dressmakers in ILGWU Local 22 increased from 600 to nearly 4,000. Maida began a lifelong career as a
strong union activist, and the Springer family's way of life was forever changed.[2]

   We were part of a social revolution. You see, the garment industry
was built by European immigrants, most of whom were victims of
oppression in their native lands. Their political opinions ranged from
Anarchism to Zionism, but communists made up the largest group.
Charles "Sasha" Zimmerman, the manager of my own Local 22, had
been an ardent communist. After the 1926 strike, which nearly destroyed the union, he turned against their ideology and became their
most bitter foe and target. The worst of it was over by 1933, but you still
had lots of problems after that. In the big local unions, you had
challenge and conflict. I was involved in all of that because the communists constituted the opposition to the union leadership. The communists were not concerned with the domestic life of the worker in
America. They had a political ideology that was destructive to improving workers' conditions.
   When the strike was settled, industry-wide, then we had to begin to
build the union. Oh, just hundreds and thousands of workers were
enrolled into the garment workers' union and this was a great excitement. My own Local 22 was one of the bigger locals. Everyone who was
not Italian belonged to Local 22, the dressmakers. We had 32 nationalities. We prided ourselves on this. We immediately began focusing
on educational work because we had all of these raw recruits. So they
began all kinds of classes—English for the non-English-speaking,
classes on parliamentary procedure, classes of all kinds to provide a
very simple, basic understanding of the union agreement. It was really
the first important agreement that we had. I began on that level as
an activist.
   You still had the Italian workers belonging to Local 89, which was
the Italian-language local—they spoke Italian. You think of Luigi
Antonini, with his flowing black tie, who looked like a great opera
impresario. He brought to the garment workers a kind of cultural

content, because any celebration meant going to the opera, or bringing the greatest of the opera stars to the garment workers. When we had our celebration in Madison Square Garden after we won the general strike, everybody from the Met was there to sing for the workers. You had the great freedom song of the Italian workers, "*Pan y Rosa*," "Bread and Roses." That's why I say that, for me, the trade union movement was always a great love affair and a great excitement.[3]

I'm a member; I work in the shop. I go and work in the shop every day from '33 until '41 or '42. But I'm active, very active, chairman of the education committee in my local during one period. I took all the courses that were required of me. Those early courses were for activists to be more intelligent and to be more informed. For those who were, I suppose, more aggressive than I, they looked forward to becoming an officer. But, on my life, this was not my concern. I could not be a member of the Committee on Prices in my local union if I did not know what I was talking about. I could not represent the shops. So I took the courses I did on the advice of my business agent so that I could be a better union member.

I was an executive board member of Local 22 and represented the union on all kinds of committees. A bread-and-butter committee, when I worked in the shop, was to settle prices. Our wages were based on the settlement of the piece rate price: what a worker would be paid for each piece completed. I was on one of the first committees of the local and I was to represent workers in structuring our base, how we settled the garment, what we were to be paid. I was elected by my shop to be their representative on the jobber's premises, the manufacturer's premises, to argue for what we would be paid for making the garment. It was complicated to learn. At first, it was most frightening, but you had the guidance of your union representative, you had training, and you and other workers who represented other shops, you met together. But the employer tried to intimidate you. This was a brand-new experience.

The union changed our way of life. I'd go off to training programs on weekends and Owen would not go. I wanted him to understand what I was trying to do in this country. I would say, "Eric needs the best chance we can give him. We only have one child, and the union has made it possible for women to be involved, to expand my opportunity." I think he resented it, which made life difficult for all of us, but he was a wonderful human being, a wonderful father. By the time Eric was ten years old, he had all kinds of involvement in activities after school, and his father came straight home from work or my mother was always close.

The New Deal

The early 1930s ushered in the Roosevelt Administration with a far-reaching labor and social legislative agenda. In 1935, the National Labor Relations Act ensured the right to organize and bargain collectively, and in 1938, the Fair Labor Standards Act provided the first national minimum wage. The ILGWU was a very progressive union, proud of its early policies against segregated locals and pay differences based on race. Maida learned to lobby and work with people in the Roosevelt Administration. In 1942, she ran unsuccessfully as a candidate for the American Labor Party for the New York State Assembly from the 21st District in Harlem.[4]

We were fighting for legislation, for all of the things that went on in the Roosevelt Administration in which labor was so closely identified. My first lobbying experience was on minimum wage. The minimum wage was thirty-seven cents an hour. I think we were asking for something like fifty cents. Well, the way those senators and congressmen talked about it, you would have thought we all had tails. This was my first exposure to government. I was so incensed for years because here I am, a proud citizen, and these people talking to us as though we're scum. One senator, he read a statement about mother love and how changing the wage structure would destroy mother love and the family. Now, what mother love had to do with wages, I don't know. Women would still have to work.

The labor movement was just beginning to be recognized. There were friends of the labor movement working for legislation to strengthen unions, like the National Labor Relations Act. After Roosevelt was elected, it became a reality. When I went to work in the garment industry it was chaotic; we did not have a strong union. In those early days, people did a lot of work at home, so that after a worker spent twelve hours in the factory, she then took work home, often to a Lower East Side apartment heated with a coal stove. It was a sweated industry indeed! But by '35, we were considered the wild ones because President Dubinsky demanded and negotiated and got a thirty-five-hour work week. This was unheard-of! Only the union printers had a thirty-five-hour work week. They said it would drive all the manufacturers out of business. It didn't, of course. Most of the manufacturers only got richer.

Innovative things were done by the trade unions in terms of health, in terms of leisure. Unity House, for example. Where could a worker go with a limited income and no money for a vacation? Unity House is a resort in the Pocono Mountains run by the ILGWU where union membership made it possible for you to go away the way a wealthy person might go. The Amalgamated Clothing Workers Union pioneered in housing and banking, establishing cooperative housing projects and banks that were available to union members. You had men of great genius and innovation who saw that union leaders had to create the climate of change and fight for housing, health care, and recreation, in addition to wages.

I would be called out of the shop, for example, to go to a meeting at lunch to represent the union. On one occasion, it was a luncheon meeting at the Waldorf-Astoria. This was a great honor. I came to work that morning in my moccasins and working clothes, you know, a heavy coat. I was a size ten then. The whole shop got involved. I was loaned somebody's pocketbook; a dress was taken off of the dress form and fitted on me, and somebody else gave me a better-looking coat than the one I had on, and I marched off to the luncheon dressed to the nines. Three women who were there, Madame Chiang Kai Shek, Madame Litvinov, and Mrs. Roosevelt—and there I was, representing my local union, representing the ILGWU in solidarity.

I went back to the shop and stitched my dresses and at six o'clock, I went to the union board meeting in my moccasins and my old coat and my tam o'shanter. There was a great howl because a few hours earlier I had been so dolled up. This was the kind of political and social atmosphere of that whole period.

Education Director, Local 132

One of the effects of World War II was a change in the work force as young men went off to war. In 1942, this change became a major challenge for Maida. To prepare her for going on the union staff, Sasha Zimmerman, general manager of the New York Dress Joint Board and a good friend and mentor, arranged for her to become education director of Local 132, the Plastic Button and Novelty Workers Union. According to Maida, the membership was 70-percent male, 30-percent female, working in metals, plastics, and materials like acetone. The union lost about 40 percent of its young male members to the war, and the new members, many more of them women, came from very diverse ethnic and racial backgrounds. Maida saw education as a key to effective interracial unionism, based on her own experiences at programs like the Harlem Labor Center and the Hudson Shore Labor School.[5] During this time, Owen went into war work and commuted during the week to a shipyard in Baltimore, where the men made good money, but shared very crowded living conditions.

I became, in 1942, the educational director of the Plastic Button and Novelty Workers Union, which was one of the accessory locals of ILGWU. It included all kinds of nationalities: Poles, Germans, Swedes, and Italians. While they hated one another sometimes, they jointly hated anything black. All these new people were coming in: the poor devils who had escaped the gas chambers of Hitler; the Negroes who had just come up from the South, who had never had a working experience in an industrial setting, in a factory; women who were strange to mass employment, housewives who were just coming to work—and a part of the training was to make all of these people understand something about the union.

So we had classes, which I initiated, two or three sessions. We had lecturers who came down and talked about the union and the contract and the union constitution and the rest of it. Well, the first thing you do is start out by indicating that they have one common bond. You didn't have to love one another, we would tell them, but you wanted decent wages, hours, conditions of work. You wanted those safety measures to affect everyone, and every worker to have a sense of responsibility to the other workers—because there were some highly dangerous materials that you worked on—the plastics and acetone and poisons and the rest of it, so that you had to be responsible for the other worker. You used some heavy machines. You could stamp off a man's hand or stamp off a woman's fingers. Also, the introduction had to include good trade unionism. For people coming from a racial community where they had never been exposed to anyone that did not look just like them, this required some doing.

For example, I would organize a weekend institute. You would have marshmallow roasting, frankfurters, and after you had pumped trade unionism and workers' education and the history of the labor move-ment over a weekend, each evening you tried to do some of the social things people did there—country dances and the rest of it. A couple of young women came to me and desperately wanted to go, but the brothers in the family said that if "niggers" were going to be there, particularly men, they could not go.

So how could I persuade their brothers? I started with the mothers. I developed some allies. Most of the mothers I won over. It had to do with a belief that I was one Negro that maybe they thought met their standards. Their standards were much lower than mine in most instances, but, again, these are the prejudices you had to deal with.

This was my first paid union responsibility. But it was a lasting experience since it was a small local union—five thousand members,

in contrast to Local 22, for example, which had 25,000 members—
and the staff was a small staff. As the educational director, I went to
the plant doors at four or five o'clock in the morning and issued
leaflets when the shifts changed. The union staff did all sorts of
things together. An interesting by-product of this, with the war on,
was that we developed a labor newspaper. It brought families together.
Brothers who were in the same army found one another when they got
this little union magazine, "The Voice of Local 132." We were all
very patriotic. The Red Cross had a blood bank, but I refused to give
blood for the reason that they segregated the blood, even though Dr.
Charles Drew, a black doctor, perfected the plasma technique so
useful during World War II. It was a union staff of five or six people.
We knew every shop steward. We knew every committee, and *we did
change some attitudes.*

Civil Rights

In 1932, before becoming a union member, Maida went to hear a
speech by A. Philip Randolph, a well-known leader in the African-
American community, president of the Brotherhood of Sleeping Car
Porters, and later vice-president of the AFL-CIO. Randolph "really
turned my head around at that meeting," she reported, "talking about
the rights of workers and the dilemma of black workers and white
workers who could be easily misused and abused . . . that there must be
a joining."[6] Randolph became a mentor and close family friend who
would have a lasting influence on Maida's interconnected commitments to the labor movement and the civil rights movement in both the
United States and Africa. While committed to helping women, she
believed "the first barrier is always race." In 1941, due in large part to
Randolph's efforts on behalf of African-American workers, President
Roosevelt signed Executive Order 8802, prohibiting job discrimination on the basis of race, creed, color, or national origin in government and the defense industry. Mass rallies were held around the
country to support establishing a permanent Fair Employment Practices Committee after the war ended. A major effort was a rally
in Madison Square Garden in 1946, and Maida became executive
secretary.[7]

We were involved in staging a Madison Square Garden rally to
establish a permanent FEPC. Mr. Randolph called Sasha Zimmerman
and President Dubinsky, and said, "We would appreciate it if you
would allow Maida to help us put this rally together." I was terrified at
the idea. The only people who could fill the Garden in those days were

the communists. In addition, I did not think I had the administrative qualifications and the fund-raising abilities to do it. You know, there were some things I was modest about.

So, to everyone he sent to me, I said, "No, I would not do it." Then Brother Randolph called and asked me to come see him. I walked in, and he said, "Now, Maida dear, the cause of social justice is at stake. We had, as you know, Executive Order 8802." Since I was prepared to march about that, I said, "Yes, sir," and he said, "Now, our colleagues in the Congress, and so and so, and Mrs. Roosevelt is going to lend her support and she will talk with Franklin." You know, I walked out of there with my head bowed and a check for a $3,000 down payment on Madison Square Garden. Billy Bowe, an officer of the Brotherhood, escorted me to the Garden to make the transaction official. The Garden in those days cost $6,000 empty.

You had to raise money and then on and on. We had good fortune. Helen Hayes, Orson Welles, and a host of others—they did the dramatic part of the program. But the building of such a program, I can't tell you. I was twenty pounds lighter and years younger, and terrified. You knew you were going to get help, but how do you stage all this, and how do you keep the momentum going as you raise money and as you do the drudgery? There was strong support from groups like the NAACP, the Urban League, people in the arts, and the churches. Max Delson, a prominent socialist lawyer in New York, did a lot of work to limit our mistakes. You got the support of trade unionists and young people from colleges. Then you were busy calling all over the country and you were busy with promoters. In terms of raising the money, I had to carry the stick for this project. Union leaders used to say to me, "Well, Springer, how much is this conversation with you going to cost?" But with a dedicated staff of people to work with, it got so that you learned in the doing.

We filled Madison Square Garden with 25,000 people, and we had a five-hundred-voice choir that no one believed was possible. I used to hang my head because they would say, "What do you mean, a five-hundred-voice choir, whoever heard of such a thing?" There was a woman who was trained, a gospel singer, choir leader. I heard about her, so I hotfooted to meet her. She liked me, and I liked her, and she said, "Yes," and we began to work. She did not have five hundred voices but she began building and building around it. The Garden was the backdrop. These men and women, the women all in their dark skirts and white blouses, and the men with their black suits and white shirts, were . . . a dramatic presence. A lot of these women worked as domestics. On the night of this rally, most of their employers were there to see them perform.

It was impressive. All of the people who came to contribute and share in that occasion were extraordinary, so it was quite an experience. If someone has faith in you, and asks you as Brother Randolph did, you try. If he had told me to walk the water, I would have tried. I tell you, I would have tried. Especially with my own union backing me up, and saying, "Yes, we want you to do this." They paid my salary for the period. The trade union movement was superb, and this was AF of L and CIO. They worked at making the rally a success. This was the meeting for the forward thrust on legislation for a permanent Fair Employment Practices Committee, the catalyst of these laws around the United States.

Business Agent, Local 22

The heart of the garment industry, and thus a major focus of the union, was the piecework system. How the work was assigned and the price paid for each piece determined wages and working conditions. Maida knew the system as a worker, a union activist, and local union education director. The next step in learning the roles and responsibilities of local union leadership was mastering the complaint process from the staff side. In 1945, she returned to Local 22 to learn the internal mechanics of the complaint department; to settle complaints about wages and grievances about working conditions, and to deal with all of the regulations which have to do with contract negotiations. In 1947, she went on the staff as a business agent, the second African-American business agent for Local 22 and the first to be responsible for a district.[8]

Well, going from an activist in the shop, when you thought you knew what you were doing, to a business agent is quite a jump, because as an activist, you think you know the instruments of the union. You walk up to the window at the complaint department office and you tell them you want this, you want that. You get a lot of action. But as a business agent, you were then the responsible person and the person who had to resolve the complaints or they would complain about *you*.

As a business agent, I had fifty-eight shops. The shops were small. The section of the industry which I was given some responsibility for was called the Better Makers because you began with the wholesale price of $10.75, which was higher-priced. You had a wide range to cover and you had to overcome the suspicion of the very talented and wise men and women who were the craftsmen in the industry. Now they had to respect you, to believe that you could resolve their grievances, and stand up to the employer and be able to defend them.

A business agent's responsibility is to see that the shop functions, and to see that the worker is treated fairly by the employer and to see that the union committees function properly. Because it's a piecework system, you had to see that the slow worker had an advantage as well as the fast worker, because the employer's tendency would be to give all of the big bundles to the fast workers and all of the rags and tags and single garments to the slower worker. He would naturally lean to what would be more profitable to him. It's a horrible system. It dehumanizes you, but I don't know what the answer is. It's a system that we grew up with and it's now expanded because the needle trade has become a multinational corporation.

Every garment shop was a small government. You had to be cognizant of the personalities that you were dealing with. After you got over the suspicion that you didn't know what you were doing and you were black and you were a woman . . . after you had overcome that, then you had to overcome the suspicion that you were probably selling the workers out to the employer. Now this had nothing to do with color or race. This just meant that you were authority and you were suspect.

You made sure that you did certain things when you walked into a shop. You greeted your unpaid elected union officers. The chairlady or chairman worked there every day and if there was a grievance, you got the chairlady and a union committee to work with you on solving it. Then you went in and sat down with the employer, but under no circumstances do you go into the employer's office in a hurry. In your anxiety to get the job done quickly, since you have a long list of shops to service, you may do that. When you walk out, the assumption might be that you have made some deal to the workers' disadvantage. You walked into a shop and sometimes by the time you're through, you've created a riot. You had to know the union contract. Your business is policing the union agreement. I did that for thirteen years. Your responsibility to the union members was every hour of your life.

You don't just start as a needle worker, a garment worker, without a good deal of discipline, and a good deal of disappointment, and a lot of inconvenience in your personal life. I've had discrimination, I've had a lot of discrimination. I've had a lot of problems. I have been rejected. There were racial hostilities in the union. I would be an awful liar if I said that there were not. We tried harder, but we suffered from all of the prejudices and disabilities of our society. Within the union there were sufficient men and women who were concerned, who tried. But there were officers of the union who really could never see the black worker or the Spanish worker, moving straight across the board. You had that to fight.

On the job there could be discrimination. It was a piece rate system. The bulk of the workers, maybe operators in the dressmakers' union, got paid for what they made, but there were certain lines. With the cheaper line, you could get a job where you just work and work and work and kill yourself to make it. With the better line, you had to be more skilled and make the whole garment. A case could be made, and was made, that people were excluded. Black people or Spanish people were excluded from the better lines. There were jobs that the men just said to themselves, "These jobs are not for women." The employer and the workers agreed that we will not let women be the tailors. There were many subtle ways it could be done. Both race and sex discrimination existed.

When I was made a member of the union staff, the manufacturers' association said that their officers would not be seen with me. I was the first black business agent. Sometimes you get sick of being the first of this and the first of that and the first of the other. But my own union leader, Zimmerman, said, "All right, nobody will function. You don't want her—you won't see her—you won't see any of us. She's an officer of our union." We won and he never told me. I found out months later that the association had officially protested. This is what always creates my constant affection and love for what a workers' organization has done to raise the sights and the sense of respect for the working men and women in the United States—which industry on its own would not do.

Role Models

While Maida was profoundly influenced by several prominent men, such as Du Bois, Randolph, Dubinsky, and Zimmerman, she also attributes much of her commitment to the labor movement and women's rights to a number of strong women activists. Among them, Mary McLeod Bethune (1875–1955), founder of the National Council of Negro Women, offered guidance and support. Her close friendship with Pauli Murray (1910–1985)—feminist, lawyer, minister—was reflected in Murray's autobiography, *Song in a Weary Throat*, which is dedicated to "Maida, incomparable companion, critic, and guide on the pilgrimage."[9] Maida worked closely with women in the Amalgamated Clothing Workers Union, such as Esther Peterson and Dolly Lowther Robinson, but perhaps most important to her development in the union were the role models from her own ILGWU, especially Pauline Newman and Fannia Cohen.[10]

I think part of the feeling I have had, my own constant passion about the labor movement with all of its bumps and warts, is because I came up at a time when there were so many role models. Pauline Newman, who was then directing one section of the health department of the ILG, this woman had been in the Triangle Shirtwaist Company fire. She was one of the giants, determined, articulate, volatile about workers' dignity and the pursuit of excellence, wherever you are. Rose Schneiderman, who headed the Women's Trade Union League, brought the women of wealth and prominence to understand the concerns, the problems of working women. Fannia Cohen was at ILGWU national headquarters in the education department. I respected her.

Fannia Cohen, Pauline Newman, and a host of others were among the rambunctious, tenacious women who made themselves heard. Talk about the uprising of the Twenty Thousand. When the men in the unions wanted to settle for less, these women garment workers were prepared to stay on strike and be hungry and to march in the winter. The men had families and other responsibilities, and felt that they ought to make the compromise, but the women felt that they had reached the point of no return, and they could do no worse. I think sometimes our madness is part of our survival. All of these women touched my life and mind, and so I did come up at a time of great transition.

In the garment workers' union, where the majority of the membership are women, deep down below I imagine there are people with those prejudices that women do not stay in the union and therefore it's harder to get them into leadership. But the majority of the members of the union, most of them women like myself, were members for twenty-five and thirty years. Even though a woman has been a member and attended meetings and done all these things and brought up a family, there is the myth that she thinks like a woman, that she's going to be away from the meetings, from serious contract negotiation—which, in fact, is not so. It's a block one has to get over, but the doors are more open now, out of pure necessity and some intelligent leadership.

International Background

Men like Sidney Hillman, president of the Amalgamated Clothing Workers Union, joined the Roosevelt Administration to help coordinate the war production effort.[11] Part of this effort was an exchange of workers to share experiences and ideas. Maida's first international experience began in 1945, when the AFL and the CIO were asked by the Office of War Information Exchange, to send four women workers to represent the American labor movement and share

wartime experiences during several weeks in England. The AFL nominated Maida and Julia O'Connor Parker from the International Brotherhood of Electrical Workers. Maida's appointment, as the first Negro
woman to represent labor abroad, was a history-making event documented in *The New York Times*.[12] While in England, she also made her
first contact with a group of young African trade unionists and the
Pan-African movement dedicated to ending colonialism and establishing independent African nations.

I remember standing up on a table in a huge factory in England
and after saying whatever I was going to say, asking them to join
me in a trade union song. The factory owner, you know, 2,000
workers, everybody stopped, and people were waving their hands
and singing. Some of their women were among the strong militants in
their unions, as were women in the United States. But insofar as being
in the top leadership of the trade union movement, the British TUC
was a male organization, just as the AF of L and CIO were male
organizations.

An opportunity to meet the Queen of England was, of course, very
exciting. We had some interesting moments, because the ladies-in-
waiting had to tell you how to behave and we had to argue among
ourselves the night before about who was going to curtsey and who
would shake hands. We were very strong about the democratic way of
doing things. But Queen Elizabeth was so utterly charming that she
just put us at ease.

My colleagues—they had problems. The CIO thought that it was the
egalitarian organization of the world, and that the AF of L was the
reactionary organization of the world. The CIO was considered more
progressive. Here you are with this black woman representing the AF
of L. The CIO ladies were horrified that the CIO had been upstaged.
My partner, Julia O'Connor Parker from the Telephone Workers
Union, had sat with Samuel Gompers in the discussions for the International Labor Organization (ILO) after World War I. She was horrified at first at the idea of having to share responsibility with this Negro
woman, but we developed mutual trust and respect. We were a good
working team. We were the conservatives. I had never considered
myself a conservative until that time.

But when doing any of our public discussions, the larger issue
was the trade union movement as a social and economic force; what
it represented to millions and millions of working people. This
was the goal, and how do you get a government and the employers to
see that the worker is not just a pair of hands, that the worker has a

mind, the worker has a home, has a family, and needs to be treated with respect, to have wages commensurate with what he or she is doing, to have a decent standard of living. If this was our goal, we had no problems.

My unofficial introduction into the politics of black Britain began at a press conference in London. George Padmore, a reporter, asked to see me. He was both an author and one of the leaders of the Pan-African Congress that had just concluded a conference in Manchester which W. E. B. Du Bois had chaired. I met Jomo Kenyatta, later president of Kenya, who asked, "Young lady, what does the American working class know about the struggle against Colonialism?" I accepted this as a challenge.

Oxford and Africa

In 1951, Maida received a scholarship from the American Scandinavian Foundation to study workers' education in Denmark and Sweden for three months. She then spent the academic year as an Urban League Fellow at Ruskin Labor College, Oxford University, England, where she made strong and lasting ties to the labor leaders of Africa also studying there. She made her first trip to Africa, on loan to the AF of L, as a delegate to the newly formed International Confederation of Free Trade Unions' (ICFTU) first seminar in Africa.[13] She worked closely with A. Philip Randolph and George Meany (1894–1980), who became president of the AFL-CIO. By this time Eric was at Oakwood, a Quaker boarding school in Poughkeepsie, New York. Owen had become one of the first black workers to secure a job in the New York transit system after the war. He was a member of the union, but was never active and never encouraged Maida in her union activities. They bought a house in Brooklyn and Maida's mother lived with them, but, by that time, she said, Owen would not discuss the year-long trip with her. They divorced in 1955.

In London, at Ruskin College, I worked with African students, and some of these men were senior labor officers. They were down at Oxford and I was at Ruskin, but I attended some of the international lectures at Rhodes House because I was interested in international affairs. So I had contact with all of these men and women from Africa—mostly men; there were very few African women in the colleges in England at the time. Many of the men were revolutionaries who, while they had a façade of accepting the status quo, were busily working at changing the status quo. We sat up at nights discussing the future of Africa.

My first trip to Africa was as a representative of the American Federation of Labor. The international labor movement, the International Confederation of Free Trade Unions (ICFTU), of which the AF of L and CIO were members, invited the American unions to send as observers two delegates to the first ICFTU meeting in Africa. This seminar in Africa was for about three weeks, and trade unionists from all over the continent who were able to come—many of them had been in jail. The emphasis was on an exchange of views, and they were talking about agriculture, mining, wages, hours, conditions of service, workers' education, the prospects of independence, and the role of labor in that world that was to come.

You must remember, this is early 1955. Ghana was the country that was preparing for independence, even though its leader, Dr. Nkrumah, had been jailed. It was very interesting that the man who jailed him, the Governor General, was the man who was at the prison gates to welcome him out to form a government. These were very exciting times. There were two delegates from the United States, one prominent officer from the United Auto Workers and myself, and there was a delegate from Canada. I was the only woman. It was a time of very serious work.

After this conference, of course, there were resolutions and a program. I came back to the United States and made some recommendations; reported to the AF of L; reported to the ILG, because I was an officer of that union simply on loan to the AF of L. One of the problems that the AF of L-CIO had was that we felt some of the decisions taken were very good on paper, but they took so long to implement. A. Philip Randolph, as a vice-president of the AF of L-CIO and president of the Brotherhood of Sleeping Car Porters, was one of the strong forces in the executive council of the AF of L-CIO. He championed actions which would more rapidly move programs to help the trade unionists be a social force for good, as we recognized and saw the transition in Africa toward independence. He made some of the most stirring addresses and worked within the AF of L-CIO Council for change.

He was kind of the catalyst, a standard for the young Africans as they attended international seminars and saw him within the leadership of the AF of L-CIO in the international labor movement. He gave a sense of dignity, courage, and intellect. He was speaking on behalf of workers who had had the least, because the Brotherhood of Sleeping Car Porters had a long and bitter struggle. He was a great example and I was fortunate to have been able to serve in some capacities as a result of Brother Randolph's help in saying that "this young woman, I believe, can share constructively."

One of the myths that I would like to lay to rest is: many Americans looked at President Meany as the conservative who only saw the status quo. He was concerned with what was good for workers and what was good for the citizen, and I don't think he's ever deviated from that. But he was an absolute optimist, and a challenger and a supporter when it came to working toward faster change in Africa. There is not a program with which I was associated subsequently, when I was on the staff of the AFL-CIO in the Department of International Affairs, that President Meany did not actively support; he put his weight behind any proposition that he felt would give the worker a fairer chance on the continent of Africa.

I could tell you intimately about the differences between President Meany and President`Randolph. They had very different approaches, and I do not pretend that Mr. Meany saw the need for the rapidity with which things had to change. They had a difference in method, and Mr. Meany had a fine Irish temper. But these two men had mutual respect and other people were angry that Mr. Meany and Mr. Randolph were not angry with each other. They disagreed on method, and Mr. Randolph felt that unions should be aggressive in combatting racial discrimination or thrown out of the AFL-CIO and the rest of it. Mr. Meany was not going to go that round. But on Africa, they had no differences. Mr. Randolph's voice on colonialism was the voice that President Meany concurred with. We were being asked by the trade unions in Africa to help them.

AFL-CIO International Representative

In 1955, the AFL and the CIO merged into one federation, consolidating their international activities. After the merger, the international department intensified its work with unions in the rest of the world. This included developing labor education programs and job training centers in Africa.[14] While there were many political and ideological reasons for labor's involvement in Africa, Maida's main concern "was to develop a cadre of trained African trade unionists who would be prepared to participate in the development of their independent countries."[15] She developed lasting friendships with men such as Tom Mboya, who became general secretary of the Kenya Federation of Labor. She was influential in interpreting their goals to the American labor movement and focusing the AFL-CIO's attention on the problems in their countries.[16] During this time, Maida remained very involved with ILGWU Local 22. In 1960, however, she joined the international staff of the AFL-CIO, and devoted her energies full time to Africa.[17]

One of my experimental projects was based on a discussion with some African leaders, one from Rhodesia and one from Nigeria. I developed a program for trade union leaders in the African needle trades or related industries. Some of us had been thinking for years that while you taught the rudiments of trade union representation and the functioning of an organization that has to function with officers and representation and writing letters properly and learning how to deal with management, there was a second phase, which I was particularly interested in. That was training workers in employment.

So, beginning in 1956, these trade unionists, these garment workers, talked to me and said, "You are our sister in the needle trades; you see the need. We need to upgrade and we need to teach ourselves. Could you help us?" Well, I tried for years and we were getting nowhere with it. I did a memorandum. This was roughly '61–'62. President Meany said, "Well, if you can put together the arrangement, this based on the request of the trade union movement in Africa, the AFL-CIO will be supportive in the ways that we need to be. You just go and work it out with President Dubinsky."

I always knew that when President Dubinsky raved and stormed, if I kept quiet, I had won. He said, "Springer, you always come with your unilateral ideas," and I said, "No, this is not a unilateral idea, it's a recommendation. I've gone to President Meany with this, and he's approved it. You have the school and I have come to ask you. . . . there are workers in our industry in Africa who need to improve the standard of their representation, as well as their knowledgeability of our standard of work." Finally, he said, "Go ahead and act," and so it came to pass. I have been singularly fortunate because the leadership of the American labor movement has always given me the kind of leeway for what was unorthodox. Well, the school is now fourteen years old. This was nation building; this was looking toward independence and looking toward a way that the trade union movement could work with the independence movement.

I worked at this with the commercial workers in Africa; worked with the motor drivers to set up a school in Nigeria. I saw the training of workers in industrial competence as a priority second to their knowledgeability on dealing with the employer and understanding the union contract and the legislation in their country.

Tom Mboya, General Secretary of the Kenyan Labor Federation, on his first trip to the United States in the fifties, was here under the auspices of the American Committee on Africa. The organization had very little money and I always offered help in my small way—a room. We had an old house in Brooklyn, a typewriter, a telephone, and food.

We didn't have money, but these were the things we shared with dozens of young Africans who were in the United States for various purposes. He was twenty-three years old when I met him in 1955. He and my son were peers in age—I don't know who was a few years younger—and so I always thought that Tom was my second son. He was probably forty-six in terms of his sense of the fitness of things, his keen perception, his composure, and his rapid mind. He was a very rare human being. He never lost his sense of humor.

In the mid-fifties, preventive detention was still the way of life in Kenya under British rule, and Africans had to be off the street by nine o'clock at night unless you had a pass. Unless you had some reason— that you were working somewhere or you were doing something—you could be arrested summarily. I have been threatened with arrest because as I walked down the street it was assumed that I was an African woman being on the street without a permit or some reason for being on the street. I've attended many meetings of local trade unions in Kenya and was careful to protect the leadership from breaking curfews and other laws that put them in jail. When it got to be nearly nine o'clock, Tom had already organized the ways in which everyone could get back home, to ensure that they were not arrested.

So Tom and I worked on many projects. I suppose the one that stands as a memorial to our work is Solidarity House, the trade union center in Nairobi; the William Green Fund contributed the first $35,000 for the building. Vice-President Randolph presented the check to the Kenya Federation of Labor. In the planning process, we had gone around to the then colonial government with a simple statement of fact. The idea was that the workers in Kenya would do something like buy a brick as their involvement and contribution to it. And so we tried to state this. We were suspect, of course, by the colonial government, but since we had nothing to hide, we gave the Kenya Federation of Labor rationale and its American counterpart supporting it, which subsequently became international support, through the International Confederation of Free Trade Unions. In July 1978, there was a seminar for women workers and the opening cere- mony was held at Solidarity House. The tradition, the history, of this workers' center continues.

The Women's Movement

Throughout her long career, Maida expanded opportunities for wo- men workers and fought discrimination on the basis of sex as well as race within both the workplace and the labor movement. She fought for women garment workers across the United States. In 1959, she advocated for a vocational school for African women and in the 1960s helped to establish the Institute for Tailoring and Cutting for women and men in the garment industry in Kenya. In 1970, she became vice-president of the National Council of Negro Women. In 1980, as a consultant to the Asian American Free Labor Institute, she helped establish the women's bureau of the Turkish Federation of Labor. Her concerns with race, women workers, and international affairs came together at the World Conference of the United Nations' Decade for Women in Mexico City, in 1975. She also came to recognize the limits of her special status. While helping with organizing drives in the South, she noted in a letter to Dubinsky that "Negro workers are aware of their need of a strong trade union movement, but we need also to believe that the trade union movement has moved from the concept of a few chosen for their high visibility to an inclusiveness which makes unionism meaningful to all the workers in industry and at all levels."[18]

I am a supporter of the women's movement. In the same way that I think the labor movement is very often misunderstood, I think that the women's movement is misunderstood. The women's movement should be here to stay. It's simply another step in our development. I am a retired member of the Coalition of Labor Union Women (CLUW). There was a need for such an organization. The National Organization for Women has settled down. Both NOW and CLUW are training grounds for building self-assurance and for participating in constructive ways.

The IWY, International Women's Year, the meeting in Mexico City, was a turning point in the historical development of the role of women. The press emphasized the conflict because that's what sells. I was in Mexico City as a part of the program of the National Council of Negro Women. I was then a vice-president of the National Council of Negro Women. We had within the conference our own program of meetings with women from Africa, the Caribbean, and Latin America. Dr. Dorothy Height, President of the National Council of Negro Women, then hosted twenty-seven of these women, who traveled with us after Mexico City, because this was part of the International Memorial Year for Mary McLeod Bethune, the beloved African-American educator and civil rights reformer, and we were celebrating Mrs. Bethune's 100th birthday. These women went to Mississippi with us to look at rural development, at the kinds of programs that are very related to the kinds of programs there are in Africa, in the Caribbean, and in Latin America.

International Women's Year, as far as I'm concerned, was a very constructive way of reaching across the world to women. There was much that was substantive and what many people forget is that we are not talking about International Women's Year, and, thank you very much, it's finished. We are talking about International Women's Decade, which is a ten-year period. There are meetings going on all around the United States, regional meetings, and there are meetings going on in many countries. There are programs as a result that are being structured.

Anything that's underfinanced is vulnerable. A women's program is almost always taken tongue-in-cheek and the assumption is "Let's get on with it and perhaps we can forget about it after." But the problem is that the women are not going to let anyone forget about it after, because every nation in the world subscribed to the document of International Women's Year and International Women's Decade. Now the fact that programmatically there has to be a great deal of effort made and funds provided for continuity, therein lies the tale. I don't think we will get 100 percent of our objective, but then nothing ever does. Oh, I'm enormously pleased and fortunate that I was one of the minor participants in the International Women's Year.

Work and Family

Long before commuter marriages, blended families, and caring for elderly parents were the subject of research, popular articles, and policy debates, Maida was living these issues. During her years working in Africa she remained based in the United States because she was the head of a household that included her son, her elderly grandmother, who moved from Panama when she was 94, her mother, and her elderly stepfather. In 1965, Maida resigned from the International Department of the AFL-CIO and returned to the ILGWU for a combination of work and family reasons. She explained that there were increasing tensions between her trade union worlds in Africa and the United States, as many African leaders focused increasingly on nation building and absorbed the labor unions, limiting the workers' freedom of association. That same year she married James Kemp, a lawyer, who was president of Local 189 of the Building Service Employees Union from 1946 to 1983. He was an active leader in the Chicago Federation of Labor and the Chicago NAACP, sharing Maida's commitment to both labor and the black community, and he very much wanted Maida to return to work in the United States. Although she and Kemp separated several years later, they stayed in contact until his death in 1983. Maida reflects on the importance of family and work in her life.

My son grew up in a period when there were still very limited opportunities for the young black intellectual. The advice I gave him was, "Pursue excellence, but be the best you know how to be. Then, whatever the context of your capabilities, always remember that you give a helping hand to someone who is striving, because there but for the grace of God, there you go. You are always one step removed from a mother who was a factory worker and from a grandmother who eventually owned a beauty parlor but before that worked as a domestic in this country. Never forget that."

I think the best contribution I have made is to have set an example for my son, who is a lawyer, but who has never forgotten that his responsibility is not only to himself and his family, but that he has a social responsibility to give back something to the society that helped to fashion his life. And to see his children now growing up with a sense of history. They have parents who are teaching them that they have a commitment—that's my best contribution.

The next is a privilege that in the labor movement, I have been able to learn and learn enough to make me humble, and always know I've got to pay back something. I'm an industrial worker and I have had some of the best training and best experience in the world. I come out of a factory. While I have attended a variety of schools, I always try to learn things. I've none of the snob labels; I've never taken myself seriously.

I haven't told you about my failures. You have a lot of those, too. You make bad judgments. I had learned early on: you have a disappointment, you get up, you wipe the blood away and go on to the next thing. Don't dwell on it. I've had my share of bloody experiences. I usually recover very quickly. As I look back on it, the bad spots were my being too highly motivated, too highly emotional about what I was doing. Very often I didn't see it from the outside, but I was so involved in what I was doing that I was blind to the motivations of others and my trust was misplaced. This happens to everybody. We wipe the blood off our noses and keep going.

In whatever field, pursue excellence; learn as much as you can about your field; do not wear your ability across your chest. If you have it, you do not need to flaunt it. Have a sense of history and do not believe that you created the wheel, because you will always learn that there were wheels there long before you came along, and that what you are doing is building. Have a sense of community identity. Give something back to society; give something back to your forbears. Never be so single-minded that you think there is only one way to live and only one choice. Learn not to be bitter about defeats and not to be arrogant about successes; each can limit you. Life is a combination of things: family; sharing; a personal relationship, which does not rob you of your self-respect and your own identity.

Always remember that the person who has done something against you—or the society, the people in that society—they are the lesser human beings than you are, or else they would not have to resort to denying you the right to opportunity. They are smaller people than you are, because in order for them to be superior they must teach you to be inferior. Never let anyone do that to you. Always remember, if bruised, you hurt; if bruised, they hurt. If cut, you bleed; if cut, they bleed. They have an Almighty that they go to in their end, as you do, and if one can get a perspective on all of this, even though you're temporarily humiliated, look at the source from which it comes, and never stop respecting yourself.

Sister Maida

In 1965, Dubinsky offered Maida a vice-presidency in the ILGWU, but without a membership base in the union, she declined and instead became a general organizer in the South. As a troubleshooter, she was involved in organizing drives in North and South Carolina, Georgia, and Florida. In 1969, she focused her attention more on the Chicago area as Midwest director of the A. Philip Randolph Institute, an organization Randolph established to work on issues of race, workers, and unions. She continued to travel to Africa on behalf of unions, African Americans, and women workers. In 1973, she returned to Africa, first joining the staff and later acting as a consultant to the AFL-CIO affiliate, the African-American Labor Center (AALC). In 1985, she attended the World Conference on the United Nations' Decade for Women in Kenya. In 1991, she spent the winter traveling in East Africa with her family and also had an opportunity to visit old friends. Today, she lives in Pittsburgh, Pennsylvania, near her son, who is a lawyer, and his family. She continues to travel and welcome visitors to her home.[19]

Maida Springer-Kemp is a remarkable woman. Some years ago, Dr. Julius Nyerere, president of Tanzania, wrote to A. Philip Randolph that "in Tanganyika she is 'Sister Maida' in more than a conventional sense. She is one of them. She is equally at home in Kenya. She has already worked a near miracle in Uganda where she helped to reunite a labour movement which was being fragmented."[20] Today, for many women and men on several continents, she remains "Sister Maida" in more than a conventional sense.

NOTES

1. The first interview documenting Maida Springer-Kemp's labor career was conducted in 1977, by oral historian Elizabeth Balanoff for the four-year, nationwide oral history project, "The Twentieth-Century Trade Union Woman: Vehicle for Social Change," sponsored by the Labor Studies Center at the University of Michigan, funded by a seed grant from the Rockefeller Family Foundation, and directed by Joyce L. Kornbluh, head of the Labor Studies Center Program on Women and Work. This project taped and transcribed over eighty interviews with women trade union rank-and-file, elected leaders, and staff in the United States and Puerto Rico. Transcripts of all the interviews are deposited at the Bentley Library at the University of Michigan. Selected transcripts, including Maida Springer-Kemp's, are also deposited at the George Meany Labor Archives, Schlesinger Library, Radcliffe College, and the Walter P. Reuther Archives on Urban and Labor Affairs, Wayne State University. Excerpts from the Balanoff interview are found in the "Black Women's Oral History Project," published by K. G. Saur, Schlesinger Library, Radcliffe College, Cambridge, Massachusetts. The project also published _Working Women's Roots: An Oral History Primer_ (Ann Arbor, 1979) and conducted workshops on oral history techniques for local union activists.

In 1994, an additional interview with Maida Springer-Kemp was conducted by Brigid O'Farrell in preparation for the book _Rocking the Boat_, forthcoming from Rutgers University Press. Related articles include the African-American Labor Center, _AALC Reporter_, Vol. 27, No. 4, 1992, and _AALC Reporter_, Vol. 28, No. 1, 1993; and ILGWU _Justice_, February 1986. The interview quotes in this article are edited from these oral history interviews and articles. Maida Springer-Kemp's papers are available at the Schlesinger Library and the Amistad Center, Tulane University, New Orleans, Louisiana.

In 1994, Dr. Yevette Richards, at the University of Pittsburgh, completed a doctoral dissertation on Maida Springer-Kemp, which she graciously shared with us. Her historical data, insights, and analyses have been enormously helpful. _"My Passionate Feeling About Africa": Maida Springer-Kemp and the American Labor Movement_, Volumes I and II: A Dissertation Presented to the Faculty of the Graduate School of Yale University (May 1994), provides over 900 pages on Maida Springer-Kemp's life, with seven chapters of background and analyses alternating with seven chapters of Dr. Richards' in-depth interviews with Maida. She provides rich detail on each of the topics in this article, plus many other important topics not covered here. For example, there is an entire chapter on South Africa. Richards concludes, "This biography enriches the scholarship on pan-African, labor, and women's histories and demonstrates the ways in which international labor relations, pan-Africanism, African independence movements, the United States Civil Rights movement, and Cold War politics are intertwined. . . . This collaborative work demonstrates the power of her oral testimony to reshape our understanding of the past (Richards, pp. 22 and 891).

We acknowledge, with appreciation, the contributions of Elizabeth Balanoff, Mary Anne Forbes, Lucile DiGirolamo, and Caitlin O'Farrell. We sincerely thank Yevette Richards for sharing her manuscript and for reviewing this article. Most importantly, we would like to thank Maida Springer-Kemp for sharing her life story with all of us.

2. The garment industry in New York, the growth of the ILGWU, and the relationship to the Communist Party is described by Philip Foner in *Women and the American Labor Movement from World War I to the Present* (New York: The Free Press, 1980).

3. Charles "Sasha" Zimmerman emigrated to the U.S. in 1913. A member of the Communist Party, he was expelled from the ILGWU in 1925. He was reinstated in the union in 1931, and served as a vice-president of the union and general manager of the New York Dress Joint Board from 1934 until he retired in 1972. Luigi Antonini (1883–1968) was general secretary of Local 89 and vice-president of the union from 1934 to 1967. See Gary Fink, *The Biographical Dictionary of American Labor Leaders* (Westport, CT: Greenwood Press, 1974).

4. The American Labor Party (ALP) was formed in 1937 by the leaders of the ILGWU and the Amalgamated Clothing Workers Union to help unite progressive people in support of Franklin D. Roosevelt. Although Maida did not seriously want to run for office, she became the first trade union member nominated from a Harlem district and won the primary on the ALP ticket. See Richards, Chapter 3, and "Maida Springer Represents New Type Leader Harlem Could Use," *New York Amsterdam News*, 1942, Maida Springer-Kemp Papers, box 1, folder 8, Schlesinger Library.

5. Richards provides a detailed history of the African American labor movement in Harlem. Chapter 2 deals with "the strong connections between the ILGWU leadership and the anti-communist black civil rights and trade union leadership" (p. 173). In 1935, 110 black and white AFL delegates organized the Negro Labor Committee, which offered organizing and education programs for the black community at their headquarters, the Harlem Labor Center. Competing programs were offered by the Garveyite Harlem Labor Union, the Father Divine Movement, and the communist-run Negro Labor Victory Assembly. The Hudson Shore Labor School was an interracial workers' education institution established by Hilda Worthington Smith in 1935 as a continuation of her work as director of the Bryn Mawr Summer School for Women Workers, started in 1921.

6. Richards, p. 247

7. For additional information on A. Philip Randolph and the rally, although not Maida's role, see Jervis Anderson, *A. Philip Randolph: A Biographical Portrait* (New York: Harcourt Brace Jovanovich, Inc., 1972). The

complicated fight by Randolph and the black community to end discrimination and achieve equality in employment in both government, the military, and the private sector during World War II is also described by Doris Kearns Goodwin in *No Ordinary Time: Franklin and Eleanor Roosevelt: The Home Front in World War II* (New York: Simon and Schuster, 1994).

8. According to Richards (p. 259), Maida was the second black business agent for Local 22 and the first to be responsible for a district. Edith Ransome was the first black business agent and the first black staff member of Local 22. She settled prices for finishers, but was not responsible for a district.

9. Richards, p. 1.

10. Peterson was a workers' educator and lobbyist for the ACWU; director of the U.S. Department of Labor Women's Bureau; and advisor to Presidents Kennedy, Johnson, and Carter. Robinson was an activist laundry worker with ACWU, who later served with Peterson at the Women's Bureau, was active with Maida at the National Council of Negro Women, and went on to receive a law degree and teach. Pauline Newman (1891–1986) was one of 20,000 shirtwaist workers in New York City who went on strike in the winter of 1909–1910, an event referred to as the Uprising of 20,000. She also survived the Triangle Shirtwaist Company fire in 1911, in which 146 workers, mostly women, were killed ("Twentieth-Century Trade Union Woman" interview). Fannia Cohen (1885–1962) was the first female vice-president of an international union. Rose Schneiderman (1884–1972) was president of the WTUL from 1926 until it disbanded in 1950. "The Twentieth-Century Trade Union Woman: Vehicle for Social Change" project includes interviews with Esther Peterson, Dollie Lowther Robinson, and Pauline Newman.

11. For an analysis of labor and the Roosevelt Administration, see Steven Fraser, *Labor Will Rule: Sidney Hillman and the Rise of American Labor* (New York: The Free Press, 1991).

12. The importance of this event, and the luncheon honoring Maida, are described in "Women Labor Leaders Are Going to England in Good-Will Exchange With 4 From There," *New York Times*, January 10, 1945, as well as the *New York Amsterdam News*, February 1945, Maida Springer-Kemp Papers, box 1, folder 8, Schlesinger Library.

13. The International Confederation of Free Trade Unions was established in 1949 in London, when many democratic unions left the communist-dominated World Federation of Trade Unions.

14. A review of the labor movement's long, complicated, and sometimes controversial history in the international arena is beyond the scope of this article. It is clear, however, that members of the Communist Party were forced out of the unions after World War II and that during the Cold War the AFL-CIO's international initiatives were guided by a strong anti-communist policy that coincided with the foreign policy of the U.S. government. Maida had rejected the communists organizing in Harlem

during the 1930s, worked closely with the leadership of the ILGWU, and supported the AFL-CIO policies during the Cold War.

15. Richards, p. 14.
16. Tom Mboya became the General Secretary of the Kenya Federation of Labor in 1953. He was assassinated on 5 July 1969, leaving Jomo Kenyatta, whom Maida had met in 1945, the undisputed leader of Kenya. See David Goldsworthy, *Tom Mboya: The Man Kenya Wanted to Forget,* (New York: Africana Publishing Company, 1982), and "Tom Mboya: In Memoriam," by Maida Springer-Kemp, "AFL-CIO Free Trade Union News," August 1969 (in Richards, p. 682).
17. During a 1958 strike, for example, she was described as a "militant Black woman" who told the strikers, "Our union will tolerate no gunka-munka business in the enforcement of future contracts!" Gunka-munka, described by President Dubinsky as a blend of dilly-dallying and monkey business by chiselers on the employer side, became the strike slogan of the 105,000 striking dressmakers. See Tracy Sugarman, "Echoes on Paper, Reflections on My Garment Workers Sketchbook, 1958," *Labor's Heritage,* Winter 1993, p. 35.
18. Richards, p. 850, letter from Springer-Kemp to Dubinsky, 23 November 1965.
19. Richards also traveled to Africa with Maida and interviewed several people familiar with Maida's life and work. For an analyses of union policy and South Africa, see "The AALC Comes to South Africa," chapter 6.
20. Richards, p. 518.

This article is adapted from a chapter in Rocking the Boat: Women Activists in the Labor Movement, *forthcoming from Rutgers University Press, edited by Brigid O'Farrell and Joyce L. Kornbluh.* **Brigid O'Farrell** *is a senior associate at the Center for Women Policy Studies. Recent publications include "Women in Blue-Collar Occupations: Traditional and Nontraditional," in* Women: A Feminist Perspective *(Mountain View, CA: Mayfield Publishing Company, 1995), co-authorship of "Unions, Hard Hats, and Women Workers," in* Women and Unions: Forging a Partnership *(Ithaca, NY: ILR Press, 1993), and co-editorship of* Work *and* Family: Policies for a Changing Work Force *(Washington, DC: National Academy Press, 1991).*

Joyce L. Kornbluh *founded and directed the Program on Women and Work at the University of Michigan Labor Studies Center. Her publications include* Rebel Voices: An IWW Anthology *(Ann Arbor: University of Michigan Press, 1963);* A New Deal for Workers Education: The Workers Service

Program 1934–1943 *(Urbana: University of Illinois Press, 1989); and, with Brigid O'Farrell, "You Can't Giddyup By Saying Whoa! Esther Peterson Remembers Her Organized Labor Years,"* Labor's Heritage, *Spring 1994 (Vol. 5, No. 4). Kornbluh currently teaches for Goddard College and for the Antioch College Degree Program in Labor Studies at the George Meany Center for Labor Studies, AFL-CIO.*

Maida Springer-Kemp (far right), International Ladies' Garment Workers' Union, AFL, was one of four women who went to England through the U.S. Office of War Information Exchange to share wartime experiences in 1945. She was the first African-American woman to represent labor abroad. Other members of the delegation were (from left to right): Grace Blackett, United Automobile Workers, CIO; Anne Murcovich, American Federation of Hosiery Workers, CIO; and Julia O'Connor Parker, International Brotherhood of Electrical Workers, AFL.

Autobiography and Reconstructing Subjectivity at the Bryn Mawr Summer School for Women Workers, 1921–1938

Karyn L. Hollis

> "Bryn Mawr has given me a new definition of internationalism and a new feeling for the word 'tolerant,' " writes . . . a cigar worker from a southern mill. "At first I thought my mother would have a fit if she knew I was going around with the cotton mill girls. Now I see that they are just as nice girls as anyone else, and I am trying to get them to come to our club [YWCA Industrial Club]. I got acquainted too with a lot of the Russian girls, and learned a lot from them."
>
> —Hilda Worthington Smith

When I first read the narratives written by students at the Bryn Mawr Summer School for Women Workers, I was moved and excited by the growth in intellect, self-confidence, and political awareness I could see in the texts before me. Clearly, these working women benefited greatly from the eight-week immersion in liberal arts and labor economics offered on a beautiful suburban college campus where, in the words of a student, "the scent of the honey suckles made us feel that we were in heaven." The Summer School was the first of four resident workers' colleges for women established in the 1920s and 1930s, and students were offered some of the luxuries their more elite counterparts experienced during the fall and spring terms. They were taken on field trips to local museums and factories, honored with teas and luncheons, taught to swim and play tennis, and treated to guest lectures by W. E. B. Du Bois, Margaret Sanger, Norman Thomas, Francis Perkins, Harold Laski, Walter Reuther, Eleanor Roosevelt, as well as many other renowned labor, political, academic, and feminist leaders. This extraordinary pedagogical experiment also offers one of the few instances in American women's history of a successful cross-class alliance among upper-, middle-, and working-class women from a variety of ethnic, religious, and geographic backgrounds.

In short, the more I learned about the Summer School, the more convinced I was of its relevance to teachers and scholars interested in improving women's lives. As women recover their history, the individuals, organizations, commitments, and struggles we unveil provide valuable examples that lend strength and understanding to our current endeavors. In the Bryn Mawr Summer School for Women Workers we find an important antecedent to the feminist and progressive pedagogies we strive to develop today.

Although I am now at work on a book that analyzes all the writing done at the school, in this essay I will look only at autobiographical narratives.[1] The women wrote copiously at the urging of the predominantly female faculty, whose student-centered pedagogy helped transform dreams, desires, and fears into demands. In their textual self-(re)presentations these working women developed more critical and powerful voices by adapting the various discursive formations culturally available to them for their own, often collective, ends. My analysis of this discursive subjectivity will be informed by literary autobiographical criticism and linked to the current composition research on gender and autobiography.

A School for Women Workers

The Bryn Mawr Summer School for Women Workers was an indirect response to the favorable climate for women's rights and worker education which prevailed during the Progressive era. Its founding was more directly due to the efforts of the National Women's Trade Union League, which in 1916 called on the women's colleges to do more to educate working women, and to two feminist educators connected to Bryn Mawr: M. Carey Thomas, suffragette and president of the college for thirty-five years; and Hilda Worthington Smith, Bryn Mawr graduate, dean, and director of the Summer School for thirteen years. During its seventeen-year history approximately fifteen hundred working women, eighty to one hundred each summer, attended the school. Appointed by Thomas to head the school, Smith attracted the upper- and middle-class Bryn Mawr alumnae to the cause of worker education through a flood of promotional publications and presentations.[2] While alumnae committees did the bulk of recruiting and fund-raising, the school was also assisted by the Industrial Department of the YWCA, the National Women's Trade Union League, labor unions, churches, corporate and private benefactors, and former Summer School student alumnae groups. The school very consciously aimed for and achieved diversity in its student body, with the largest number of working women coming from the needle trades of the Northeast. Many were fairly recent immigrants from Russia or Eastern Europe. The school required an eighth-grade education and recruited women eighteen to thirty-five years old, with the average age being twenty-five.

As years passed, students and faculty pushed for a stronger alliance with progressive elements of organized labor. By 1938 the connection to labor had alienated a great many Bryn Mawr trustees and alumnae. After an incident in which the school was falsely accused of supporting a strike (forbidden in the administrative agreement with the college), it was asked to leave the Bryn Mawr campus. The school then moved to the Smith family estate in upstate New York and continued there as the coeducational Hudson Shore Labor College. The college closed its doors in 1952, as workers turned to short-term classes offered by unions, university residential and nonresidential courses, and university labor education programs to meet their educational needs.

Developing a Pedagogy: Faculty and Students Together

It was quite an honor to teach at the Summer School. Included among the faculty were distinguished professors from colleges and universities across the nation who gave up their summer research opportunities to come to the Bryn Mawr campus; others were high school teachers or YWCA Industrial Department administrators; still others had eschewed traditional educational careers to devote themselves year round to worker instruction. The majority were women with a strong commitment to women's education. They formed a close-knit, cooperative academic community, drawing on one another for disciplinary knowledge, teaching techniques, and administrative skills.

Democratic participation in administrative and curricular matters by faculty and students alike was a cornerstone of the workers' education movement much promoted by Smith, and students were given an equal vote on all governing committees.[3] The policy-making Joint Administration Committee adopted the mission statement of the Summer School in 1923, according to which, the school was to provide

> young women in industry opportunities to study liberal subjects and to train themselves in clear thinking; to stimulate an active and continued interest in the problems of our economic order; to develop a desire for study as a means of understanding and of enjoyment in life. The School is not committed to any theory or dogma.

> The teaching is carried on by instructors who have an understanding
> of the students' practical experience in industry and of the labor
> movement. It is conducted in a spirit of impartial inquiry, with
> freedom of discussion and teaching. It is expected that thus the
> students will gain a truer insight into the problems of industry, and
> feel a more vital responsibility for their solution (Smith, *Women
> Workers* 7).

In attempting to carry out these aims, the faculty developed a pedagogy derived from several sources: the worker and adult education
movements in the United States and abroad, Deweyan educational
philosophy, leftist and liberal social thought, and, to a certain extent,
feminist principles. Faculty often worked individually with the wom-
en, and undergraduate assistants from the other eastern women's
colleges participated in various capacities, from tutors to typists.

Curriculum committees met almost daily during the summer session and frequently during the year to work on issues of instruction at
the school. The curriculum was critiqued and amended in response to
student suggestions and criticisms as well as faculty's perceptions of
what worked and didn't work. One basic principle, however, remained
constant: that workers' own experiences should be central to their
education. Regarding the importance of using workers' own lives as a
starting point for intellectual inquiry, Smith wrote that "it may seem
like an illogical arrangement of material," but "learning is strangely
illogical." "It is only teaching which aims to be logical and in so doing
it often misses the necessary contact which results in learning. The
contact must be with the experience of the worker and the starting
point—logical or illogical—must be there" (*Education* 25). Smith and
other faculty believed workers had a right to an education that revealed their personal role in economic production and which would
help them improve their daily lives.

Women Workers and the Autobiographical Assignment

Since personal experience was to play such a key role in the course of
instruction at the Summer School, it is not surprising that writing an
autobiography was one of the first tasks the women were assigned in
their English composition class (Heller, "Blue Stockings" 119) Indeed,
when interviewed, former instructor Alice Hansen Cook emphasized
the importance the faculty gave to the autobiography assignment and
stressed that the assignment "was something that we all did."

Today some feminist and poststructuralist critics express a certain
distrust of autobiography, and, as I will discuss, some compositionists

have warned of the gender-related problems inherent in this genre (see Rose; Flynn; Sirc; and Peterson). Sidonie Smith maintains that, "during the past five hundred years, autobiography has assumed a central position in the personal and literary life of the West precisely because it serves as one of those generic contracts that reproduces the patrilineage and its ideologies of gender" (*A Poetics* 44). In other words, autobiographical subjectivity is compromised by andro-centric illusions of a unified, autonomous self that "valorizes individual integrity and separateness and devalues personal and communal interdependency" (39).

While faculty working at the Summer School in the 1920s and 1930s could not have had a contemporary poststructuralist understanding of subjectivity, they were not entirely uncritical of bourgeois subjectivity either. Judging from their assignments, faculty saw autobiography as a way to represent the reconstruction of a subjectivity that was able to be both self-critical and critical of the status quo. Perhaps because of their close association with their working-class students, faculty came to understand the needs and perspectives of these "Others." In fact, the faculty also seemed aware of the disadvantages their own class background imposed on their ability to know their students. In her book on worker education Smith wrote:

> The first concern of the teacher should be to discover the special interests and the occupational backgrounds of his students. . . . Without this background of detailed knowledge . . . the teacher may plan instruction which is remote from any real significance in their daily lives (*Education* 25).

Smith and her faculty thus regarded the student autobiographies as a source of information crucial to their classroom success. Another benefit of the autobiographical assignment, therefore, was that it helped the faculty understand whom they were teaching.

In a relevant study of Victorian working-class autobiography Regina Gagnier has shown the unfortunate results that can occur when working-class autobiographical subjects, both male and female in this case, do not go beyond prevailing autobiographical conventions. Those working-class subjects—who attempted to construct a subjectivity in terms of bourgeois norms such as close family upbringing, lengthy schooling, romantic love and marriage, and a progressively successful career—often experienced both narrative and psychological breakdowns because of the disparity between what has often happened to them and what they believe should have happened in bourgeois ideological terms. Gagnier finds that a happier outcome occurs when the working-class writer recognizes the difficulty, if not the impossibility, of *embourgeoisement* and critiques the inequities of working-class life, gaining strength through the representation of a collective subjectivity (114).

Typical of the English composition instructors at the Summer School was longtime faculty member Ellen Kennan. Teaching at the school from 1925 to 1938, she began all her classes with an auto-biographical assignment, which, as we will see, was modified over the years in ways that took her students' life experiences into account and required a more critical response from her students. The two versions of the assignment which follow reflect Kennan's growing awareness that worker's lives did not mirror the ideal bourgeois life pattern of familial nurturing, uninterrupted schooling, romantic love, and career but, instead, likely involved truncated schooling and economically strained family relationships.[4]

Kennan's 1926 Autobiography Assignment

The first assignment is to write an essay about yourself. The following questions are not designed as a kind of third degree. They are suggestions merely. Please answer as many of them as you will and add anything in your life which seems to you to have influenced you.

What is your age?
Where were you born?
How far did you go in school?
What studying have you done since you left school?
What work do you do now?
At what age did you begin?
How did you happen to take up that kind of work?
Do you like it?
What work would you like to do if you had your choice and the training for it? What would be your second choice?
How did you happen to come to this school?
What do you want to get from the school?
Name the three books which you have read which you enjoyed the most.
What amusements are you fond of?
What things in your training (either from your parents or teachers) are you beginning to feel doubtful about?

Even in this early version of the assignment Kennan clearly wanted her students to take a critical perspective on their lives. "Do you like it [your work]?" she prompts, and "What work would you like to do if you had your choice and the training for it?" With a final question such as "What things in your training are you beginning to feel doubtful about?" she avoids encouraging received opinions about how her students' lives should be unfolding.

Kennan's 1934 Autobiography Assignment

First Composition
I. Family and Background
II. Childhood:
> What is the first thing that you can remember?
> What do you remember that you wish you could forget?
> Did you have a grandmother?
> What thing in your childhood are you glad about?

III. Education
> What schools did you go to?
> What did you get outside of schools?
> What did you fail to get?
> What did you get that you later found untrue?
> What friends did you have? Were they lasting ones?

IV. Work
> Did you choose it?
> Do you like it?
> What work would you do if you had your choice?

V. What do you do for fun?
> (Do you read, for example? What sort of books? Do you go to plays? Do you enjoy games, music, dancing?
> Note: Don't take any of these questions as commands. Answer what you please. Tell everything about yourself that you will and can.

If you do not wish to write an autobiography, the following questions may suggest a different kind of composition:
I. What kind of life would you live if you could arrange your life just as you wished—if you could do as you wish and be what you wish?
II. What beliefs and ideas that you have grown up in [*sic*] are you beginning to question? What ones have you cast aside entirely? What first caused you to question accepted ideas? Do you now challenge some things that you formerly considered sacred?
III. If there is a particular subject that you have in mind and wish to write upon, you may do it, regardless of the other suggestions.

Eight years later Kennan has expanded the assignment and divided it into five parts. Even though the categories may reflect bourgeois life patterns, the questions asked encourage a critical examination of these patterns. Omitted from the 1934 assignment are the specific inquiries about age and birthplace, perhaps because this information was easily obtained from the lengthy application forms available on each student or perhaps because such facts were not pertinent to the tasks ahead. We see that Kennan now invites her students to write on "Family and Background" as well as "Childhood." Perhaps she wanted to help students understand how these culturally derived constructs or discourses shaped the selves or subjectivities they were representing in their autobiographies. One can only speculate, but she may have found that workers tended to neglect these categories if their experiences hadn't been as "happy" as prevailing ideology required. And, true to her critical aims, she also asks, "What do you remember [about your childhood] that you wish you could forget?" Similarly, Kennan wants a critical perspective on education. She prompts: "What did you get *outside* of schools?" "What did you *fail* to get?" "What did you get that you later found untrue?" (emphasis added). Under the "Childhood" category the question about having a "grandmother" (as opposed to a grandfather) may reveal Kennan's hope for a more woman-centered investigation of family ancestry. Finally, Kennan conveys a more contemporary distrust of autobiographical subjectivity as she recommends that students: "Tell everything that you *will and can.*" Thus, Summer School faculty seem to have believed that the autobiographical assignment could help students discursively move beyond a static, limited version of the self.

Women Workers Writing Autobiographical Narratives

The narratives that follow appeared in *Shop and School*, the student magazine published during every Summer School term. *Shop and School* contained prose, poetry, humor, and labor drama. I examined 163 narratives appearing in the last ten issues of *Shop and School* from 1928 to 1938,[5] the period when the students and faculty were organized into the effective, interdisciplinary "unit system" described earlier. Since many teachers at the school assigned autobiographies, I have not been able to determine who these students' English teachers were. But, while I cannot say for certain that the texts I examined were written for Kennan, the narratives they tell fall readily into the categories set up by her autobiography assignment.[6]

By far the most popular topic among the female students concerned some aspect of their work lives. More than half of the pieces I examined were of this type. Titles include "Waste in My Shop," "My Start in

Industry," "A Working Girl Speaks," "An Incident in My Shop," "Piece Work System," "The Long Arm of the Job," and "My First Experience as an Organizer." As the economic hardships and labor struggles of the 1930s increased, the titles begin to reflect more of this conflict and the resultant difficulties in workers' lives: "A Day Searching for a Job," "The New York Elevator Strike," "My First Arrest," "On the Picket Line," "The 1931 Hosiery Strike in Philadelphia," "An Experience with a Sweatshop Boss," and "The Effect of Unemployment on One's Health."

The next most popular category was education. About 16 percent of the narratives dealt with this topic, whether stressing the value of the Bryn Mawr experience, the need for more workers' education projects, or a critique of earlier educational experiences. Another 15 percent of the pieces in the sample I read concerned "Family and Background." Many of these narratives told how the economic conditions of the times had led to extreme deprivations. Typical titles include: "A Mining Village," "Motherless," "Homeless in Russia," and "My Childhood during the War." As the Depression wore on, workers wrote less about their early childhood experiences and family backgrounds and more about their current economic difficulties in the context of the family— for example, "The Pressure of High Rent" and "The Effect of Unemployment on My Family."

The remaining narratives could be placed for the most part into Kennan's second group of topics. Some students wrote utopian descriptions of lives they would like to lead; others criticized forms of organized religion they had begun to doubt or wrote of a recently acquired sympathy for Southerners, Northerners, African Americans, Jews or immigrant women they had met at the Summer School; or they wrote about how they had begun to think of themselves as public speakers or activists. Still others described the "Funeral of Sacco and Vanzetti," making a speech to the Pennsylvania House of Representatives, a racist incident in a restaurant, or the Pennsylvania Amish. Incidentally, the "fun" category was hardly ever chosen. Smith comments that many workers had to be taught recreation while at the school, never having had the opportunity for it before (*Women Workers* 164).

Narratives on Family and Childhood

The narratives on family, background, and childhood reveal a variety of subject positions, which the writers often represented as evolving into collective narratives of desire and demands. Beulah Parrish, a student at the Summer School in 1930, wrote this brief narrative about life in a southern mill town. A white student from Durham,

North Carolina, Parrish's application revealed that she was twenty-one-years-old when she attended the school. She had never voted and was not a union member, but she was a leader in her church and YWCA Industrial Club. She left school at age thirteen to work in a hosiery mill.

Those Mill Villages
by Beulah Parrish, 1930

> For three years I lived in a southern mill village. I found it very unpleasant. An employer may shout "Cheap Rent" all he wants to, but what do we get for our cheap rent?
>
> The streets of the village are usually narrow and muddy. Sometimes they are poorly lighted. Most of the houses are small and have no bathtubs. In the village where I lived we were not allowed to have telephones. Our lights were turned off at certain hour every night. They were turned on again early in the morning, and then turned off at daylight. The lights were turned on for one day each week so that we could do our ironing.
>
> It seems as though there were always more children in a mill village than anywhere else. Many of the mothers have to work in the mill. Their children, having no one to take care of them, roam about the streets wherever they please.
>
> People are inclined to look down on the people who live in a mill village. The employer seems to think he more or less has control over the people. We workers do not want our employers to give us community houses and cheap rent, with lights and water free. We want wages that will enable us to live in better houses on better streets and to pay for our own amusements. We should feel much more independent—and that is how everybody wants to feel.

Notice how Parrish first represents her subjectivity: " 'I' lived in a southern mill village. 'I' found it very unpleasant." This first-person singular narration is the conventional narrative device for autobiographies. Smith argues that this "narrated I" typically presents a singular, unitary consciousness, the bourgeois subjectivity, which reflects on a painful past to be vanquished as the narrative progresses. As Parrish's example and others show, however, this pattern is not typical of the autobiographical narratives written at the Summer School. Parrish turns over her narrative to a narrating "we," a narrator of participation, a much stronger and more confident collective subject, which, as noted earlier, Gagnier has found to be beneficial to working-class writers. "We workers do not want our employers to give us community houses and cheap rent," writes Parrish. "We want wages that will enable us to live in better houses on better streets." As is typical of this discursive move, the shift in person is often accompanied by a shift in tense. Thus, the exploited "I" is left in the past, while the "we" becomes an active subject of the present or future and plays a public, adversarial role on behalf of all mill village workers. As is also typical, the "we" carries the more resistant stance of the narration. The narrated "I" is critical of her surroundings, but the narrated "we" offers solutions to the exploitation. While "I" generally belongs in the private sphere, "we" ventures into the "public domain." This shift in person, tense, and discursive domain occurred in three-fourths of the narratives I examined, and there is no evidence that such shifts were prompted by the assignment.

As is typical of these working women, Parrish does not seem to have been exposed to a feminist critique of her work or home life, or, if exposed to such a critique, she chose not to make it part of her own discourse. She does not denounce the fact that the female workers she describes probably earned less than the men or that the women most likely returned from mill work to do a shift of housework. Although women's issues of shelter and family predominate in her narrative, they are presented in terms of prevailing cultural standards. For example, her use of the Victorian domestic discourse of woman as nurturer and homemaker legitimizes her struggle for "finer things" in culturally acceptable terms. In another discursive expropriation she uses the androcentric discourse of worker empowerment to achieve a strengthened collective voice. This melding of discourses in her text, and in others that follow, offer examples of Bakhtin's "heteroglossia," amalgams of various social discourses in dialogic interaction. That the women use and exploit various discourses for their own ends, incorporating them with personal discourses connected to their needs of work and family life, corresponds to the notion of "constructed knowledge." Belenky, Clinchy, Goldberger, Matluck, and Tarule argue that women attain constructed knowledge when they welcome, rather than feel threatened by, the thoughts of others, integrating them with subjective information and feelings into a personally meaningful set of beliefs.

The following text was written by an African-American student.

Looking Back
by Eloise Fickland, 1933

> If it were possible for me to turn and look back along the years of some six generations, I'd see my mother's maternal and paternal ancestors in this America.

My mother's mother was a slave. Four generations of these slaves had served four generations of one family. My mother is the result of the joining of the two families. We never knew my father's people. We never saw them and heard very little, for he died before we were old enough to be interested and to ask questions.

My maternal grandmother told many tales of the slave life, and *The War*. Some of these stories were very sad.

From the time I was able to sit on the floor and hold my sister I have had the responsibility of "the children." I was the one to whom each child came with all cares from a scratch to a fight; all secrets I kept, notes from teachers even; all kinds of trouble.

Well do I remember, once, when my next oldest sister and I had to act Santa. My father was away, and my mother was too ill to help. We had just finished trimming the tree, putting around the presents, and filling the stockings when we had to hide as my brother and next sister came down to take a look around. It was a narrow escape.

We were a happy group of youngsters. A group that was so sheltered that it has proven a handicap to some of us.

It is nearly nineteen years now since my father died. Ah! the awful change that death made. My oldest brother had just married. Yes, there was a little insurance. A methodist minister, how can he pay for a large policy with nine children to support?

Depression! The depression started nineteen years ago with us.

Eloise Fickland's autobiographical piece illustrates many characteristics that scholars have found typical of black autobiography. Margo Culley writes that, "for most black women, as for most black men, the foundational category [of being] is race" (8). Thus, Fickland begins her narrative by emphasizing her lengthy roots in this country and identifying herself as a descendant of slaves, an African American. She probably knew that few if any in her audience of predominantly white schoolmates could claim to have had family in the United States for six generations, and this gave her a birthright and legitimacy that may have surprised them.

In another important article, "In Search of the Black Female Self," Regina Blackburn locates three interrelated tasks essential to black women's autobiographies: the first is defining the black self; the second is valuing that self; and the third is achieving an awareness of the double bind that being black and female imposes (136). True to the first of these tasks, Fickland defines herself matrilinearly through her African-American female ancestors and inherits a character and strength that her narrated "I" values greatly. Elizabeth Fox-Genovese has found that black female autobiographers make frequent reference to the love "felt for and felt from their female elders: mothers, aunts, grandmothers" (71). And William L. Andrews has traced this tradition back to the nineteenth-century female slave narratives. "In general, nineteenth-century black autobiographers single out their mothers, sisters and grandmothers for special praise," he writes (227). He continues, however, that, because these autobiographers wanted "to reconcile an absolute moral standard for womanly virtue prescribed by white culture with the actual circumstances of a slave woman's complex lived experience," a certain ambivalence is found in their narratives (230). Perhaps a similar ambivalence motivated Fickland's rather oblique reference to her mother's conception as "the result of the joining of the two families."

Like Parrish, Fickland is concerned with traditional women's issues: the home, mothering, children. Both use the conventions of Victorian domesticity for their own ends. Fickland appropriates this domestic discourse as she presents a self that others in her family come to for solace and comfort. She was a mother with "children" before her time and derives a great deal of self-esteem and self-respect from this role. Fickland offers her experiences, and those of her forebears, as evidence of her authenticity as a woman, again having to legitimize herself, as Fox-Genovese writes, in terms of "bourgeois women's domestic discourse" (83). Neither Parrish nor Fickland explicitly critique this discourse of womanhood, but each use it as a means to get what they want—material comfort, respect, and justice. Fickland, because she is black, must reassure her readers that she approximates the feminine ideal. Parrish, because she is white, can, in this instance, take her gender for granted and directly protest the injustice of being denied middle-class comforts.

Fickland, however, has had to go well beyond the bounds of the white bourgeois or working-class mother and temporarily assume a role traditionally reserved for men. At Christmastime she has played Santa, the mythical male provider, implying what others have stated more explicitly: that black women's status as women has not shielded them from "man's" work. Thus, Blackburn's third theme is present in an emergent form here. Like the other female African-American autobiographers Blackburn studied, Fickland shows an awareness of the double oppression that being both black and female imposes.

Her narration then slips into "we," but not the androcentric, narrating "we" of Parrish, which collectively confronts an oppressive situation in the present. Her "we" is familial, woven in and out of her narrative, firmly connected to her past "I" by close ties of kinship. "We were a happy group of youngsters" she writes, perhaps too "sheltered" to confront successfully the racism of white culture. Suffering has long been a part of this family's collective experience: always present under the surface, it forces its way out in the narrative's bitter ending. Severe deprivation didn't begin with the Depression, as it may have in the white culture. For her family "the depression started nineteen years ago," with the death of her father and the "loss" of her older brother. In earnest, then, Fickland has permanently taken up the role of male provider for her family.

Perhaps Fickland does not use the collective, androcentric voice of worker empowerment because, as the daughter of a minister, she considered herself middle-class, or perhaps she had never been exposed to this rhetoric, or perhaps she rejected it. Since racial discrimination was the overriding historical factor contributing to Fickland's oppression, any discourse that did not give race prime consideration would not likely be adopted by her. Fox-Genovese argues that "the tension at the heart of black women's autobiography derives in large part from the chasm between an autobiographer's intuitive sense of herself and her attitude toward her probable readers" (74). We feel this tension in Fickland's references to her mother's problematic conception, her having to play Santa, her overly sheltered family, and her last overly controlled, embittered statement.

Narratives of Work and Union

In her study of contemporary working-class women's writing Janet Zandy finds that reference to historical events can trigger the narrative response (11). She mentions that several contemporary women poets have written about the great "Triangle Fire" of 1911. Similarly, one of the women at Bryn Mawr wrote about when, as a young woman working nearby in Manhattan, she first learned of the fire.

Sacrifice
by Rose Greenstein, 1930

> The most panic-stricken moment of my life was at the time of the Triangle fire in 1912 [*sic*], when I saw one hundred and fifty-four of my fellow-workers burned to death in a non-union dress shop. But it is not of my own sick horror that I want to tell you. It is of the revelation that that fire brought to all workers, everywhere.
>
> The Triangle Waist and Dress Company was one of the largest of its kind at that time. The firm employed about three hundred people, mostly girls. During the historic strike of the Ladies Waist and Dressmakers' Union of 1909, we did not succeed in organizing that shop, though the workers put up one of the most heroic fights in the

history of the trade. They were out on the streets twenty-six long and bitter weeks, and, finally, broken down by the brutality of the place, they gave up, but with an unbroken spirit. They decided to go back to work, but only to prepare themselves for a renewed struggle, in which they, and not the employers, should be victorious. To the sorrow of the working class, they did not live to see that day.

After the rest of the workers in the garment industry had won for themselves a fifty-hour week, and were working on Saturdays only until one o'clock, the Triangle factory still worked fifty-nine hours. And so it happened that one Saturday a crowd of us, going home at one o'clock from our shop across the street, called up to them a cheerful good-bye. It had become almost a tradition with us to cry out to them: "So long, until the victory is yours!"

But that Saturday was the last time we called. Nor did we ever see those glorious fighters again, for that very day, before five o'clock, they were smothered to death in a blaze that did barely any damage to the building or to the employers. Later, definite proof was brought forward that the doors had been bolted to keep out inspectors and interfering union members, and it was revealed that those who were not actually burned were found huddled together on the floor against locked doors. They had died of suffocation.

Since then, you are sure to find, on the third Sunday in March of every year, a group of workers from the Dressmakers' Union gathered around a grave in Brooklyn. They are honoring twenty-four unidentified victims, who fell in the workers' cause.

In his pioneering essay on working-class women's writing Paul Lauter has pointed to the "instrumental" nature of much working-class women's writing, which, unlike bourgeois autobiography, does not reflect on the path to success followed by an individual but, instead, shows how a collectivity has struggled, and must continue to struggle, for a better life. Lauter also points out that a rich intertextuality links working-class women's narratives to other popular cultural forms and artifacts such as songs, workplace narratives, broadsides, political fables, union banners (18), and, I might add, the Bible and political theory. "Sacrifice," is an example of such a richly intertextual and multivocal construction. Again, Bakhtin's notion of heteroglossia is helpful here, as we notice the various discourses that assist the writer in telling her story.

From her first horrific statement concerning the burned women workers, Greenstein leaves the narrated "I," or "unitary subject," behind. She forcefully refuses to reflect on her "self" or on her unique response to this event: "It is not of my own sick horror that I want to tell you. It is of the revelation that that fire brought to all workers, everywhere." The author then records the history of a working-class struggle for fair wages from the inside, as one worker among many. Her first two paragraphs set the background for the tragedy in terms that reveal a familiarity with organizing tactics and collective, worker-centered interpretations of labor history. "During the historic strike of the Ladies Waist and Dressmakers' Union of 1909, we did not succeed in organizing that shop, though the workers put up one of the most heroic fights in the history of the trade." Greenstein's slightly unidiomatic "Until the victory is yours!" marks her as a recent immigrant, carrying strains of another sociolinguistic experience steeped in European, leftist ideology. Greenstein's phrasing also reveals her familiarity with left-wing texts of worker empowerment: "all workers, everywhere," "to the sorrow of the working class," the "renewed struggle in which they . . . should be victorious." An allusion to messianic revelation and sacrifice is also found in the text. Greenstein says her narrative is about the " 'revelation' that that fire brought to all workers, everywhere"; "It was revealed that those who were not actually burned were found huddled together on the floor against the locked doors." Thus, these young women workers, died together as they worked together, collectively to the bitter end, giving their lives in the fight for workers' rights.

Greenstein shifts into a collective voice similar to Parrish's: "A crowd of us . . . called up to them a cheerful goodbye" and later "Nor did we ever see those glorious fighters again." This is the narrative "we" of worker empowerment, a discourse the writer was familiar with through union and political work. The narrative inclusivity continues with a direct address to the reader, "Since then, you are sure to find. . . ." And she ends with a tribute to the twenty-four unidentified victims, the "nameless," or Others, who fell for the still deferred "workers' cause." Again, it is the narrating "we" that participates in an example of active public resistance.

The next text offers one of the few critiques I found of sexism in unions. The writer, Sarah Gordon, was a Jewish immigrant with family in Russia and Poland. She was thirty-nine years old and had been in the United States for twenty years when she wrote this piece. She spoke Yiddish, Russian, and English. She worked as a hat trimmer and was a member of the Cap and Millinery Workers Union. She had already lost one job and had been blacklisted after a very successful organizing drive among women workers in the glove trade. She had taken courses in literature and economics at the Rand School of Social Science and reports that she read "various daily papers" and "some magazines." Where she acquired her feminism is not evident; perhaps it was from her teachers at the Rand School. Or perhaps some feminism had been instilled in her union by organizers with ties to leftist political parties. For, although rife with sexism themselves, these parties did at least address "the Woman Question" (Coiner 164).

A Typical Day in My Life
by Sarah Gordon, 1929

What does a day in the life of a working girl mean? It seems so insignificant and yet it means so much. I have a habit of saying when I start out in the morning that I am going to war, for war it is for a worker, in an unorganized trade especially. We must always be on the defensive because we never can tell how our day will end; it depends on the mood of our employer. I will however try and describe one of the average days in my life.

I start the day wondering why the car company was allowed to raise the fare and was not made to add one or two cars so that the early morning passengers should at least have a seat. But I have found that there is an advantage in hanging on a strap shaking to and fro; it gives me an opportunity to observe my fellow passengers.

I love to observe people's faces; it is almost like reading books. I always wonder what is going on beyond their calm exteriors. I also like to observe what people are reading, for almost everybody is reading in the train. I have learned to classify people by their reading.

In the morning paper the average girl is reading the novel first, the young man the sports page, the middle-aged business man turns to the stock exchange news, and the elderly, tired-looking man tries to solve the crossword puzzle, probably as a means of relaxation, but very few people read the editorials, or the news of the day unless there is a big headline about a murder, a scandal, or a society wedding.

But I? I read all these people. Out of the train I come up to my shop, full of impressions. I would be glad if I were given work and were allowed to work my day through peacefully. But no!

Just one look at the boss who always wears a grouch on his face, another look at the boy who deals out the work, and at the girls who have come before me, and I instantly feel that there is trouble in the air. I do not question immediately but wait for developments.

In the meantime I have a feeling as though I were sitting on a slumbering volcano, I can never tell on which side the lava will break out. I do not have to wait very long before it comes. The boss cannot forgive the girls for making him pay three or five cents more on a hat. He begins picking at the work; he accuses them of unfairness, the girls defending themselves; there is general confusion.

A little later a heated argument among the girls about the unequal distribution of work, endless talk, some bitter words, general resentment, but who is to blame? The system, the struggle for existence.

Lunch hour—I eat my lunch in a hurry, and go out to the "corner" that is the "labor market" of the trade. There I meet the girls from other shops, also some union officials. We discuss conditions in the trade; we get some information as to what is happening in different places, but the most heated discussions are about the split in the organization. This is now the most vital question of the day.

I come back to work usually under the impression of the argument started on the street and am compelled to continue it, because half of the workers of our shop, that is, the men workers, belong to the opposition and are responsible for the break in our organization. These arguments take on very violent and in many cases dangerous forms. It is a very difficult life for us girls in these days; we have to fight our boss on one side, our union that should otherwise protect us on the other, and we are crushed between the two.

Under such physical and mental strain I finish my day's work.

And then the evening! That much desired evening! I straighten up my shoulders, walk out on the street, sniff some fresh air, and go to eat in a place where I can meet friends. We eat and talk about current events, and then we go to a lecture or a meeting or to see some good play, or to the Symphony Concert according to the day. This the antitoxin which must counteract the poisonous effects of the day in the shop.

As in the other autobiographical narratives, Gordon makes use of a narrative "we" in the present tense and the public domain. But this time the "we" represents women's collective voice: "We have to fight our boss on one side, our union that should otherwise protect us on the other." Another salient characteristic of this piece is the frequent reference to physical violence, with an emphasis on bodily harm. In Gordon's narrative men are the source of this violence, and it is directed at women. She compares a working girl's life with "war." She sits on "slumbering lava" in fear of vitriolic eruptions from her boss as "he begins picking at their work and accus[ing] them of unfairness." Arguments with men in her union take on "violent" and "dangerous" forms. The women are "crushed" between their union and the boss. Sidonie Smith maintains that in bourgeois, androcentric autobiography—whether written by men or women—woman's sexuality, woman's body, her desire, is written out of the text, erased. When female autobiographers begin to address this lack, a new type of subjectivity may be created. In other words, this emphasis on the physicality of woman's experience in autobiography is a resistant, counterhegemonic move, a way to subvert the "metaphysical self" of disembodied, androcentric autobiography ("Resisting" 77). Smith speculates that "with that new subjectivity may come a new system of values, a new kind of language and narrative form, perhaps even a new discourse, an alternative to the prevailing ideology of gender" (*Poetics* 59). While we are now beginning to see that new discourse in the writing of French feminist critics and others, here we see a similar attempt by an American working-class woman as she inserts a language of woman's desire into the previously male-centered discourse of worker collectivity. In her final comment we sense the important regenerative power she experiences when meeting both physical and intellectual needs.

The last self-(re)presentation is by an African-American woman whose experience at the Summer School seems to have changed her life quite dramatically.

It Set Me Thinking
by Marion Jackson, 1937

When first I learned of Bryn Mawr's Summer School for Women Workers in Industry, immediately I decided I would like to attend. I never once took into consideration the true purpose of the school. I have always had a craving for knowledge, but I have never had time or money enough to complete my education; so, when at a YWCA conference I found out about this school, I thought, "Oh, how nice! Now, here's a chance for me to learn a little something. Who knows? Someday it may come in handy."

I have always felt one should learn all one can at every possible opportunity. I am terribly ashamed to say that I thought only of my own selfish gain. I was thinking of a possible chance of getting a better job, and I believe that foremost in my mind was money.

I am a piece-worker in a dress factory. My work is seasonal. It is not a very comfortable feeling when you realize that the end of the season is nigh, and soon your income will cease while your obligations will go on. For that reason I have always hoped for a steady job with steady pay, or, shall I say, secure employment.

I knew that this school was neither a trade nor a vocational one, but I believed that it gave one prestige to attend the school and meant much in one's favor when seeking employment. I therefore set out to gain admittance to Bryn Mawr.

On Monday, June 15, at the official opening exercises, I listened with profound interest to President Park. She related the origin of the school. It was a vision of former president M. Carey Thomas that led her to create a place where women working in industry might go to prepare themselves to meet any problems that might confront them in their field.

Dr. Susan Kingsbury in her address very clearly pointed out that any woman receiving this training should, when she has returned to her home, feel it her duty to render a service to fellow workers through leadership or individual service. There were many more interesting and important facts brought out through these and other speakers—far too numerous for me to mention.

This meeting to me was really an awakening! The true purpose of the school was unfolded.

It set me thinking. I have been asking myself, "What can I, in my small way, do to contribute to labor or humanity? I am only one little insignificant person among a multitude."

At such a time one has a feeling of inferiority, realizing the lack of training and experience; obviously one feels hopeless.

I come from the large and prosperous city of Philadelphia. There we have our trade unions, workers' education, adult education, peace conferences, youth congress groups, churches, and other civic organizations all seemingly well organized and fairly advanced in their movements, and so I still wondered what then could I do?

I was walking through the hall in Denbigh on Tuesday afternoon when the girl in room 13 called to me. She wanted to know what I could tell her about the Scottsboro case and about Angelo Herndon, the Negro organizer. I am a Negro; still I was forced to confess that there was very little I could tell her. Many of us feel that the Negro problem is a tremendous one and we feel so helpless in regard to it that we take the easiest way out and shut our eyes to much of the real suffering of our people. Of course, we know that this is the wrong way to look upon the matter; but then too we often feel that we are only one tenth of the population, and that is a very small minority. Then the girl in Room 13 reminded me of the fact that nearly 90% of the Negro population were workers, and the workers are the masses. Therefore we need only to unite our forces and we will bring about a betterment of conditions for all. Through unity of forces we can break down race discrimination and class discrimination.

I am glad my sister student called me into her room that day. She set me thinking in an entirely different direction. I no longer think in terms of dollars and cents. I think in terms of what I can do for my class and my race. I feel that I too can do my part, be it ever so small. I feel that I will have accomplished a great deal if I am able to convince other Negroes that we as a race must stop sitting down and taking it on the chin, so to speak.

We must stop looking for the path of easiness, for we must face facts and learn truths—know the cause in order to find a cure.

> I intend therefore on returning home to connect myself with the National Negro Congress and to learn Negro history, since what education I do have I have received in the public schools and any favorable facts pertaining to the Negro were very intentionally omitted.
> I have then to thank Bryn Mawr for putting me on the right track.
> I have Bryn Mawr to thank for making me race and class conscious.

Similar to Eloise Fickland, Marion Jackson concentrates on the tasks of defining and assigning value to a black self in her narrative. Details of the interactions between the writer, college administrators, and a white student illustrate Jackson's awakening and growth from self-interested individualism to racial pride and working-class solidarity. Although Jackson mentions no ties to left-wing political organizations, this type of "working-class success story" was common among European socialist autobiographers in the early 1900s (Maynes, "Gender" 110). She admits that her first reason for coming to Bryn Mawr was the desire to complete her education for "my own selfish gain." Motivated by bourgeois values, Jackson's narrated "I" believed "that it gave one prestige to attend the school and meant much in one's favor when seeking employment." It wasn't until the opening exercises that she learned from President Park the true purpose of the school: "to render service to fellow workers through leadership or individual service." Park and other speakers motivated the narrated "I" to a certain extent, and Jackson came away committed to seeking change for "labor [and] humanity." She still felt, however, that she was "only one little insignificant person among a multitude." This feeling of unimportance has been commonly voiced by white working-class writers, male and female. In Gagnier's study of the ways white Victorian working-class autobiographies differed from those written by members of the white middle-class, she describes the "social atom" phenomenon, in which for a variety of reasons the narrative begins with a "statement of the author's ordinariness." This is not the case for the conventional bourgeois autobiographer, who frequently begins with family lineage or a birthdate (103).

Continuing to describe her past subjectivity, Jackson creates a narrated "we" that begins to identify with many of the Philadelphia movements for civic and worker improvement. "There we have our trade unions, workers' education, adult education, peace conferences." But this collective "we" is not an empowered one. Jackson "still wonder[s] what then could I do?" Up to this point in the narrative Jackson has not yet dealt with her blackness. Perhaps the source of her powerlessness lies in the fact that her "we" is still racially unaware.

Blackburn has written that "most African-American female autobiographers confess to one incident in their early years that awakened
them to their color; this recognition scene evoke[s] an awareness of
their blackness and of its significance, and it had a lasting influence on
their lives" (134). The incident involving the "girl in room 13" serves
this purpose for Jackson. Although the girl subsumes the black cause
in the white one, she "reminds" Jackson "of the fact that nearly 90% of
the Negro population were workers, and the workers are the masses,"
powerful in their numbers. For Jackson there is no assimilating the
black cause in the white one. She separates the issues of race and class.
Although she is willing to join forces with white workers, she keeps
racial equality a separate and distinct goal. Like Fickland, Jackson's
subjectivity slips back and forth between "I" and "we." On returning
home, "I" intends to join the "National Negro Congress and to learn
Negro history." Thus, she is motivated to act only when she does so as
an African American in a larger workers' movement.

Similar to most of her white counterparts in the school, Jackson
does not discuss her problems from a gendered perspective. Many
reasons have been given for American working-class women's lack of a
feminist consciousness. The women's movement of the early twentieth
century and beyond has been criticized for its mainly upper- and
middle-class constituency. Working women, in general, had little access to feminist rhetoric as such, and the Bryn Mawr Summer School
experience proved to be no exception. When interviewed by Marion
W. Roydhouse on the issue, Hilda Worthington Smith said that "at the
Bryn Mawr Summer School [we] never talked directly of women's
problems 'because these were women, and we knew they were women,
and we knew what they'd come for.' " Roydhouse nevertheless argues
that "the Summer Schools were certainly feminist in the early years,"
because the students and faculty did discuss disparities in wage scales
or the difficulties faced by married women in the work force, "but they
viewed these issues within the context of needed change in the industrial system, rather than as problems resulting from a male-dominated
society" (203).[7] Roydhouse further maintains that the feminism of the
Summer Schools was based on an idealistic belief in women's potential for fuller participation in society, rather than in the kind of
commitment that led to the introduction of the ERA during the same
period" (203). Scholars have termed this approach "social feminist."[8]
At any rate it seems clear that the feminism operating at the school was
one of equality, not difference.

Others scholars have argued that gender may not be so decisive a
factor in working-class women's lives as it is for the middle class. In her

analysis of gender and class in early-twentieth-century German working women's autobiography, Maynes concludes that "gender oppression was not regarded as primary by any of the female autobiographers":

> Whether socialist or apolitical, whether writing for a working-class audience or a middle-class one, whether positing collective or individual solutions to their problems, or no solution at all, these autobiographers all seem to agree that it is mostly because they are poor and reliant on their labor that they suffer. . . . While their identity as women is certainly central to their accounts of their life courses, they do not regard solidarity with women, across class lines, as a possible or desirable tactic for improvement ("Gender and Class" 243–44).

It may be that, since these working-class women were well aware of the brutality of working-class men's lives, as Beulah Parrish indicates, they did not aspire to equality with them but, instead, to a more humanized world for everyone—men included.

In conclusion we can see that in the context of the Bryn Mawr Summer School the autobiographical assignment was often successful in encouraging the women workers to represent empowered, collective subject positions through their narratives and, occasionally, to take up feminist positions. Through their autobiographies the working women were offered the opportunity to represent newly acquired versions of more powerful selves. Although these ideas of empowered selfhood were usually derived from androcentric configurations offered to workers in their Bryn Mawr classroom as well as in institutions of working-class culture, the women often used this rhetoric to win better working conditions and more respect on the job for female workers. Follow up studies of alumnae also attest to the fact that many went back to their communities and became civic, church, and union leaders. In my view these accomplishments were remarkable indeed.

Women and Autobiography: Workers and Students, Past and Present

Important implications for writing instructors can be drawn from a comparison of the Bryn Mawr autobiographers, literary autobiographers, and studies of today's student autobiographers. The research on autobiography by literary critics and composition theorists alike finds that women focus on human relationships in their writing to a greater extent than men. This finding tends to hold true across race and class—at least in the United States. For example, in her groundbreaking study of female autobiographers, Estelle C. Jelinek found that these writers concentrate on "personal lives—domestic details, family difficulties, close friends, and especially people who influenced them" (8). Compositionist Elizabeth Flynn reports that the narratives of her female college students are "stories of interaction, of connection, or of frustrated connection" (428). Similarly, Linda H. Peterson notes that "the topics that women students choose are almost always 'relational'—i.e., they focus on the relationship of the writer with some other person or group" (173). The same focus on relationships is present in the Bryn Mawr narratives by both black and white women and in Zandy's anthology of contemporary working-class women writers.

In explaining women's greater concern with human interactions, researchers in both scholarly groups tend to rely on social constructivist readings of Nancy Chodorow's theories and/or Carol Gilligan's extension of them (see S. Smith, Friedman, Rose, Flynn, Peterson, and Sirc). Friedman asserts that applying Chodorow's theories of selfhood (as well as those of Sheila Rowbotham) "to women's autobiographical texts—particularly those by women who also belong to racial, ethnic, sexual and religious minorities"—helps expand the autobiographical canon by deemphasizing the androcentric or conventional focus on the individual self (35). Quoting Chodorow, Friedman asserts that "we can anticipate finding in women's texts a consciousness of self in which 'the individual does not oppose herself to all others,' nor 'feel herself to exist outside of others, but very much with others in an interdependent existence' " (41). Since many women have been found to write in this manner, their focus on relationship and their deemphasis of the individual ego need not—indeed, must not—be devalued in academic writing. As Peterson cautions, "Evaluation of personal essays should not privilege certain gender-specific modes of self-representation, nor penalize others" (175).

Another point shared by both compositionists writing about autobiography and literary critics of autobiography is their emphasis on the poststructuralist notion of a discursive or textual construction of subjectivity. They argue that gender is a social construction, which the individual acquires through cultural beliefs, values, and attitudes—all "texts," in their language-constitutive nature. These texts motivate the behaviors marking gender. For example, Sidonie Smith writes that the tropes an autobiographer uses in self-(re)presentation "are always cast in language and are always motivated by cultural expectations, habits and systems of interpretation pressing on her at the scene of writing" (*A Poetics* 47). Similarly, Sirc argues that "any occasion for the actual production of written discourse is going to reflect the way that the writer (as well as the text) has been inscribed into the forms of gender's discourse" (4). Since, in our culture, conventional discourses of gender, race, and class are not equal in the opportunities they provide individuals, the activity of reconstructing subjectivity through autobiography for more powerful self-(re)presentation is a valuable assignment in a writing class whose aim is, among other things, to build self-confidence and social equality.

It also seems clear from research by compositionists and from the evidence provided by the Summer School autobiographies that certain textual and extratextual conditions for autobiographical writing produce more empowered subjectivities than others. Sirc's assignment to "recreate for me in words a single incident in which you were involved or which you witnessed" provides a good example of unempowering textual conditions (5). This topic did not result, for the most part, in self-(re)presentations of strength for his female students. Sirc reports that most of their written responses did, indeed, include scenarios of nurturing or of providing care (7); he also found, however, that the female students "were more likely to picture themselves as confused and out of control" than his male writers (8). When women's traditional focus on others is accompanied by an autobiographical subjectivity that is devalued, subservient, or exploited, instructors who are teaching for the empowerment of women need to reevaluate their assignments and provide textual contexts (readings, assignments, discussions) which are conducive to personal growth. As Sidonie Smith maintains, "To write an autobiography from that speaking posture, [oppressed] does not . . . liberate woman from the fictions that bind her; indeed, it may embed her even more deeply in them since it promotes identification with the very essentialist ideology that renders woman's story a story of silence, powerlessness, self-effacement" (*A Poetics* 53). Sirc (8), Flynn (434), and Peterson (173) voice a similar concern.

The fact that the texts written by the women workers are so strikingly different from Sirc's further underscores this point. There were almost no voices of confusion or disorientation among the Bryn Mawr narratives I examined, and I maintain that one reason for their strength lies in the textual context for writing encountered at the Bryn Mawr Summer School—in unions, the YWCA, and progressive churches in which these women came into contact with empowering discourses. Also, as we have seen, the Kennan assignment asked for a critical appraisal of the workers' life situations. Thus, the Bryn Mawr project teaches the importance of exposing students to an array of empowering voices so that they are better able to meld those voices with their own. Several feminist scholars support this contention. Chris Weedon argues that "women need access to the different subject positions offered in imaginative alternatives to the present, in humorous critiques and even by positive heroines" to reconstruct more appropriate subjectivities for themselves (172). Peterson recommends that "the readings suggested as models for the [autobiographical] assignment should include examples by and about both masculine and feminine subjects" (175). And Patricia Bizzell has recently advocated a pedagogy for the composition class which will "generate egalitarian social power relations" (55). She urges compositionists to offer readings "that are not simply pluralistic, but politically engaged in a variety of ways; and . . . to try to get students into these texts even if they initially seem very uncongenial" (67). Of course, as Bizzell implies, our focus need not solely be on women. Members of the working class and minorities can benefit from reading discourse about collective strength and control.

The use of a collective subjectivity ("we") marks the most significant difference between the student autobiographical writing reported on by compositionists and that of the Bryn Mawr writers. The crucial factor that produced this striking stylistic feature was likely the extratextual context in which the working women were writing. I have argued elsewhere for the importance of the wider social, economic, and political context in producing critical literacy (Hollis). Both text and subjectivity have a dialectical relationship with material conditions such as the economy in which they occur, and both respond to and influence these conditions in the culture at large. As Weedon writes, "discursive practices are embedded in material power relations which also require transformation for change to be realized," yet these "material power relations constitute and inhere within discursive practices" (106). When people believe that better lives are possible through writing, their writing will reflect this expectation. The theories and practices of worker empowerment offered at Bryn Mawr and in other collective movements of the time may have led the women workers to believe that their lives could be improved through school and writing, organizing and protesting. Such worker "texts" did in turn influence the social, economic, and political context of the period. The shift in the Bryn Mawr narratives from the private "I" to the more public "we" likely arose from this more public arena for the students' collective writing and actions.

Writing about working women in the early 1900s, Gagnier concludes that, "contrary to the claims on behalf of a room of one's own, workers' autobiographies suggest that writing women were those whose work took them out of the home" (100). This supports findings by social historians that "the process of 'self discovery' and emergence of a group consciousness for early 20th century women depended on employment outside the home" (Eisenstein 9). This group consciousness is indeed very crucial to women's empowerment, but I would add that history also shows us that, unless women and other oppressed groups are provided with the discourse of collective experience, protest, and power, they will likely remain in a weakened individualist frame of mind. In the manner of the Bryn Mawr educators I think we need to study our students through their autobiographies and other means and strive to create textual and even extratextual contexts that lead them to greater self- and group confidence. Occasionally, requiring students to write in a collective voice might change their perceptions of themselves as isolated individuals with disparate problems to a powerful collectivity with legitimate rights and demands. If students learn to write as "we," instructors may find them better able to appreciate the benefits of collective endeavor. We may even re-encounter the raised consciousness and liberating discourse that characterized the students at the Bryn Mawr Summer School back in the 1920s and 1930s.

NOTES

1. The book is scheduled for publication in Prentice-Hall's Writing and Culture series in 1995.
2. Much of the following background information comes from Hilda Worthington Smith's 1929 book describing the school's early success, *Women Workers at the Bryn Mawr Summer School*. My account is also based on records of the school's various administrative and curricular activities, which Smith and subsequent directors carefully preserved. These records as well as student publications, application forms, course syllabi, and committee minutes are found in archival collections located at Bryn Mawr, Rutgers, Cornell, and the University of Wisconsin. In addition, I received much inspiration and information from Rita Heller's definitive dissertation study of the school as well as the film she produced, *Women of Summer*, which depicts the history of the school, and a moving 1984 reunion of many of the Summer School faculty and students. I also obtained information from interviews with eighty-nine-year-old Alice Hansen Cook, former Summer School faculty member, and two Summer School students, Garineh Narzakian and Mary Scafidi, now well into their seventies, who live in the Philadelphia area.
3. See Smith, "Student and Teacher in Workers Education," *Education and the Worker-Student* and *The Bryn Mawr Summer School for Women Workers* (41).

4. Kennan's syllabi and assignments are located in a set of files containing business records, correspondence, publications, course materials, curricula, student works, and photographs donated by Hilda Worthington Smith to the Institute of Management and Labor Relations, Rutgers University.
5. Because of a dispute with the Bryn Mawr College Board of Directors, the Summer School was not on the Bryn Mawr campus in 1935. I have not been able to obtain an issue of *Shop and School* for that year.
6. Similar assignments were found in Dorothy Weil's English syllabus of 1927 and William Card's syllabus of 1936.
7. In fact, economist Amy Hewes and her students published several pamphlets on such issues. Published in the U.S. Department of Labor's *Bulletin of the Women's Bureau,* they include: "Women Workers and Family Support: A Study Made by Students in the Economics Course at the Bryn Mawr Summer School" (1925); "The Industrial Experience of Women Workers at the Summer Schools, 1928–1930" (1931); and "Women Workers in the Third Year of the Depression" (1933).
8. Roydhouse cites Stanley Lemon, *The Woman Citizen: Social Feminism in the 1920s.* (Urbana: University of Illinois Press, 1973), for more on the issue of social feminism.

REFERENCES

Andrews, William L. "The Changing Moral Discourse of Nineteenth-Century African American Women's Autobiography: Harriet Jacobs and Elizabeth Keckley." In *De/Colonizing the Subject.* Ed. Sidonie and Julia Watson Smith. Minneapolis: University of Minnesota Press, 1992.

Bakhtin, M. M. *The Dialogic Imagination.* Austin: University of Texas Press, 1981.

Belenky, Mary Field, and Blythe McVicker Clinchy, Nancy Rule Goldberger, and Jill Mattuck Tarule. In *Women's Ways of Knowing: The Development of Self, Voice and Mind.* New York: Basic, 1986.

Bizzell, Patricia. "Power, Authority, and Critical Pedagogy." *Journal of Basic Writing* 1, no. 2 (1991): 54–70.

Blackburn, Regina. "In Search of the Black Female Self: African-American Women's Autobiographies and Ethnicity." In *Women's Autobiography: Essays in Criticism.* Ed. Estelle C. Jelinek, 133–48. Bloomington: Indiana University Press, 1980.

Carter, Jean, and Hilda W. Smith. *Education and the Worker-Student.* New York: Affiliated Schools for Workers, 1934.

Coiner, Constance. "Literature of Resistance: The Intersection of Feminism and the Communist Left in Meridel Le Sueur and Tillie Olsen." In *Left Politics and the Literary Profession.* Ed. Leonard J. Davis and M. Bella Mirabella, 162–85. New York: Columbia University Press, 1990.

Eisenstein, Sarah. *Give Us Bread but Give Us Roses: Working Women's Consciousness in the United States, 1890 to the First World War.* London: Routledge and Kegan Paul, 1983.

Fickland, Eloise. "Looking Back." *Shop and School* (1933): 32.

Flynn, Elizabeth A. "Composing as a Woman." *College Composition and Communication* 39 (1988): 423–35.

Fox-Genovese, Elizabeth. "My Statue, My Self: Autobiographical Writings of Afro-American Women." In *The Private Self: Theory and Practice of Women's Autobiographical Writings*. Ed. Shari Benstock, 63–89. Chapel Hill: University of North Carolina Press, 1988.

Friedman, Susan Stanford. "Women's Autobiographical Selves: Theory and Practice." In *The Private Self: Theory and Practice of Women's Autobiographical Writings*. Ed. Shari Benstock, 34–63. Chapel Hill: University of North Carolina Press, 1988.

Gagnier, Regina. "The Literary Standard, Working-Class Autobiography, and Gender." In *Revealing Lives: Autobiography, Biography and Gender*. Ed. Susan Groag Bell and Marilyn Yalom, 93–114. Albany: State University of New York Press, 1990.

Gordon, Sarah. "A Typical Day in My Life." *Shop and School* (1929): 27–28.

Greenstein, Rose. "Sacrifice." *Shop and School* (1930): 30–31.

Hansen, Alice. Personal interview, 16 June 1992.

Heller, Rita. "Blue Collars and Blue Stockings: The Bryn Mawr School for Women Workers, 1921–1938." In *Sisterhood and Solidarity: Workers Education for Women, 1914–1984*, 110–45. Philadelphia: Temple University Press, 1984.

———. "The Women of Summer: The Bryn Mawr Summer School for Women Workers, 1921–1938." Ph.D. diss., State University of New Jersey, 1986.

———. *The Women of Summer*. Film. National Endowment for the Humanities. 1985.

Hollis, Karyn L. "Literacy Theory, Teaching Composition and Feminist Response." *Pre-Text* (Spring 1993). 103–116.

Jackson, Marion. "It Set Me Thinking." *Shop and School* (1936): 9–10.

Jelinek, Estelle C. *The Tradition of Women's Autobiography: From Antiquity to the Present*. Boston: Twayne Publishers, 1986.

Kennan, Ellen. "Autobiography." *English Syllabus*. Bryn Mawr: Bryn Mawr Summer School for Women Workers, 1926.

———. "Autobiography." *English Syllabus*. Bryn Mawr Summer School for Women Workers, 1934.

Lauter, Paul. "Working-Class Women's Literature: An Introduction to Study." *Radical Teacher*. March (1980): 16–26.

Maynes, Mary Jo. "Gender and Class in Working-Class Women's Autobiographies." In *German Women in the Eighteenth and Nineteenth Centuries: A Social and Literary History*. Ed. Ruth-Ellen B. Joeres and Mary Jo Maynes, 230–46. Bloomington: Indiana University Press, 1986.

———. "Gender and Narrative Form in French and German Working-Class Narratives." In *Interpreting Lives: Feminist Theory and Personal Narratives*. Ed. Personal Narratives Group, 103–17. Bloomington: Indiana University Press, 1989.

Parrish, Beulah. "Those Mill Villages." *Shop and School* (1930): 6.

Peterson, Linda H. "Gender and the Autobiographical Essay: Research Perspectives, Pedagogical Practices." *College Composition and Communication* 42 (May 1991): 171–83.

Rose, Shirley K. "Reading Representative Anecdotes of Literacy Practice; or 'See Dick and Jane read and write!' " *Rhetoric Review* 8 (Spring 1990): 244–59.

Rowbotham, Sheila. *Woman's Consciousness, Man's World.* London: Penguin, 1973.

Roydhouse, Marion W. "Partners in Progress: The Affiliated Schools for Women Workers, 1928–1939." In *Sisterhood and Solidarity: Worker's Education for Women, 1914–1984.* Ed. Joyce L. Kornbluh and Mary Frederickson, 189–221. Philadelphia: Temple University Press, 1984.

Sirc, Geoffrey. "Gender and 'Writing Formations' in First-Year Narratives." *Freshman English News* 18 (Fall 1989): 4–11.

Smith, Hilda Worthington. "The Student and Teacher in Workers' Education." In *Workers' Education in the United States.* Ed. Theodore Brameld, 181–202. New York: Harper and Brothers, 1941.

———. *Women Workers at the Bryn Mawr Summer School.* New York: Affiated Summer Schools for Women Workers in Industry and American Association for Adult Education, 1929.

Smith, Sidonie. *A Poetics of Women's Autobiography: Marginality and the Fictions of Self-Representation.* Bloomington: Indiana University Press, 1987.

———. "Resisting the Gaze of Embodiment: Women's Autobiography in the Nineteenth Century." In *American Women's Autobiography: Fea(s)ts of Memory.* Ed. Margo Culley, 75–110. Madison: University of Wisconsin Press, 1992.

Weedon, Chris. *Feminist Practice and Poststructuralist Theory.* Oxford: Basil Blackwell, 1987.

Zandy, Janet, ed. *Calling Home: Working-Class Women's Writings—An Anthology.* New Brunswick, N.J.: Rutgers University Press, 1990.

Karyn L. Hollis *is Assistant Professor of English and Director of the Writing across the Curriculum Program at Villanova University. Her book,* Liberating Voices: Writing at the Bryn Mawr Summer School for Women Workers, 1921–1938, *will appear in Prentice-Hall's Writing and Culture series in 1995.*

Working Class Consciousness in Jo Sinclair's *The Seasons* [1]

Florence Howe

I want first to explain the impulse behind this essay. As publisher of more than one hundred books over the past twenty-two years, I have only twice before been moved to write a critical paper. Janet has asked me to reflect on this fact, as though to move from experience to theorizing working-class literature. The subjects, each time I was moved to write, were working-class books—*Daughter of Earth*, an auto-biographical novel, and *The Maimie Papers*, a collection of correspondence that can be read as memoir. Both are rarities in form and substance. *The Seasons: Death and Transfiguration* joins them and, in terms of form and substance, takes another leap. Like Smedley's fiction and Maimie's correspondence, Sinclair's memoir tries to make sense of a would-be writer's life. [2]

And not one life only: the immediate impulse for Sinclair's book is the death of her beloved Helen Buchman, the person who rescued the twenty-five-year-old part-time working-class writer and who, for the next twenty-five years, provided a middle-class family setting, a room of Jo's own, and comforts for a full-time writing life. It is the story of what Jo calls "levels," a word she uses to suggest moving from her working-class place into a middle-class life and which she then uses to mean carrying the sense of the past in the present, and especially feeling the present pain in the memory of the pleasures of the past.

Although I did not see the manuscript of *The Seasons* until the late 1980s, the memoir reads as though it was written in 1969, thus "covering" the thirty-one years between then and 1938, when Jo and Helen first met. The memoir is divided into three unequal chronological periods: first, the twenty-five-year "journal of life," Jo's second quarter of a century—from age twenty-five to fifty—the joy with which she credits Helen for transforming the "tough ghetto kid" who wore her hair unusually clipped, walked funny, and even talked funny into the successful writer who lived for more than twenty years with Helen Buchman, her husband, Mort, and their two children in three different houses, two in Cleveland and one thirteen miles into the countryside. Second, the "journal of death," the final nine months of

Helen's life, in which Jo becomes the strong, life-giving person, and Helen the frightened, sick one. And third, the six years after Helen's death when Jo must struggle alone to reclaim the will to live and to write.

The form of the book (and much of its substance) comes organically from the tool that wise Helen knew would bring spiritual health to Jo and great pleasure to both of them, and many others: the garden. This is not your ordinary small city or suburban plot: around the third house they move into together, the "garden" is a small farm, the fruits, vegetables, and flowers sufficient for many families. Partly with the aid of two found journals, the memoir moves through *the seasons* of grow- ing from spring to winter three times: first, with respect to the life of twenty-five years together; second, with respect to the death—Helen's first stroke occurs in the spring of 1963, the fifth at the end of December that same year; and, third, with respect to the six years following Helen's death.

So the book is at once the story of a twenty-five-year daily relation- ship, the story of an early death (Helen was fifty-four in 1963), and the story of loss and recovery. In it, of course, Jo Sinclair tells us much about herself, even glimpses of the twenty-five years without Helen in her life, and it is that young, class-bound Jo who reappears after Helen's death. Jo Sinclair has to fulfill two purposes: she wants us to know this person who made such a difference in her life, and she wants us to know the dimensions of the difference. That last purpose means she needs to weave into the chapters of life and loss the making of herself as writer, for, as Jo sees it, Helen's belief in Jo's ability was essential to the production of Jo's novels, stories, and plays. We hear Helen's refrain, even after her death "Ruthie, go write me a book." Thus, into key positions within the book's narrative of the death, as well as the life, Jo Sinclair places flashbacks that testify to Helen's belief in her as a writer and to her own need, as a writer, of Helen's supportive presence. These flashbacks, present in the "Journal of Death," serve especially to prolong and make more poignant the loss of Helen Buchman, who seems to have become not only Jo's friend, mentor, beloved intimate, but symbiotically, her alter ego. Helen's physical death is Jo's "creative death," only to be released when written out through the pain.

To accomplish both of these purposes Jo Sinclair *works* class con- sciousness into her text, in three different ways, which I want to outline here. First, Helen is Jo's "teacher" and, in fact, for two years, the person Jo calls her "green thumb psychiatrist." During that period, before Jo moves into the house, she sees Helen daily for "therapy" and lunch. Not

surprisingly, the lists of "she taught me" are, at first, dominated by material goods: linen napkins, napkin rings, foods the ghetto kid had
never eaten ("Shrimp salad on Bibb and watercress, Southern biscuits
in a basket—wrapped in a huge damask dinner napkin to keep them
hot . . . [50]), then by culture—music, art (Kaethe Kollwitz and Vincent
Van Gogh become her favorites), and writers outside the United States
("I read all about Oscar Wilde in prison, and knew all over again how
confused and ignorant and fearful my psyche had been before Helen"
[52]).[3] Later in the volume, during the partial recovery after the first
stroke, there is this dialogue:

> ME: "Do you realize that I had never heard of a counter-tenor before I
> met you?"
> HELEN: "Do you realize that I had never heard of a bagel or a potato
> knish before you?"

Yes, Helen is Jewish, as is Mort, but they are so very different from Jews
I could recognize that Jo had to correct my assumption that they were
Christian, thus demonstrating the significance of class.

At least as important as food and culture; Helen teaches Jo that it's
all right, even lovely, to express affection through touching, kissing,
even language, though only Helen uses the tender endearments. For
example, she calls Jo/Ruth "*toi*," the familiar French pronoun reserved
for intimates and perhaps reminiscent of Jo the "tough kid," the
"toughie." Helen extends the lessons to Jo's mother, her sisters: "My
little mother—who ever kissed her in Russia, or in rotten Brooklyn, or
all the years in Cleveland? Helen and the kids are really kissers! And
Ma kind of pushes at them, but she loves it" (115).

My second point: Jo emphasizes the contrasting moods in which the
two begin their relationship, seeming at first to define thereby their
social class: the earth-bound pessimist of a Jo; the stargazing dreamer
of an optimist Helen. Jo expects defeat when her first novel is declined
by a publisher; Helen then sends *Wasteland* off again, and it wins the
$10,000 Harper prize. Honest Jo would not leave the portrait uncom-
plicated by reality; she reminds us that her sister Fannie is also an
optimist, a joyous, happy person, though someone without Jo's aspira-
tions. I would theorize that the mood difference sharpens when a
working-class person is either crossing the boundary of her class or
understands enough about class to want to do so. How do I know this? I
know it from my own experience. Here is a brief example: at age
twenty, living in my first middle-class setting, an elegant mansion
housing twenty-eight graduate students at Smith College in 1950, I was

told by the housemother that I was "clearly an unhappy person," that I would be "depressed" all my life. I thought she was magical to know how I felt, but, of course, both she and I were blind to class differences. I was the only working-class person in the house.

I cannot review in detail the class-bound fights about money that occur with some regularity in *The Seasons* or in the varying reactions to Helen's medical treatment. In general, however, Jo's response is fury, often mingled with suspicion. The key word, and feeling, so familiar to my own working-class emotions, is *unfair*. It is unfair that Helen be cursed with so wounded a body; it is unfair that she does not have superior, really knowledgeable medical treatment that might have saved her life.

Third, and most important, is the tool for all the rest, the language in which Jo and Helen speak to each other over a twenty-five-year period: their voices, their diction and metaphor, are class bound. I should say at once that *The Seasons* is filled with dialogue. In one place Jo describes Helen as a voice teacher: "Well, a person is a kind of instrument, too. And whatever voice or song lies within is dependent, so often, on a teacher." Not in imitation. Jo continues: "And of course, the person-instrument is always different. What fashioned this particular one?—or who? Where was it created? And the final question (for Jo in the volume and for us as readers of Jo Sinclair today), "How can an instrument go mute again, after so many years of singing? Her kind of teacher should have left permanence in an ardent student like me" (82–8).

And, of course, I must at least mention the idea of "permanence," so important to the fifty-year-old Jo mourning the friend who first gave her the sense of even the possibility of permanence. And we both understand the significance of class here: as a working-class person, my whole body vibrated to that desire for permanence and for the keeping of Helen's promise, that she would not "leave" Jo. Dying, of course, breaks her promise.

For dozens of pages early in the volume Jo distinguishes between her vocabulary and Helen's, often in language invented for their shared experience of gardening/farming. And these words are often class bound: Jo's "chiselings," for example, for plants borrowed or taken from other places; Helen's "Johnny" for the woodchuck, named after a character in a children's book Jo had "never even herd of." "But" also, I am quoting, "oh, Christ, our vocabularies are one language, so often" (22). Perhaps the single best example can be found in another of the volume's refrains: Jo's description of herself "touring the joint," meaning a long walk through several gardens that surround the house down to and around the pond, to note not only the growth of plants and bloomings of trees and shrubs but also the life of animals and birds. And, of course, to report all of this—once Helen is ill and bed- or house-ridden—in detail to Helen.

To conclude I must return the question of how I knew what I did about this book: how I read what was suggested under the surface, how it was that I could theorize about working-class language and sensibility, how I knew especially about the need for affirmation, the lack of confidence as a given. I used to think that my own lack of confidence stemmed chiefly from gender, but I know otherwise now, and perhaps that is why *The Seasons* spoke so deeply to me. The need for support and affirmation may be doubled by gender, but the dimensions particular to Jo Sinclair (and to me) are rooted in class. I am theorizing now: the need Jo has for support, assurance, belief, affirmation, formed during the first twenty-five years of her life, does not disappear, but simply retreats from dominance, during the second twenty-five years of her life. And then it returns. To state the idea somewhat differently, without a single Helen Buchman, one would continue to need many versions of Helen Buchman. I never even tried to write, never even believed enough in myself to try, until, by accident, I wrote a long piece about Mississippi's Freedom Summer, which, also by accident, was published to small acclaim. That was 1965. Even today, I am "surprised" when some different "Helen" declares my work (which is, in fact, the way I refer to my writing) to be worthwhile. So, I understand— from the inside—Jo's need for affirmation, though that is only half the story: the loss of twenty-five years of sustained love and friendship warrants its own kind of mourning. Beyond mourning this book ultimately affirms Jo Sinclair's ability to capture and inscribe the memoir with her unmistakable literary working-class hand and voice. We are grateful to her (and thus to Helen) for a text that honestly evokes, neither exalting nor diminishing, the making of a working-class writer.

NOTES

1. This essay was read as part of a panel at a session on Working-Class Literature, chaired by Janet Zandy, at the Modern Language Association's meetings in December, 1992. I am grateful to Janet Zandy for her generous encouragement and her insightful criticism.
2. The memoir also explains why, although Jo Sinclair wrote and published four novels between 1940 and 1960, there were no more after that. The novels were: *Wasteland,* 1946; *Sing at My Wake,* 1952; *The Changelings,* 1955; *Anna Teller,* 1960. The latter two books have been republished by The Feminist Press.

3. All page numbers are from *The Seasons: Death and Transfiguration*, a Memoir by Jo Sinclair (The Feminist Press, 1993).

Florence Howe is Director of The Feminist Press at The City University of New York and Professor of English at City College and the Graduate Center, CUNY. She has recently edited the revised edition of No More Masks! An Anthology of Twentieth-Century American Women Poets *(1993).*

The Writing on the Wall, or Where Did That Dead Head Come From?

Cy-Thea Sand

Class Connections

The dragon slayer looks up, alerted by a subtle shift of energy. Something has changed here as the day's light dims into darkness. She looks beyond her shield and gasps with disgust. The monster suddenly has another head, and it is dangling obscenely from Dragon-Lady's thick neck. Depression. The face of Depression. A Dead Head, yellowish brown with scorched and shriveled scales. Its tongue distends from a cavernous mouth, thick and ugly, and its eyes are vacuous and remote. Old ideas and loss of spirit register here as lethargy. The eyes weep pus. The dragon slayer's angry protest against Anxiety's fiery dictates falters, tripped up by fatigue. The Dead Head invites the dragon slayer to read the writing on the wall as Despair.

I have worried over the years that I would lose my mind from the stress of Dead Head's oppressive tactics against me. I once asked friends with whom I shared a communal home to sign a statement promising that they would never let me be taken to a psychiatric ward. Several years ago I wrote that I hesitate to call myself a writer in part because "I identify with the millions of women rocking back and forth, shuffling down hallways or staring out of windows. Scrapes of last night's supper have crusted on the housecoats they pull closer to themselves. Few of them speak. The ones who do usually shout or force the odd syllable from drug-swollen tongues."[1] In my imagination these women are fat and poor and hate themselves just like me. We are all driven mad by a self-rejection that is so deeply inscribed that its origins are erased. The Dead Head has colonized our bodies and minds, and we are too tired to break free.

Brick by brick, brick by brick, the writing on the wall gets writ.

The Dead Head of Depression invites me to classify, measure, compare, differentiate, judge, and qualify myself, in short, to back myself up against a wall of constructed madness and impoverished ideas that gnaw at the beauty and splendidness of my life. Its tongue is swollen with lies, with old, bloated, useless ideas about me. Its eyes are shut, blind to my resourcefulness and power to overcome the passivity it embodies.

I mention my close escape from confinement in the Allan Memorial Hospital in Montreal, where Dr. Ewen Cameron conducted his horrific, de-patterning experiments on people suffering under the influence of Anxiety and Depression. While I am entering my adolescent years in the Verdun district of Montreal, several women and a few men are subjected to Cameron's "concentration camp techniques" of brainwashing. The Allan Memorial is housed in a cold, stone mansion once known as Ravenscrag on Mount Royal. Ravenscrag used to be the family mansion of ship-building millionaires near the district of Westmount, where my great-aunt and my father's sisters worked as domestic servants in the 1930s. As I grow into womanhood a half-hour bus ride away, a Gothic house of horrors muffles the screams of patients tortured by prolonged drugged sleep, LSD, and electroshock "treatments." A son of one of Cameron's victims has written that Ravenscrag was "once a place of elegant parties, of the English elite in a French city, now for us, it was a mansion of despair."[2] Cameron once kept a woman—who was under the influence of the Dead Head of Depression—in a sealed room for thirty-five days, her eyes blindfolded, her ears blocked, her hands and feet padded.[3] Isolation and sensory deprivation were Cameron's cure for psychic pain.

Raven scrag. *Scrag* is a slang word for an ugly girl in Verdun, as I grow up in its cement and brick world of sweltering summers and Arctic winters. I grow up in the landscape of an urban consciousness saturated with ideas about how working-class women should look and act and be. Ewen Cameron performed those operations on the mind and psyches of imprisoned women while I am growing into adolescence just miles from the horror. I see myself standing in the schoolyard of Verdun High School, chatting with my best friend, tense with self-consciousness and worry. It is the early 1960s. The Dead Head of Depression has stalked me since I was about eight years old: I am frightened by the despair of the people around me, especially my father's. I feel helpless and powerless over his chronic irritability, sullenness, and worries about money.

In 1963, while I am chatting with my girlfriend in the schoolyard, I already have years of experience with feelings of despair, hopelessness, and immobility. I look like a cool teenager, but I already know a monster of tremendous power exists. It seems to feed on the unhappiness in my family. I don't understand it. I just know it's there, and I live in fear of it. I look up at the Verdun Aqueduct, a canal that links

Lachine and Verdun with the city of Montreal. The water drifts along in the direction of the horror house of Ravenscrag. I am a working-class girl in deep psychic pain because I can read the writing on the wall: girls aren't as important as boys, and they just grow up and get married and have kids—my value is in direct proportion to my looks because I am just a girl, and I am supposed to find a man with a good job and get married and have kids. That man can't be French or black though. And that man can't be a woman. The writing also says that people who work for others never get ahead and are always worried about money, and *that* never changes. You do the best you can and drink when you're not working. I know how bad the world can get, how hate can manifest, because I read books about the Holocaust. I know there's no hope because, when I talk to my parents about my concern, they always say the same thing: "It's human nature, and you can't change it. Notions about change are ridiculous."

The writing on the wall is penned with the indelible ink of dread. I am not in command of my feelings: anger, shame, and frustration eat me up as I shut down deep within myself. I feel shy and unconfident. I am terrified of the world beyond my family, but I am dying to escape the borders of the existence I see here in Verdun. Feelings overwhelm me and begin writing the story I have lived within until very recently, the story that I am tense, nervous, and deeply morose. Depressed. When I swallow a bottle of pills at eighteen, too frightened to face an audience and speak, my doctor and family send me to a psychiatrist. Dr. Striker or Straker, I can't remember. But I like the way the "Strike-*Her*" pronunciation sums up my experience of the experience. I am so terrified of him and his huge, dark, wood-paneled, uptown office that I cannot speak. He calls my mother into his office and recommends that I be put in the hospital right away. But I refuse to go. I recruit my rage into effective action and vow to finish my undergraduate degree. "Fuck him, I'm going to finish my courses," I told my brother in a dragon slayer–like protest against Strike*Her's* pathologizing the effects of gender, class, and familial oppression on me.

While I am growing up female and working-class in a world that worships maleness and money, "the godfather of Canadian psychiatry"[4] is dreaming up ways to erase impressions, memories, and insights that cause his patients suffering. A few years later, when Dr. Strike*Her* wants to send me off to Ravenscrag, Dr. Ewen Cameron is two years dead, but his dangerous ideas are alive and well in psychiatric circles. I guess I was a dragon slayer in training back then because I defied my worried parents and an imposing medical authority. I knew Dr. Strike*Her's* drugs would imprison me as effectively if not more than the brick and wood and concrete I'd be kept in. I could read the writing on the wall. I knew that commitment to a mental hospital would devastate my already precarious self-esteem. I knew that suppressing the feelings that were overwhelming me was not the way to liberation. The dragon slayer in me intuits that Freedom's door cannot be opened by silenced and controlled pain.

The idea behind my book is that I have deconstructed my emotional life and liberated myself from the devastating problems of Anxiety and Depression by using a therapeutic technique informed by postmodern thought. The idea behind this book is that ideas are powerful and really do have a life of their own. I have always loved ideas. Big ideas like socialism and feminism and the belief that human consciousness is evolving more and more toward liberation. Maybe it was time for me to use radical concepts and perspectives to transform my own inner world so I could write again and in order for my passion to dare to wake up. What I want to celebrate with you is that the narrative approach to therapy is a big wonderful grand idea in my life. It is a therapy of metaphor and respect. It is a way of working with problems and with language which invites me to flaunt my success all over these pages.

With this narrative about the narrative, this story of a therapeutic approach to the forces that threatened to annihilate my spirit, I am creating a story around my ideas of what feminism, class analysis, and a narrative approach to therapy mean to the resurrection of my creativity, to my "awesome lust for life," to my "hunger growing and growing inside the earth for centuries on end!" to honor Anne Hebert's description of women's relentless persistence about life and freedom. Here I interview myself and make public my private story with the passion of a poet, the clarity of a critic, and the curiosity of an investigative journalist. I have accepted Nicole Brossard's invitation to become my own mistress, and with this offering I play in a place of experiment and dare to take a risk. To my own story I apply a few of the skills expected in the literary world, such as the ability to research; interview; define concept and structure, narrative and dialogue, voice and stance. I also develop a skill expected in the academic world—that is, to take information and notes from various sources and then synthesize this study into a coherent whole or thesis. The idea, as I understand it, is to add to a *body* of knowledge with original conclusions or analyses. In other words, a student must read all the authorities on a given subject and then produce something new, a piece of work which builds on the ideas and perspectives of other thinkers.

With this rhetorical pastiche, this postmodern auto*body*graphy, I visualize theory into a narrative of expertise about the meaning of *my own experience*. In it I play with postmodern ideas and alter the text of my life. I consult myself as source in an exploration of the effects of class and gender oppression on my body, on my voice, and on my stance in the world. Writer and critic Susan Crean encouraged me to write a book about class during the summer of 1988, when she was my instructor in a Creative Documentary course at a women's writing retreat here in Vancouver, British Columbia. Susan suggested that I gather together all the material I had been exploring over the years I wrote about class as an issue in feminist political theory and in women's literary production. This is the book I must birth first. In this text I disrupt my old fixed identity, the old story of domination. I play with the script. I learn to perform my own meaning as I become my own referent and a sovereign with many subjects. This is the project that breathes life into the possibility of others.

In 1992 I was invited by narrative therapy practitioners to consider that Anxiety and Depression could be understood as *external* forces that were *subjugating me*. An Australian therapist explains the basis of narrative therapeutic thought in this way:

> The body of ideas known as postmodern or constructivist thought presents a perspective on the construction of our reality that allows us to see how we have been recruited into particular ways of being that may or may not be useful or helpful. The possibility of developing new ways of being, that are more in line with what we would prefer, is opened up. We give meaning to our lives by interpreting the experiences we have in the light of the beliefs that we have about ourselves, and we largely dismiss those experiences which do not fit these beliefs. But these beliefs can be changed, they are not fixed or based on any essential truth about human nature.[5]

In other words, each of us can write a preferred story of who we are in opposition to ideas about ourselves which oppress or limit us—ideas that undermine the delicious text of our existence, what theologian Matthew Fox calls the original blessing of our lives. In her novel *Borderlines* Janette Turner Hospital writes that the past is a capricious and discontinuous narrative and the present an infinite number of fictions. The narrative therapeutic idea thrives in this realm of the imagination, in the rich, playful realm of possibilities. The heart of the narrative idea is political; it's about power and possibility. It's about the idea, the passionate idea, that I can separate my life and my relationships from ideas about myself which hurt and oppress me. As a person, I am distinct from my problems. I am a person, and a problem is a problem.

Narrative therapeutic practice is based on the belief that reality is cocreated within a cultural discourse and that problems can be deconstructed *away from a person's identity* or sense of who they are. People and problems are two separate entities. The narrative is about *externalizing* the problems. This has turned out to be a transformative technique for me. This is the big idea that has birthed my emotional freedom. The problem does not reside in me. The problem is the problem, or, more specifically, the *effects* of the problem is the problem. I am invited to resist notions of determinism and the paralyzing impact of pathologizing that informs the medical model of dis-ease in this culture. The narrative approach to human struggles invites me to resist the idea that somehow to be anxious and depressed is part of my essential self or of an indelible problem-saturated story of my life. I am invited to resist the domination of Anxiety and Depression and to have more of a say in the direction my life is going.

The magic in the metaphor began for me when I was able to see Anxiety outside of me in the shape of a fire-breathing dragon that kept threatening to incinerate me. The panic attacks I suffered felt like I was burning alive, and, as the metaphor became more and more real to me, I was able to gradually separate myself from its domineering influence and to name it Dragon-Lady. My life gradually and sometimes dramatically transformed, and I began to write again after several years of silence. Then one day the dragon appeared as a *two-*headed monster, and the Dead Head manifested in my imagination. The tongue on the second head hung from a cracked-lipped mouth, a putrid profusion of passivity. I knew what that swollen tongue was silencing. Working on this piece, my chapter about Depression, had become a struggle. I gazed at the Dead Head of Depression before me, and I knew it was *its* voice telling me that I am too tired to handle the stress of looking for work *and* the focus and discipline needed to write this story. "How can you write the second chapter of a book?" Dead Head laughs at me, opening its mouth just wide enough to expel its venom. "I will tire you out!"

Dead Head dangles loosely from the dragon's thick neck, its eyes closed, a putrid, swollen tongue dominates its flaccid mouth. William Stryon describes the word *Depression* as slivering "innocuously through the language like a slug, leaving little trace of its intrinsic malevolence."[6] But Depression's malevolence and deadly grip are clearly manifested in my imagination in this moment, and I know I have

externalized the problem of Depression in proportion to its dominance in my life. It is not just a scale on Dragon-Lady's tail. It is not just
doing a bit part in the old story. It is not just a *syllable* in the problem-
saturated discourse of femininity. It is its language system, its life-
support system. It is a big problem, a big life-threatening problem.

Women describe its effects on their lives as overpowering; it fosters
a feeling of helplessness and loss of control over one's life. People
under the influence of Depression have six times more marital failures, three times more serious problems in school, and are more likely
to be alcoholics than the general population. They suffer two to three
times more heart attacks and are significantly more likely to die of
cancer or suicide.[7] Furthermore, women receive shock treatment twice
as often as men do and are prescribed 72 percent of all mental
health–related medications.[8]

Dragon-Lady's attacks on me are an immediate challenge, an ad-
renaline rush that forces me to move, to act to save myself. But the
Dead Head of Depression is a weightier matter. I feel breathless in its
bloated presence. It makes me tired and tricks me into thinking I need
to sleep or eat. What's the point of writing or studying or taking
photographs, anyway? Who cares? What difference does it make? It
interrogates me with life-draining questions over and over, over and
over. My Muse, my Maenad, my creative inner child, who loves to play
with words and images, suffers a broken heart and my days and nights
are submerged in passivity and powerlessness. How I look is not good
enough, what I do or think is not good enough, and the sparkle and
magic of existence is extinguished. I drag myself from chore to chore,
forgetting to laugh, oblivious to the kaleidoscope of color outside my
kitchen window. I don't care if the purple finches come or not.

Dead Head is Dragon-Lady's twisted twin. Dragon-Lady's tongue
spits fire, and the Dead Head spews news and views that gag me, that
cut off my breath, that leave me too breathless to speak or write. (Don't
be too creative, too passionate, too intelligent.) Depression is the
consequence of Anxiety: I feel trapped, victimized, and paralyzed by
the toll fear and tension extract from my spirit and from my body. I
wake up in the middle of the night; my stomach is nervous, and I am
tired out. I want to hide from the challenge of living and breathing. My
turbulent history of fear and nervousness has me rocking back and
forth on the bed enveloped by a quilt and the cold cruelty of despair. I
am afraid of being publicly shamed if I voice these thoughts.

Depression used to be a wail of a tale in my mind's eye, but no more.
This scale carries too much weight. Its ideas continue to oppress me
and keep me in my place by comparing me to others and torturing me

with repetitious nonsense, with stories of failure and loss. Brick by brick, brick by brick, the writing on the wall gets writ. (If my own father appears to hate me, how can I possibly matter? Don't relax, don't trust, don't be happy, don't poke out the eye of the ever-watchful double-headed monster.) Dead Head disentitles me to a life of my own, sculpted by care and compassion. It demands allegiance to passivity and people pleasing. The importance of my voice and my life fade away. I feel lost in a fog of fatigue, and I can't seem to make it matter.

Maybe Dead Head appears between the need to belong and the demands of conformity. Maybe Dead Head lives in the distance between dreams and possibilities. After all, a 1978 British study theorized that working-class women were four times more likely to become depressed than women from middle-class homes.[9] Lack of money leads to fewer ways to cope with stress and that old helpless feeling. Poverty devours hope in this story much like Dragon-Lady devoured my energy, focus, and vision. And another study argues that, as a society, we cannot improve women's mental health until we improve their status.[10]

I grew up in Verdun, roller-skating, skipping rope, walking fences. The red and gray brick of Verdun cemented my options: stay, marry, or work as a clerk or secretary and help your folks out. The wall of my childhood was a place referred to in the sociological jargon of the 1930s as an immigrant colony or catch-basin of poor and working-class people. My father's parents immigrated from Scotland in 1929 and settled here in Verdun, a district of Montreal in the province of Quebec. (Brick by brick, brick by brick, the writing on the wall gets writ.) The black iron railings of Verdun extend like tentacles along the quarter-mile of brick flats, side by side, creating a density, a closed atmosphere, a containment. Poverty and hardship are main characters in this scene.

I remember my Great-aunt Nan stooped over, an exhausted expression on her tiny-featured face, her neatly styled hair, her eyes small, blue, intense. She works as a cook in the wealthy district of Westmount, Quebec. When she can leave her employer's kitchen, my mother's simple meals soothe and nourish her like the brown vinyl hassock under her aching legs.

Nan sits in her favorite armchair slightly bent over and intent on her television program. She is enjoying her half-day off from live-in domestic service, relaxing in our living room. She has a half-day off. Thursdays and Sundays were her rest times, according to my mother, who welcomes her husband's aunt into our tiny Verdun flat. My mother babysits neighbors' children, my father works as a supplies clerk, the two paternal aunts who live with us work in the same company; one is a factory worker, the other spends her days upstairs in the office work-ing for an erratic boss, who is under the influence of alcohol most of the time. My aunt makes many crucial decisions for him which her paycheck never reflects. During the evenings our pet budgie pulls bobby pins out of my aunts' hair, as they set their hair in 1950s fashion and laugh as the budgie dips his beak in the glass of water beside the pins.

The outside world for my family is one of bosses and landlords, us and them, the privileged ones and our family, who works for them as a matter of course, as a matter of fact, as a matter of history. Ameri-can archivist and activist Joan Nestle argues that the feminist dictate that the personal is political can be expanded to embrace the notion that the more personal is, in fact, historical. In the preface to her book *A Restricted Country* Nestle writes that the more personal de-mands attention be paid to how we fill our days and our nights as we participate in any given economic system. This idea reflects what the British working-class sociologist Caroline Steedman calls the drama of class, the process of working-class autobiography. I approach history as Tillie Olsen defines it as both a personal past, which gives one a continuous identity, and a social legacy, which links genera-tions. My tension comes from knowing that history's paradigms do not include servants, factory or office workers, and the private world of domesticity. Charlotte Perkins Gilman noted that all the distinctive lines of human progress lie outside this private realm of household management.

In 1987 I traveled to Montreal on a Canada Council grant to inter-view my aunts, who all worked as domestic servants in Montreal during the 1930s and 1940s, before getting better work in factory, sales, or office jobs (except Aunt Nan, who worked in service all her life). As I travel from Westmount to Verdun in a taxi I feel the geogra-phy of class in my bones, as sharp and persistent as fatigue. As I drive into Verdun's density of brick row housing far away from the West-mount spaciousness my aunts served, I feel disquiet. Carolyn Steed-man writes that "accounts of working class life are told by tension and ambiguity out on the borderlands,"[11] and her words gnaw at my insides: Will my aunts remember enough details for me to build a narrative? Will I be able to sift through the family silences to catch a glimpse of my aunts as young immigrant workers? The inherent/in/ herited maid-in-me feels awkward riding in a taxi from Westmount to Verdun, the fare paid from Canada Council coffers. Aunt Nan rode the bus, after all.

How did I begin this work, this story of my aunts as workers? It began in my academic voice, the voice that approached the Canada Council for an explorations grant to search for radical Canadian women writers of the 1920s and 1930s using a feminist cultural framework informed by both a class and historical perspective on writing by women. I wrote that I wanted to search for the Canadian equivalents of Tillie Olsen and Meridel Le Sueur as well as for evidence of the lives of female domestic servants in Montreal during the 1920s and 1930s. I wanted to know if any records were left of their lives and whether or not any of them wrote. I wanted to understand what limited these women's creative expression. I could not accept Canadian poet Sharon Stevenson's perspective that "the working class works, and the owning class directs the affairs of the country. The class in between writes."[12]

But Sharon was right, of course. And I think the main reason I had such a need to search out evidence specifically of domestic workers who wrote is the memory of my Aunt Nan. She loved literature and used to recite the classics to me, like Coleridge's *The Rime of the Ancient Mariner,* her voice soft, her face etched with the exhaustion of working long and hard hours for the luxury of others. But her crinkled, lined countenance seemed to soften as the sounds of the words echoed around our tiny bedroom.

Nan had access to the tremendous libraries of her wealthy employers in Westmount and brought their books home to Verdun with her when she came to rest on her days off or for longer periods, when she was on holiday. Often when I left for school in the morning I would notice where she was in her book and be amazed when I returned home for lunch just how much she had read. A half-read novel on my aunt's lap cheered me somehow: the world seemed less dreary, less limited by the demands of the laboring life I witnessed everyday in the eyes and gestures of my family members. I imagined Nan retreating to her room in her employer's large house with a book of prose or poetry in her hand, and somehow this idea comforted me.

I even embellished this story because I liked it so much. I dared to wonder if my aunt ever wanted to write? Did she resist her role as servant at all in her imagination? Did she feel excluded from the dominant culture of the white men who produced the fine literary work she read so lovingly? One (female) professor was outraged at my questions when she read them in my funding application. She insisted that they denoted "a subjective phenomenelogical thrust that is antipolitical, possibly dangerously so. Whatever her subjectivity, and despite her subjectivity, your aunt was excluded, she was not capable of writing in the discourse that has been defined culturally as 'literature,' she was defined for her employers and their friends and on government documents as a servant. People like your aunt are exploited whether they think so or not."

I let this response silence me for awhile—a long while. Haunted by my own misgivings about the value of my nonmainstream work, I let this reasoned statement of the nature of reality undermine my confidence. I forgot that academics can be dangerous. Ideas and musings seldom are. I felt directionless. I felt dominated by Shame. I felt silly about wondering if Aunt Nan ever thought of writing. Still, I think it was these questions that coached me to fill out a Canada Council application form in the first place and to declare boldly that "I am committed to a full-length study of Canadian women's literary production from both a materialist and feminist viewpoint and am interested in what critics Wendy Frost and Michelle Valiquette call the 'specificity of women's writing'—the social, cultural, historical and economic contexts in which it is produced." If my aunt and other well-read domestic servants like her left evidence of their writing, perhaps in their work I could find a kind of tradition to sustain me in my tortuous ambivalence about academe: I love ideas but am repulsed by academe's inaccessibility, its language and arrogant assumptions about what is worth considering, about whose lives and ideas are worthy of attention and care.

My aunt Nan was the closest I got to the power of the word, the power of language to transport me out of the economic, social, and emotional confines of being a girl in a working-class family. My uncle Steve loved literature, too, but the slaughter and chaos of World War II left its topography on him: he recited poetry in the frenetic language of skid row despair.

Imagining my aunt in a library of her own may be a way I ask for permission to write. Imagining my aunt away from the culinary details of someone else's kitchen may be my way of asking for clues, for comfort, for support—a kind of reaching into my family's history for permission to write, for permission to even consider myself someone with public authority. With this narrative I escort my family into the public domain of what is considered to be history.

The Dead Head of Depression appears at night and writes nightmares on garage walls and the sides of buildings in Verdun. I read them each morning as I board the bus from Verdun to a downtown university with a language all its own.

But this is a postcolonial text. To externalize Depression as an effect of oppression that is informed by subjugating ideas about gender and class *and* to witness its manifestation as a moribund protrusion of a metaphoric monster is salvific and fun. With it I oppose the Dead Head's subjugation of my imagination. I awaken from its hypnotic chant of inadequacy. I cut out its tongue with my pen as mighty as the sword, and I speak against its impoverishing ideas. If I believe that Depression is a part of me—a biochemical quirk or disorder or an emotional tendency—*I* become the problem to be controlled and fixed. If I believe that Depression is not me, I am invited to separate myself from its strategies and sneaky, insidious ways. I am invited to defy it. The most powerful element of this radical conversation is the not-me aspect of externalizing. To fully understand that Depression is *not-me*, that I am not a depressed person, is a tactic against Depression. I may have been immobilized By the spirit-stealing grip of Depression for most of my life. Dead Head may still try to take over my imagination at times, but *I* am not depressed.

In the light of all this, it's my royal duty now to end Dead Head's occupation of my mind, to tear down the walls, brick by brick. The subject of my life can no longer be contained. I have taken charge of the meaning of my suffering. I have taken charge with a pen/sword, and I now cut off the Dead Head whenever I need to. It's my mind, it's my imagination, and the sharp effectiveness of rewriting my life script pleases this duchess.

I like to live in the heart of lightheartedness. Did I mention that I am a duchess as well as a dragon slayer? The Duchess of Verdun, a friend humorously named me a few years ago, as we hiked through the woods and I marveled aloud at the comforts that the money I long for could buy. My friend saw how I love luxury and long for elegance. But I grew up in the working-class district of Montreal, where my people sat on porches to drink beer and tea so they could wake up the next morning to work for others. Poverty has stalked the duchess most of her life. But now I am the subject and sovereign of my life.[13] I love pleasure. I take delight in my own skin. There is a friendly takeover in progress. I have suffered long enough with the cellular memories of occupation, of severe takeovers of my self. I am in charge of my realm now, my body, my mind. The light is on, and I'm at home with myself. I can no longer leave my life to the double-headed dragon of Anxiety and Depression. I can no longer leave my body to suffer the *effects* of oppression on it. I prefer to intervene on my own behalf and have more of a say in the direction my life is going in. I reclaim my imagination as my own playground which thrives at a safe distance from ideas that want to incarcerate it.

NOTES

This piece is an excerpt entitled "Class Connections" from the second chapter of a book-in-progress by Cy-Thea Sand. Her working title is *Magic in a Metaphor; A Dragon-Slayin' Tale about Narrative Therapy.* The first chapter describes how she became a dragon slayer and defeated Anxiety. It was published in the *White Rock Journal of Family Therapy* in November 1993. This segment tells a story about the Dead Head of Depression and how it began to stalk her from the very beginnings of her life as a working-class woman.

Cy-Thea's lyrical documentary prose explores the theory and practice of deconstruction and its application to a form of therapy known as the narrative. Its power lies in the fact that Cy-Thea has liberated herself from Anxiety and Depression after suffering under their abusive power for most of her life. She has become a dragon slayer extraordinaire. To become conscious of the forces operating against her was the beginning of her ability to speak on her own behalf, to argue for her preferred story. Cy-Thea believes that she could not give effective, transformative voice to her opposition to the forces of Anxiety and Depression until there *was* an opposition, a double description, of dragon slayer and dragon.

1. "A Question of Identity," *Fireweed*, 25 (July 1987).
2. Harvey Weinstein, *A Father, a Son and the CIA*, 5.
3. *Vancouver Sun*, 17 January 1984.
4. *Vancouver Sun*, 17 January 1984.
5. Maggie Carey, "Perspectives on the Men's Movement," *Dulwich Centre Newsletter,* nos. 3–4 (1992): 71.
6. William Styron, *Darkness Visible*, 37.
7. Pat Leidl, "Poor Job Prospects Linked to Older Women's Depression," *Vancouver Sun*, 26 September 1988.
8. Jane O'Hara, "The Agony of Depression," *McLeans' Magazine*, 19 March 1994.
9. O'Hara, "Agony of Depression."
10. Leidl, "Poor Job Prospects."
11. Carolyn Steedman, *Landscape for a Good Woman*, 22.
12. Sharon Stevenson committed suicide. In the introduction to Sharon's book of poetry, *Gold Earrings*, Robin Endres writes that the contradictions Sharon experienced as a working-class woman and a writer invited her to meet them with both strength and self-assertion and paralyzing self-denial.
13. I have photographs to prove I'm the Duchess of Verdun. Kathleen Symmons, who calls herself the Baroness of Burnaby, is my dear friend, who is an anti-Anxiety activist as well as an artist. She took photographs of my duchess persona for a project for one of her classes at the Emily Carr School of Art and Design here in Vancouver. Kathleen calls her project *Frame of Mind* and it includes photographs of four working-class women, including herself, her mother, her roommate at the time, and yours truly, the Duchess of Verdun. Kathleen describes her work "as a project to

empower *us*, in a sense to deconstruct the dominant story based on gender and class issues or play with the dominant story to externalize this story and see what our gender, our class/cultural beliefs and family of origin assign to us and how this dictates our position, place, and power. This project plays with my belief in the horizontal connectedness of all people and demystifies and disempowers the existing vertical hierarchy of the patriarchy."

Cy-Thea Sand *has begun work on a play called* The Sylvia Plath of Verdun. *She says that "the Duchess of Verdun just may sneak into it."*

Autobiographies by American Working-Class Women: An Annotated Bibliography

Cheryl Cline

I believe that the study of women's autobiographical writings, of our lives, is better served by a more elastic definition of *autobiography* than by one too narrowly defined. Working-class women's writing, especially, too often finds itself on the wrong side of the borders used to separate autobiography from other literary forms, and it violates rules set down to define autobiography as an expression of the self—that is, an expression of *one*self, written *by* oneself. Much of women's autobiography is oral history, taken down from women who may be illiterate or at least not of a literary bent. Women may also, often as not, write their autobiographies into collective histories, whether it be labor struggles, the history of their own ethnic group in the United States, regional culture, or family history.

Therefore, this bibliography includes not only formal autobiographies but also memoirs, diaries, oral histories, and interviews. It includes "as told to" autobiographies by celebrities and common working women alike: country singers and cotton mill girls, actresses and labor leaders. I have also listed a number of recent experiments in autobiography which weave together fiction and fact and collections of writings in which it is difficult to draw the line between personal narrative, political writing, and poetry. I have also included a few texts that are as much documentary as autobiography but which serve to ground the writer's experience in her culture.

Anthologies, Oral Histories, and Documentary Histories

Andrews, William L., ed. *Sisters of the Spirit: Three Black Women's Autobiographies of the Nineteenth Century*. Bloomington: Indiana University Press, 1986. 245pp. Reprints, with footnotes and commentary, *The Life and Religious Experience of Jarena Lee* (1836), *A Brand Plucked from the Fire* by Julia Foote (1879) and *The Memoirs of the Life, Religious Experience, Ministerial Travels and Labours of Mrs. Zilpha Elaw* (1846).

Buss, Frances Leeper. *Dignity: Lower Income Women Tell of Their Lives and Struggles: Oral Histories*. Introduction by Susan Contratto. Ann Arbor: University of Michigan Press, 1985. 290pp.

Byerly, Victoria. *Hard Times Cotton Mill Girls: Personal Histories of Women and Poverty in the South, as Told to Victoria Byerly*. Introduction by Cletus E. Daniel. Ithaca: Cornell University Press, 1986. 223pp.

Hourwich, Andria Taylor, and Gladys L. Palmer, eds. *I Am a Woman Worker: A Scrapbook of Autobiographies*. New York: Affiliated School for Workers, 1936. 152pp. Facsimile reprint, Arno Press, 1974. 152pp.

Kahn, Kathy. *Hillbilly Women*. Photos by Al Clayton. Migrant photos by Franck Blechman, Jr. Garden City, N.Y.: Doubleday, 1973. 230pp.

Martin, Molly. *Hard-Hatted Women: Stories of Struggle and Success in the Trades*. Seattle: Seal Press, 1988. 265pp.

Moraga, Cherríe, and Gloria Anzaldúa. *This Bridge Called My Back: Writings by Radical Women of Color*. 1981. With an introduction by Toni Cade Bambara. Watertown, Mass.: Persephone Press. Reprint, Latham, N.Y.: Kitchen Table/Women of Color Press, 1984. 261pp.

Myerhoff, Barbara. *Number Our Days*. New York: Dutton, 1978. 306pp. New York: Simon and Schuster, Touchstone, 1980. 306pp.

Seiffer, Nancy. *Nobody Speaks for Me! Self-Portraits of American Working-Class Women*. New York: Simon and Schuster, 1976. 477pp.

Seller, Maxine Schwartz, ed. *Immigrant Women*. Philadelphia: Temple University Press, 1981. 347pp.

Sheth, Jagdish, and David A. Heffner, eds. *Voice with a Smile: True Stories from American Telephone Operators*. Barrington, Ill.: PERQ Publications, 1993.

Sternsher, Bernard, and Judith Sealander, eds. *Women of Valor: The Struggle against the Great Depression as Told in Their Own Life Stories*. Chicago: Ivan R. Dee, 1990. 312pp.

Thomas, Sherry. *We Didn't Have Much, but We Sure Had Plenty: Stories of Rural Women*. New York: Doubleday, Anchor, 1981. 185pp. (Second ed. subtitled "Rural Women in Their Own Words.")

Tucker, Susan, comp. *Telling Memories among Southern Women: Domestic Workers and Their Employers in the Segregated South*. Baton Rouge: Louisiana State University Press, 1988. Paperback ed. New York: Schocken Books, and Toronto: Random House of Canada, 1988. 278pp.

Wetherby, Terry. *Conversations: Working Women Talk about Doing a "Man's" Job*. Millbrae, Calif.: Les Femmes, 1977. 269pp.

Zandy, Janet, ed. *Calling Home: Working Class Women's Writings*. New Brunswick and London: Rutgers University Press, 1990. 366pp.

Individual Works

Abbot, Shirley. *The Bookmaker's Daughter: A Memory Unbound*. New York: Ticknor and Fields, 1991. 290pp.

———. *Womenfolks: Growing Up Down South*. New York: Ticknor and Fields, 1983. 210pp.

Ahern, Nell Giles. *Punch In, Susie! A Woman's War Factory Diary*. Drawings by Alan Dunn. New York and London: Harper Brothers, 1943. 143pp.

Allison, Dorothy. *Skin: Talking about Sex, Class & Literature*. Ithaca: Firebrand Books, 1994. 261pp.

Anderson, Mary. *Women at Work: The Autobiography of Mary Anderson*. As told to Mary Winslow. Minneapolis: University of Minnesota, 1951. 266pp.

Angelou, Maya. *All God's Children Need Traveling Shoes*. New York: Random House, 1986. 210pp.

———. *Gather Together in My Name*. New York: Random House, 1974. 214pp.

———. *The Heart of a Woman*. New York: Random House, 1981. 272pp.

———. *I Know Why the Caged Bird Sings*. New York: Random House, 1969. 281pp.

———. *Singin' and Swingin' and Gettin' Merry like Christmas*. New York: Random House, 1976. 269pp.

Anon. *Four Years in the Underbrush: Adventures as a Working Girl in New York*. New York: Charles Scribner's Sons, 1921. 315pp.

Anzaldúa, Gloria. *Borderlands / La Frontera: The New Mestiza*. San Francisco: Spinsters / Aunt Lute, 1987. 203pp.

Barber, Olive. *The Lady and the Lumberjack*. Introduction by Stewart H. Holbrook. New York: Crowell, 1952.

Barr, Roseanne. *Roseanne: My Life as a Woman*. New York: Harper and Row, 1989. 202pp.

Bloor, Ella. *We Are Many: An Autobiography*. New York: International Publishers, 1940. 319pp.

Box-Car Bertha. *Sister of the Road: The Autobiography of Box-Car Bertha*. As told to Dr. Ben L. Reitman. Sheridan House, 1937. 314pp. Reprint. Harper and Row (Harper Colophon), 1975. 314pp. Reprint, with an introduction by Kathy Acker and an afterword by Roger Bruns. New York: AMOK Press, 1988. 285pp.

Brant, Beth [Degonwadonti]. *Mohawk Trail*. Ithaca, N.Y.: Firebrand, 1985. 94pp.

Burrow, Brunettie. *Angels in White*. San Antonio: Naylor, 1959. 132pp. (Memoir of a nurse.)

———. *I Lay Down My Cap*. San Antonio: Naylor, 1961. 96pp.

Caldwell, Taylor. *On Growing Up Tough*. Old Greenwich, Conn.: Devin-Adair, 1971. 159pp.

[Carpenter, Arie]. *Aunt Arie: A Foxfire Portrait*. Edited by Linda Garland Page and Eliot Wigginton. New York: E. P. Dutton, 1983. 216pp. (Arie Carpenter lived from 1885 to 1978.)

Caudill, Rebecca. *My Appalachia: A Reminiscence*. New York: Holt, Rinehart and Winston, 1966. 90pp.

Cavalleri, Rosa. *The Life of an Italian Immigrant*. Edited by Marie Hall Ets. Foreword by Rudolph J. Vecoli. Minneapolis: University of Minnesota Press, 1970. 254pp.

Cochran, Jacqueline. *The Stars at Noon*. Boston: Little, Brown, 1954. 274pp.

Cuero, Delfina. *The Autobiography of Delfina Cuero, a Diegueno Indian,* as told to Florence C. Shipek. Los Angeles: Dawson's Book Shop, 1968. 67pp.

Davis, Alice Pauline. *Bayou Boats*. New York: New Voices Publishing, 1950. 143pp.

Day, Dorothy. *The Long Loneliness: An Autobiography*. Illustrated by Fritz Eichenberg. New York: Harper, 1952. 288pp. Reprinted with an introduction by Daniel Berrigan, San Francisco: Harper and Row, 1952, 1981. 288pp.

Day, Helen Caldwell. *Color, Ebony*. New York: Sheed and Ward, 1951. 182pp.

DeForest, Elsie Davis. *Out of My Cabin*. Boston: Christopher, 1956. 186pp.

Dodge, Helen Carmichael. *My Childhood in the Canadian Wilderness.* New York: Vantage, 1961. 77pp.

Durbin, Marina. *Lima Beans and City Chicken: A Memoir of the Open Hearth.* New York: E. P. Dutton, 1989. 172pp.

East, Lorecia. *The Boomers: The Autobiography of a Roughneck's Wife.* Baton Rouge: Legacy Publishing, 1976. 63pp.

Ellis, Anne. *The Life of an Ordinary Woman.* With an introduction by Lucy Fitch Perkins. Boston: Houghton Mifflin, 1929. 300pp. Reprint. New York, Arno Press, 1974. Reprint, with a foreword by Elliott West. Lincoln: University of Nebraska Press, 1980. 300pp.

———. *Plain Anne Ellis: More about the Life of an Ordinary Woman.* Boston and New York: Houghton Mifflin, 1931. 264pp. Reprint. Lincoln: University of Nebraska Press, 1984. 264pp.

———. *Sunshine Preferred: The Philosophy of an Ordinary Woman.* Boston and New York: Houghton Mifflin, 1934. 248pp. Reprint. Lincoln: University of Nebraska Press, 1984.

Emerson, Irma Lee, with Jean Muir. *The Woods Were Full of Men.* New York: David McKay, 1963. 242pp.

Engle, Ada M. *It Happened at 1001.* New York: Vantage Press, 1959. 80pp.

[Erickson, Gail, pseud.] *The Whole Works: The Autobiography of a Young American Couple.* By Bruce and Gail Erickson, as recorded by Starry Krueger. New York: Random House, 1973. 205pp.

Erwin, Carol. *The Orderly Disorderly House.* With Floyd Miller. Garden City, N.Y.: Doubleday, 1960. 284pp.

Evert, Gertrude S. *My Twenty-eight Years as an Army Nurse.* New York: Exposition Press, 1959. 84pp.

Ferris, Louanne [pseud.]. *I'm Done Crying.* As told to Beth Day. New York: M. Evans, 1969. 275pp.

Findlay, Mary. *Tooth and Nail: The Story of a Daughter of the Depression.* Wellington: A. H. and A. W. Reed, 1974. 267pp.

Flynn, Elizabeth Gurley. *I Speak My Own Piece: Autobiography of "The Rebel Girl."* New York: Masses and Mainstream, 1955. 326pp. Revised edition published under the title *The Rebel Girl: An Autobiography. My First Life (1906–1926).* New York: International Publishers, 1973. 351pp.

French, Emily. *Emily, the Diary of a Hard-Worked Woman.* Edited by Janet Lecompte. Lincoln: University of Nebraska Press, 1987. 166pp.

Gazaway, Rena. *The Longest Mile*. Garden City, N.Y.: Doubleday, 1969. 348pp.

Gerken, Mabel. R. *Ladies in Pants: A Home Front Diary*. New York: Exposition Press, 1949. 96pp.

Giles, Janice Holt. *Forty Acres and No Mule*. Second edition, with a new prologue by the author. Boston: Houghton Mifflin, 1967. 239pp.

Gilfillan, Lauren [pseud. for Harriet Woodbridge Gilfillan]. *I Went to Pit College*. New York: Viking Press, 1934. 288pp.

Golden, Marita. *Long Distance Life*. Garden City, N.Y.: Doubleday, 1989. 321pp.

————. *Migrations of the Heart: An Autobiography*. Garden City, N.Y.: Doubleday/Anchor Press, 1983. 234pp.

Goldman, Emma. *Living My Life*. 2 vols. New York: Alfred A. Knopf, 1931. Reprint, with an introduction by Sheila Rowbotham. London: Pluto Press, 1986. 2 vols.

Goodwin, Ruby Berkley. *It's Good to Be Black*. Garden City, N.Y.: Doubleday, 1953. 256pp.

Guffy, Ossie. *Ossie: The Autobiography of a Black Woman*. As told to Caryl Ledner. New York: W. W. Norton, 1971. 224pp.

Guillory, "Queen" Ida. *Cookin' with Queen Ida: "Bon Temps" Creole Recipes (and Stories) from the Queen of Zydeco Music*. Queen Ida Guillory with Naomi Wise. Interviews by Michael Goodwin and Irene Namkung. Rocklin, Calif.: Prima Publishing, 1990. 240pp.

Hasanovitz, Elizabeth. *One of Them: Chapters from a Passionate Autobiography*. Boston: Houghton Mifflin, 1918. 33pp.

hooks, bell. *Talking Back: Thinking Feminist / Thinking Black*. Boston: South End Press, 1989. 184pp.

Hurston, Zora Neale. *Dust Tracks on a Road*. Boston: J. B. Lippincott, 1942. 294pp. Reprint, with an introduction by Larry Neal. Boston, J. B. Lippincott, 1971. 286pp. New edition, edited and with an introduction by Robert Hemenway. Urbana: University of Illinois Press, 1971, 1984. Reprint, with a new foreword by Maya Angelou. New York: Harper/Perennial, 1991. 278pp.

Huttman, Barbara. *Code Blue: A Nurse's True Life Story*. New York: William Morrow, 1982. 280pp.

Jacobs, Harriet A. *Incidents in the Life of a Slave Girl. Written by herself. . . .* Edited by L. Maria Child. Boston, Published for the author,

1861. 306pp. Reprinted with an introduction by Valerie Smith. New York: Oxford University Press, 1988. 306pp. New edition edited and with an introduction by Jean Fagan Yellin. Cambridge: Harvard University Press, 1987. 306pp.

Jackson, Nannie Stillwell. *Vinegar Pie and Chicken Bread: A Woman's Diary of Life in the Rural South, 1890–1891.* Edited with an introduction by Margaret Jones Bolsterli. Fayetteville: University of Arkansas Press, 1982. 108pp.

Kingston, Maxine Hong. *China Men.* New York: Alfred A. Knopf, 1980. 308pp.

———. *Woman Warrior: Memoirs of a Girlhood among Ghosts.* New York: Alfred A. Knopf, 1976. 209pp.

Kunkler, Anita. *Hardscrabble: A Narrative of the California Hill Country.* Edited, with commentaries and notes, by Wilbur S. Shepperson. Reno: University of Nevada Press, 1975. 252pp.

Larcom, Lucy. *Letters of Lucy Larcom to the Whittiers.* Edited by Grace F. Shepard. Baltimore: Southworth Press, 1930. 20pp. Reprinted from *New England Quarterly 3*, 3 (1930).

———. *Lucy Larcom: Her Life, Letters and Diary.* Daniel Dulany Addison. Boston and New York: Houghton Mifflin, and Cambridge: Riverside Press, facsimile reprint, 1894. 295pp.

———. *A New England Girlhood, Outlined from Memory.* Boston and New York: Houghton Mifflin, 1889. 274pp. Facsimile reprint. New York: Arno Press, 1974. Reprint, with a foreword by Nancy Cott. Boston: Northeastern University Press, 1986. 274pp.

Le Sueur, Meridel. *Ripening: Selected Work, 1927–1980.* Edited and with an introduction by Elaine Hedges. Old Westbury, N.Y.: The Feminist Press, 1982. 291pp. Second edition, with a new afterword, by Meridel Le Sueur. New York: The Feminist Press, 1990. 295pp.

Lorde, Audre. *The Cancer Journals.* Argyle, N.Y.: Spinster's Ink, 1980. 77pp.

———. *Zami, A New Spelling of My Name: A Biomythography by Audre Lorde.* Freedom, Calif.: Crossing Press, 1982. 256pp.

Lucas, María Elena. *Forged under the Sun / Forjada Bajo el Sol: The Life of Maria Elena Lucas.* Edited with an introduction by Fran Leeper Buss. Ann Arbor: University of Michigan Press, 1993. 314pp.

Lynn, Loretta, with George Vecsey. *Coal Miner's Daughter.* Chicago: Regnery, 1976. 204pp. Reprint. New York: Warner Books, 1980. 269pp.

McConnell, Roberta. *Never Marry a Ranger*. New York: Prentice-Hall, 1950. 261pp.

McGarvey, Lois. *Along Alaska Trails*. New York: Vantage Press, 1960. 200pp.

Mitchell, Dorothea. *Lady Lumberjack*. Vancouver: Mitchell Press, 1967. 135pp.

Moody, Ann. *Coming of Age in Mississippi*. New York: Dial Press, 1968. 348pp.

Moraga, Cherríe. *Loving in the War Years: Lo que Nunca Pasó sus Labios*. Boston: South End Press, 1983. 152pp.

Mother Jones. *The Autobiography of Mother Jones*. Edited by Mary Field Parton. Introduction by Clarence Darrow. Chicago: C. H. Kerr, 1925. 245pp. Reprint. New York: Arno Press, 1969. Reprint, with an introduction and bibliography by Fred Thompson. Chicago: Published for the Illinois Labor History Society by C. H. Kerr, 1972. 242pp.

———. *Mother Jones Speaks: Collected Writings and Speeches*. Edited by Philip S. Foner. New York: Monad Press (distributed by Pathfinder Press), 1983. 724pp.

Murray, Pauli. *Proud Shoes: The Story of an American Family*. New York: Harper, 1956. 276pp.

Nestor, Agnes. *Woman's Labor Leader: An Autobiography*. Rockford, Ill.: Bellevue Books, 1954. 307pp.

Nieman, Linda. *Boomer: Railroad Memoirs*. Berkeley: University of California Press, 1990. 252pp.

Padow, Mollie Potter. *A Saga of Eighty Years of Living*. Philadelphia: Dorrance, 1971. 228pp.

Parker, Sybil Rosa. *Working Stewardess to Captain's Lady: My Life on the Luxury Liners*. Los Alamitos, Calif.: Hwong Publishing, 1979. 195pp.

Pesotta, Rose. *Bread upon the Waters*. Edited by John Nicholas Beffel. New York: Dodd, Mead, 1944. 435pp. Reprint, with a new introduction by Ann Schofield. Ithaca: ILR Press, 1987. 435pp.

———. *Days of Our Lives*. Boston: Excelsior, 1958. 262pp.

Pinzer, Maimie. *The Maimie Papers*. Edited by Ruth Rosen and Sue Davidson. Old Westbury, N.Y.: The Feminist Press, 1977. Paperback ed., 1981. 439pp.

Ritchie, Jean. *Singing Family of the Cumberlands.* Including words and music for forty-two songs. Illustrated by Maurice Sendak. New York: Oak Publications, 1963. Reprint of 1955 edition. 258pp.

Rodriguez, Rosalie. Oh! *For the Life of a Stewardess.* New York: Comet Press, 1953. 123pp.

Ruby, Edna R. *Shorthand with Champagne.* Cleveland: World, 1965. 246pp.

Rutland, Eva. *The Trouble with Being a Mama.* New York: Abingdon, 1964. 143pp.

Scarborough, Mary Grossman, 1895–. *Whirlwinds of Danger: The Memoirs of Mary Grossman Scarborough.* With a foreword by William McAdoo. New York: David Walker Press, 1990. 187pp.

Schneiderman, Rose, with Lucy Goldwaite. *All for One.* New York: Paul S. Ericksson, 1967. 264pp.

Sinclair, Jo. *The Seasons: Death and Transfiguration.* New York: The Feminist Press, 1993. 279pp.

Strainchamps, Ethel Reed. *Don't Never Say Cain't.* Garden City, N.Y.: Doubleday, 1965. 168pp.

Stewart, Elinore Pruitt. *Letters of a Woman Homesteader.* Boston and New York: Houghton Mifflin, 1914. 281pp. Reprint, with a foreword by Jessamyn West. Lincoln: University of Nebraska Press, 1961. 282pp.

Stokes, Rose Pastor. *I Belong to the Working Class: The Unfinished Autobiography of Rose Pastor Stokes.* Edited by Herbert Shapiro and David L. Sterling. Athens: University of Georgia Press, 1992. 173pp.

Tam, Augusta. *By Dim and Flaring Lamps.* Transcribed by Katherine Boies McCallen. New York: Vantage Press, 1964. 143pp.

Tarbell, Ida Minerva. *All in the Day's Work: An Autobiography.* New York: Macmillan, 1939. 412pp.

Terrell, Mary Church. *A Colored Woman in a White World.* Washington, D.C.: Ransdell, 1940. 436pp. Reprint: Washington, D.C.: National Association of Colored Women's Clubs, 1968. 545pp. Reprint. New York: Arno Press, 1980. 436pp. Reprint. Salem, N.H.: Ayer, 1986. 436pp.

Van Vorst, Mrs. John, and Marie Van Vorst. *The Woman Who Toils. Being the Experience of Two Gentlewomen as Factory Girls.* New York: Doubleday, Page, 1903. 303pp.

Vorse, Mary Heaton. *The Autobiography of an Elderly Woman.* Boston and New York: Houghton Mifflin, 1911. 269pp. Reprint. New York: Arno Press, 1974. 269pp.

———. *Footnote to Folly: Reminiscences of Mary Heaton Vorse.* New York: Farrar and Rinehart, 1934. 407pp. Reprint. Arno Press, 1980. 407pp.

Walker, Alice. *In Search of Our Mother's Gardens: Womanist Prose.* San Diego: Harcourt Brace Jovanovich, 1983. 397pp.

Walker, Margaret. *How I Wrote Jubilee.* Chicago: Third World Press, 1972. 36pp. Reprinted in *How I Wrote Jubilee and Other Essays on Life and Literature.* New York: The Feminist Press, 1990. 157pp.

Waterman, Sherry. *From Another Island: Adventures and Misadventures of an Airline Stewardess.* Philadelphia: Chilton Books, 1962. 206pp.

Weisbord, Vera Buch. *A Radical Life.* Bloomington and London: Indiana University Press, 1977. 384pp.

Williamson, Anne A. *Fifty Years in Starch.* Culver City, Calif.: Murray and Gee, 1948. 245pp.

Yamauchi, Wakako. *Songs My Mother Taught Me: Stories, Plays and Memoir.* New York: The Feminist Press, 1994. 257pp.

Cheryl Cline is a writer interested in working-class autobiography and literature. She is the author of Women's Diaries, Letters, and Journals: A Bibliography (1989). *She publishes* Twangin', *a small magazine about Country music, and is currently working on* Payday, *a newsletter devoted to working-class writing to begin publication in the fall. (For information, write to 2230 Huron Drive, Concord, CA 94519; or e-mail to cline@well.sf.ca.us).*

Reclaiming Our Working-Class Identities: Teaching Working-Class Studies in a Blue-Collar Community

Linda Strom

> We struggle to live.
> We strive for more.
> We struggle for more.
> To begin where we started.
> We start at the bottom.
> To work our way up.
> When things fall apart,
> We move on
> and start
> at the bottom
> again.
>
> —*W. Kay W., "The Cycle"*

The cycle the writer describes in this epigraph was once a familiar one to me. Before entering college at the age of thirty, I worked a string of low-paying pink-collar jobs that left me frustrated and struggling from paycheck to paycheck to make ends meet. I longed for meaningful work that would be valued by me and by others. Education seemed like the way to break the cycle and to find work that mattered.

In the beginning the strong work ethic instilled in me by my parents and the years of working an eight-hour day translated well into the academic world. I approached school like a job, putting in a day's work and finding myself rewarded with praise and good grades. Soon, however, I discovered that, the longer I stayed in school, the more separated I felt from the first thirty years of my life. The signs of separation were all around me. I now had two distinct groups of friends—those I had made while working and those I had made while in school—and, like my two lives, those two groups of friends never mixed. My family, while supportive, also began to feel like I was growing away from them. My father and brother once told my mother that they thought that, because of my education, we no longer had anything in common.[1]

I began to notice, too, a growing anxiety in myself. I did not know what world I belonged in anymore.[2] The turning point for me occurred while I was attending the 1990 Women's Studies Conference in Akron. Janet Zandy was chairing a panel made up of contributors to her anthology of working-class women writers entitled *Calling Home*.[3] Zandy and Victoria Byerly, who wrote *Hard Time Cotton Mill Girls*, discussed their struggle to reclaim and to integrate their working-class backgrounds with their present academic lives.[4] When Zandy opened up the discussion and invited us all to join in, I was amazed to find myself in a room full of women who shared a similar feeling of pride and shame in their working-class roots. Hearing their stories and hearing myself speak, for the first time, about my two separate lives made me realize that much of the experience and the story of working-class people has been, until recently, invisible in the academic world.

Recent scholars such as Zandy, Paul Lauter, Deborah Rosenfelt, and Tillie Olsen, who have helped make visible the forgotten or silenced literary history of the working class, can be seen as the pioneers in defining the field of working-class studies. With the publication of *Yonnondio: From the Thirties* and *Silences*, Olsen not only rekindled an interest in writers of the 1930s but also an interest in working-class fiction.[5] Rosenfelt's essay entitled "From the Thirties: Tillie Olsen and the Radical Tradition" reconnected Olsen's *Yonnondio* with the literary and cultural history that produced the text.[6] Until that essay the importance of Olsen's early political work in the Communist Party and her working-class background had not been sufficiently acknowledged.[7] In 1980 Paul Lauter's essay "Women's Literature: An Introduction to Study" provided a much needed bibliography, which sketched out the beginnings of a literary history of working-class women writers.[8] Zandy's *Calling Home* continued that history by showing us the themes and issues that concern twentieth-century working-class female writers. The notion of reclaiming and legitimizing our working-class past—illustrated by the work of Olsen, Rosenfelt, Lauter, and Zandy—became the focus of a class I teach entitled "Working-Class Women Writers."

My primary concern when I was designing the course was to connect the themes and issues of the various works by women with the students' own personal experiences and backgrounds. I teach at Youngstown State University, where the majority of students come from blue-collar families. The university is surrounded by deserted steel mills— mills that, when they were in full production, "made Youngstown's steelworkers one of the most productive, best-paid, and seemingly secure industrial labor forces in the world." When the mills began closing in 1977, Youngstown went from "the prototypical industrial city" to "the prototypical city in economic crisis." In less than three years over ten thousand jobs were permanently eliminated within the metropolitan area.[9] In response to the crisis the local union, the rank and file, and the people in the Youngstown community organized the Ecumenical Coalition of Mahoning Valley and attempted to buy back one of the mills and make it an employee-run operation.[10] The plan failed, but it is only one example in a long history of the community's labor struggle. As Staughton Lynd, a labor lawyer and a political activist, writes, "[Youngstown] is a strong union town."[11]

Although it seems at times that the shutdown of the mills has overshadowed the powerful history of Youngstown's working class, in the course that I teach students begin to make connections between their current struggle to work, in some cases full-time, and to attend school with the struggle of past laborers within the community— laborers who are often their parents, grandparents, or relatives. As the course progresses, we begin to construct a communal history that is then woven together with the history of working-class people represented in *Coming Home*, which is the main text for the course.[12]

To help the students make the connection between their personal histories and the larger political history of working-class people, I frame the course with the students' own writing, asking them to keep a journal and, at the end of the term, to submit a creative piece of writing—an essay, a poem, or a short story—which reflects the themes discussed throughout the term. These writings are then gathered together into a class book, which is edited and assembled by the students. Ideas for the final creative piece often take shape in the first journal assignment, in which I ask the students to write the story of their work histories. To get them started I begin class the same way I began this essay—by describing my family background, my work history, and my experiences in college. By writing their own and their family's work histories, the students feel empowered by their working-class experiences and begin to take pride in their class background.

During the second class session the students read their autobiographies aloud. The stories are amazing. They tell of men and women who organize unions, go on strike and walk picket lines, file charges against employers who have sexually harassed them, go to work as teenagers to help support the family, and struggle to make life better for themselves and their families. Individually or collectively, they create an impressive story of working-class life within the community.

Writing and hearing the stories help students identify themselves as members of the same socioeconomic class while also showing them how differences such as race, gender, sexual preference, and income level can complicate that identity. Their differences inflect their auto-biographies, their readings, and their final creative projects.

As we begin discussing the readings in *Calling Home*, I encourage the students to write their own experiences into their analyses of the readings. I want their voices to interrupt and to intersect with the voices in the text, thus providing a continual link with the issues and themes of other working-class people. For most of the students the extreme poverty and the oppressive home and working conditions that shaped many of the women's lives in *Calling Home* fall outside their perceptions of growing up in a working-class home. Although, as one woman put it, while she personally had not experienced the pain and suffering documented in the readings, every reading made her remember someone in her life who had.

The final collaborative class book becomes an important step for collecting memories of family, of childhood, and of work experiences. Everyone is asked to submit a piece of writing for the book, and the last two weeks are spent editing the submissions, writing the introduction, and deciding how to organize the writing into sections of shared themes. The students are often inspired by a piece they read in *Calling Home* and go on to write about a similar experience.

For example, after reading Donna Langston's poem "Down on the Strike Line with My Children," Laura Kollat recalls the time her mother packed up all the children and took them down to join their father on the picket line.[13] Kollat writes about the importance of this memory in an essay entitled "My Mother Is a Working Woman":

> I remember my mom in the traditional role of mother and wife, caretaker and nurturer. I remember her cleaning the house, helping with the homework, making dinner, and doing laundry. There was a time, however, when she was much more to our family—a time I sometimes forget.
>
> It was almost winter, and I was only seven years old the first time my father went out on strike with his union. I didn't understand what it meant, I only knew that mother got a job and became a member of the "working society."[14]

Her mother "found work at Montgomery Ward's, a department store on the other side of town," working "long days and even longer nights, taking as many hours as the management would give her." In her mother's absence Kollat learned "to clip coupons" and "make soup from left-over chicken bones." All throughout this family crisis Kollat is impressed with her mother's resourcefulness: "My mother was a wonder at making what little money we had stretch far beyond what it should. Yet, despite all her worries about not having enough, she never let my brother and me know just how much of a financial bind we were in."

The hard work and sacrifice of mothers is a constant theme in the students' writing. In "Second Helpings" Tracy Coleman writes that, as a child, she used to complain to her mother "that [she] was sick and tired of being poor." Her mother never told her how much her complaining hurt her until Coleman was an adult: "She says that back then, I may have been sick and tired of being poor, but she was just plain sick and tired—and she didn't have the time or energy to explain or to make me understand that a single woman with three children couldn't work any harder."[15] In her poem "Image of My Mother" Sherry T. celebrates her mother's years of laboring in other people's houses to support Sherry and her sister and, like in Kollat's essay, her mother's resourcefulness:

> Glancing downward I look at my mother's hands,
> how they toiled to make dollars too few . . .
> Cleaning houses for others, and ironing clothes,
> accepting hand-me-downs; making them look new.[16]

Along with celebrating the hard work and the sacrifices of their mothers, the students also acknowledge their own struggles. They write about the tedious jobs they must hold to support themselves and to pay for their schooling. For example, in her poem entitled "The Line" W. Kay W. writes about what it's like to work on an assembly line day after day:

> I punch in at the clock
> on my way to the line.
> I pick up an order
> and the top one is mine.
> I follow the order
> one thing at a time.
> Place it all in the box—
> send it on down the line.
> I return to the bin
> and again from the top
> I repeat the whole process
> which seems never to stop.[17]

Denise Bowell, in her poem entitled "Everyday," describes a similar kind of daily monotony:

> Everyday she walks into the same
> workplace, punches in the same timecard,
> works the same job, and sees the same
> people.
>
> Everyday while she works, she wonders to
> herself, "am I working to live, or
> am I living to work?"[18]

While the students' writings describe their daily struggles to work and go to school, the writing also reveals their determination not to let the work they must do destroy their spirits. Sherry Buzzard writes in her poem "They Don't Have Me!" that, while her employers "may have 9 hrs of my day / They don't have me!" She ends the poem by claiming her power: "They will never take away / my dignity or my will to do better in life!"[19]

In the introduction to *Calling Home* Zandy writes that working-class "lives are obscured and erased; their work is barely visible. And their writing is not read in literature classes."[20] As the field of working-class studies grows, the experiences and literary history of working-class people and culture begin to come into focus. Reclaiming the past is an important first step not only for the students, teachers, and scholars who work in the field but also for those of us who come from working-class backgrounds. Our pasts have taught us that we must have what Pam Limbert describes in the introduction to *Our Voyage toward Life* as "searching eyes—eyes that delved back to where it all began for each, and enabled each to stretch forward to see, to discover, what lies beyond what each thought possible."[21]

NOTES

Epigraph: This poem is taken from the first-class book entitled *Hidden Treasures: The Discovery of Working-Class Identities* (March 1994). I will explain the process and the significance of putting this book together later in the article.

1. Richard Rodriquez describes a similar feeling of alienation from his family in his essay entitled "The Achievement of Desire," *Hunger of Memory: The Education of Richard Rodriquez* (Boston: Godine, 1981). See also the introduction to *Working-Class Women in the Academy: Laborers in the Knowledge Factory*, ed. Michelle M. Tokarczyk and Elizabeth A. Fay, 3–24 (Amherst: University of Massachusetts Press, 1993), for a description of that feeling in working-class women academics.

2. My anxiety took the form of what Tokarczyk and Fay describe as the "imposter complex": "As outsiders in academia, many [working-class women academics] have an imposter complex; they fear they've scammed others into giving them doctorates and academic positions" (17).

3. Janet Zandy, ed., *Calling Home: Working-Class Women's Writing—An Anthology* (New Brunswick, N.J.: Rutgers University Press, 1990).

4. Victoria Byerly, *Hard Times Cotton Mill Girls* (Ithaca: Cornell University Press, 1986).

5. Tillie Olsen, *Yonnondio: From the Thirties* (New York: Dell, 1975); and *Silences* (New York: Dell, 1978).

6. Deborah Rosenfelt, "From the Thirties: Tillie Olsen and the Radical Tradition," *Feminist Studies* 7 (1981): 371–406.

7. See, for instance, Selma Burkom and Margaret Williams, "De-Riddling Tillie Olsen's Writings," *San Jose Studies* 2 (1976): 64–83, who refer to Olsen as a humanist.

8. Paul Lauter, "Working-Class Women's Literature: An Introduction to Study," *Radical Teacher* 15 (1980): 16–26.

9. Terry F. Buss and F. Stevens Redburn, *Shutdown at Youngstown: Public Policy for Mass Employment* (Albany: State University of New York Press, 1983), 2, 1.

10. For a more complete history of the community's response to the closing of the steel mills, see Staughton Lynd's *The Fight against Shutdowns: Youngstown's Steel Mill Closing* (San Pedro: Singlejack Books, 1982). Lynd was the attorney for the coalition. See also Thomas G. Fuechtmann, *Steeples and Stacks: Religion and Steel Crisis in Youngstown* (New York: Cambridge University Press, 1989).

11. Lynd, *Fight against Shutdowns*, 5.

12. Along with Zandy, *Calling Home*, I also use *If I Had a Hammer: Women's Work in Poetry, Fiction, and Photographs*, ed. Sandra Martz (Watsonville: Paper-Mache Press, 1990); and either Agnes Smedley's *Daughter of Earth* (New York: The Feminist Press, 1976); or Dorthy Allison's *Bastard out of Carolina* (New York: Plume, 1993).

13. Zandy, *Calling Home*, 281.

14. Laura Kollat, "My Mother Is a Working Woman" in *Our Voyage toward Light* (May 1994). In the contributors' list Kollat describes herself as "coming from a great family, trying to create a great family, so that there may be a great family to come."

15. *Our Voyage toward Light*.

16. Ibid. Sherry T. describes herself in the list of contributors as "a full time student, with a full time job, a mother and a grandmother attempting to educate, hoping to elevate and praying her efforts will not be in vain."

17. From *Hidden Treasures: The Discovery of Working-Class Identities*. W. Kay W. writes in the list of contributors that she "has had many different jobs, all blue-collar or minimum wage, the longest lasting of which was working on a warehouse line. She claims to have learned a lot from her job experience, mainly what she does not want to do forever: run a cash register, sell food,

work in meat packing, work in a nursing home, or work in a warehouse for the next forty years."

18. Ibid. Bowell writes in the list of contributors that she "began work at sixteen and has been working since."

19. *Our Voyage toward Light.*

20. Zandy, *Calling Home,* 5.

21. In the list of contributors Limbert writes that she is "daughter, sister, wife, Mother, teacher, student, volunteer, Citizen of the Universe."

Linda Strom *is an Assistant Professor of English at Youngstown State University, where she is currently working to develop a Working-Class Resource Center.*

APPENDIX

Course Syllabus: Working-Class Women Writers

Required Texts

Dorothy Allison, *Bastard out of Carolina*
Janet Zandy, ed., *Calling Home: Working Class Women's Writing*
Hidden Treasures: The Discovery of Working-Class Identities

Course Description

Through our discussion of our own personal and work histories we will create a framework for reading and analyzing works written by or about working-class women. Implicit in our discussion will be the consideration of the effects socioeconomic class have on women's lives and the conflict women feel when they move from one class to another. The format of the course will be discussion, group presentations, and a final collaborative project.

Course Requirements

Journal.   This is a place for you to respond to the readings and the class discussions. There should be a journal entry for every reading assignment and another entry after we have discussed the readings. There will also be various assignments in addition to responding to the readings and class discussion. Use the journal to note insights, to raise questions and concerns, and to suggest issues that you feel are important and which perhaps we overlooked in our initial discussion. Bring your journal to every class meeting. Your grade will be based on the quality of your responses. You will lose one full grade for every missing journal entry.

Group Presentations.   Each student will participate in a group presentation. On that day you and your group will be responsible for leading class discussion. Creative approaches are encouraged and welcomed.

Two Midterm Exams.   There will be two midterms exams (open book): the first one is on *Calling Home,* and the second one is on *Bastard out of Carolina.* Questions for these exams will be taken from our class discussions. Except in cases of documented catastrophe, there will be no makeup exams.

Final Creative Project.   This final project is meant to be enjoyable and personally rewarding. After reading about other women's personal and work experiences, you will have the opportunity to express your feelings and attitudes about working-class life in a poem, a short story, a play, a drawing, a photograph, a short autobiography, or an essay. It is also possible to write about someone else whose personal history or experience has influenced or had an impact on your life.

Collaborative Class Book.   During the eighth week of class we will work together in groups to put together a collection of our final projects. For collaboration to be successful everyone must show up and do their parts; consequently, any student who misses class during this time will loose credit for that portion of the grade.

Course Syllabus: Working-Class Experiences in American Fiction

> One characteristic of working-class writing is that we often pile up many events within a small amount of space rather than detailing the many implications of one or two events. This means that our lives are chock full of action and also that we are bursting with stories which haven't been printed, made into novels, dictionaries, philosophies.
>   —Judy Grahn

Required Texts

Tillie Olsen, *Yonnondio*
Clifford Odets, *Six Plays of Clifford Odets*
Carlos Bulosan, *American Is in the Heart*
Harriette Arnow, *The Doll Maker*
Lorraine Hansberry, *A Raisin in the Sun*
Alice Lynd and Staughton Lynd, eds., *Rank and File: Personal Histories by Working-Class Organizers*

Course Description

This class is meant to introduce you to the "lives" of the working class in American literature. Its purpose is to acquaint you with working-class literature written in this century and to increase your skill in reading and interpreting poems, novels, plays, films, and personal histories. Your thorough preparation and active participation will be crucial to the success of the class.

Course Requirements

Two Short Critical Papers.   Topics will be generated from the class discussion of the various works. Rough drafts of these two papers will be presented to a small group, for help with revisions. These essays should be approximately five typed, doubled-spaced pages.

Weekly Position Papers.   These shorter papers will give you a chance to try out ideas for the two longer critical papers and will be shared with a small group. Some of these papers will be written in class, and some will be written out of class. I will let you know at the beginning of each week which option we will use that week.

Group Presentation.   Each student will participate in a group presentation. On that day your group will be responsible for leading the class discussion of a text. The purpose of the presentation is to enhance our understanding of the text. Creative approaches are encouraged and welcomed. I will pass out a sign-up sheet the second week of class, and we will discuss possible ideas for the presentation at that time.

Reading and Attendance.   Because this is a discussion class, it is important that you keep up with the reading, attend class, and contribute to discussions. For each class for which we have a reading assignment, I will ask you to write two thought-provoking questions (TPQs) for discussion. These questions will be collected at the beginning of the class period and will be used to generate class discussion.

Schedule of Events

Week 1 Clifford Odets
"Waiting for Lefty"
"Awake and Sing!"
2 Tillie Olsen *Yonnondio*
3 Poets of the 1930s: Handouts
4 Charlie Chaplin *Modern Times* (film)
Rough draft workshop of the first essay
First Critical Essay Due
5 Carlos Bulosan *American Is in the Heart*
6 Harriette Arnow *The Doll Maker*
7 Lorraine Hansberry *A Raisin in the Sun*
8 Selections from Alice Lynd and Staughton Lynd, eds.: *Rank and File: Personal Histories by Working-Class Organizers*
9 Poetry handouts (Judy Grahn, Philip Levine, James Wright, and selections from *Calling Home*)
10 *Last Exit to Brooklyn* (film)
Rough draft workshop of the final essay
Final Critical Essay Due

NELLIE LANGFORD ROWELL LIBRARY

A Wealth of Possibilities: Workers, Texts, and Reforming the English Department

Laura Hapke

Every human being . . . is a millionaire in emotions.

—Isaac Bashevis Singer

A few years ago, having completed the extended compliance with authority which began by coloring my robin red and ended with a promotion to professor, I began to breathe the heady air of liberty. I had been taking in lung fulls of the stuff since the early 1970s, when I was a graduate assistant at a campus of the City University of New York, where I found a streetwise student body receptive to the rebellious literary naturalism and so-called lower depths subject matter of Dreiser, Norris, and Crane. (Of course, these authors, though fascinated by labor-class themes, were not worker-writers: I had yet to discover Agnes Smedley and Anzia Yezierska, Jack Conroy and Meridel Le Sueur.) Even in my part-time teaching days my syllabi clung tenaciously to *Sister Carrie*, Dreiser's unfashionable, poignant ode to the urban down-and-out. To other skeptical graduate students I defended *McTeague*, Norris's forgotten tale of simple people destroyed by nature, nurture, and social indifference. And, in halting conversations with those unmoved movers, my graduate professors, I inserted allusions to the not-yet-resurrected Crane (praised then, only occasionally, for *Red Badge of Courage*) and his experimental melodrama of blue-collar womanhood, *Maggie: A Girl of the Streets*.

But it was only when I was strapped into tenure and a professorship, above desire and beyond reproach, that I turned my department's suggested syllabi into rejected ones. I offered, instead, a series of courses about labor fiction in general and proletarian literature in particular, whose titles included "Classics of Working-Class Literature" and "Blue Collar: The Worker in City Fiction from the Civil War to the Present." (When, by no choice of my own, the course had a less defiant label such as "Introduction to Writing," I used my own titles as subheadings.)

Repeatedly, I found that the students seated so passively at semester's opening—as if with the same compliance I had so recently abandoned—were completely unfamiliar with the literary imagination of manual and industrial labor.[1] Yet soon they became interested and, in some cases, intrigued. I found that my colleagues, seated politely at my brief department talk on teaching working-class literature, were familiar at least in passing with this body of fiction—and completely uninterested. Or, in the way of academics wary of a new approach, their collective response reminded me of my old thesis advisor's rejoinder to my request for a bibliography: "It doesn't matter what books we read as long as we read the same books."

Clearly, the subjects of my departmental talk, Chicago-based Jack Conroy's Bottom Dogs saga of heavy industry, *The Disinherited* (1933); Agnes Smedley's passionately autobiographical *Daughter of Earth* (1928; 1935), the radical coming of age of a Colorado mining town girl; and *Love on the Dole* (1933), Walter Greenwood's classic of British mill town unemployment, were not on that list. Was not, my colleagues inquired, the 1930s radical novel, and any leftist fiction for that matter, "lacking in playfulness"? Were there any *real* writers among the cohorts of proletarian author Mike Gold (not to mention that ur–Communist Party (CP) member, Gold himself)? In today's United States, "was there even a working class" about which literature could now be produced? And who cared about texts that were not high art, anyway?

Naively, somewhere in my remarks I quoted a snooty British critic in an effort to stir debate. "Virtually no writing of literary importance," he wrote, "came out of the working class during the [British] 1930s" (and, by implication, the American 1930s as well). Yet I was unprepared for the department's acid concurrence with that critical view or for the colleague who presented an elegant paper after my informal talk. He took up the cudgel for ever-aristocratic Virginia Woolf, whom he lauded for her honest understanding of social class.

After his well-received presentation two feminist scholars who employ texts by Le Sueur and Yezierska in their courses on American literature briefly turned the discussion to the value of such assignments, but no one picked up that lead, and soon we recessed.

Two days later my talk received a final, belated response—a short, ambivalent note from one of my most scholarly colleagues. He wrote that I was probably right about the value of labor texts, which the department should assign if it was "capable."

The *Encyclopedia of the American Left* reminds us that "intellectual disfavor of radical literature became the norm in universities when . . . English professors adopted a 'New Criticism' that devalued writing that was politically committed."[2] Furthermore, particularly at a business-oriented university like mine, the post–House Un-American Activities Committee (HUAC) fallout remains, and the Stalinism (and Nazi-Soviet pactism) which a Mike Gold embraced philosophically is wrongly conflated with the radicalism of his thinking on literature.[3] But the careful frostiness that greeted my apologia for working-class texts may have a deeper cause. Literary theories superseding New Critical ones and empowering feminist, black, and multicultural literatures are now in place, while working-class literary studies are still in their infancy. Perhaps the task of assigning fictive texts that pay compassionate attention to the factory worker denied his or her right to strike or the plight of the urban transient involves too drastic a shift from the aesthetic to the humanistic or a relocation of the aesthetic in what Janet Zandy aptly terms the "collective sensibility."[4] Nor, partially excepting the brief spurt of late-nineteenth-century American literary naturalism, if that lone colleague who was fitfully considering my new classroom agenda had really wished to survey labor fiction from the American Revolution onward, would he have found in classic literature prior to the 1930s any balanced or even extended descriptions of the laboring experience? Although with the rise of the novel, American authors of the magnitude of Melville and James did not simply relegate the working class to the status of Shakespeare's "rude mechanicals," neither did they pay much, or respectful, attention to the subject. Indeed, from "Bartleby" to *Princess Casamassima*, from "Paradise of Bachelors" to *The American*, portrayals of the clerking, shopgirl, servant, and garment trades classes resonate with the prejudices of bourgeois literary production. The lower orders, laboring or otherwise, are variously comic, eccentric, vulgar, manic, or, worst of all, awash in Dickensian sentiment.

Thus, as the departmental silence on my topic suggested, it is not surprising that modern critic-teachers, already little motivated to hunt out less stereotyped portrayals, often choose to omit the blue-collar classes and their importance to noncanonical world literature from inquiry and reading lists for the undergraduate classroom. Even a text billed by its publisher, the Modern Language Association (MLA), as a "groundbreaking volume" the newly published collection *Redrawing the Boundaries: The Transformation of English and American Literary Studies*, includes essays on gender and African-American criticism but nothing on labor studies.

The flowering of labor studies among the new social historians, the proposed establishment of a permanent MLA section on working-class literature, and the publication of works such as Paul Lauter's

Canons and Contexts (1991) and *Left Politics and the Literary Profession* (1990), edited by Lennard J. Davis and M. Bella Mirabella, all broaden the somewhat weary definition of "the Humanities" to include ne-glected, lost, and maligned texts of the laboring life.

To join this still modest revolution I offer here some proposals for curricular change. They are based on a transformation of my own university's Introductory Literature and Basic Composition require-ments, with their devotion to traditional readings, into courses cen-tered on the crucial social and literary questions such readings inspire. In creating these courses, I was concerned to select classics of labor fiction (and, to provide a historical context, of social documen-tary nonfiction). By their very nature they challenge the goals of the new consumer-oriented urban university, whose largely first-generation college students, for good or ill, perceive education as vocational training. I found it not as difficult as I had thought to balance the college/student agendas with my need to awaken my captive audience to the realities of class difference, the underside of the American Dream, and the democratic eloquence of working-class fiction. By appealing to the fundamental sense of fairness in young people whose own parents' ascension to lower-middle-class security was recent enough, any instructor can interest students in the unoffi-cial history of the United States, that of the laboring classes, and in so doing help awake in them a compassion for those at the bottom of the socioeconomic barrel.

In a 1977 *Radical Teacher* account of his Boston University course on the history of work in modern America, Marc Miller wrote that he hoped to convey why the struggle of workers to create unions was an important one. To his disappointment he found students in the main "hostile to the concept of organized labor," even though some of them worked at jobs not far removed from the hardships or monotonies of mass-production work.[5] Miller implied that, while his course did much to prod students to examine the industrial job site beyond what might be termed the "local color" side of work life, there was a general "failure to go beyond description to analysis" (30). My aims were less ambitious. As my university, though it includes a school of Arts and Sciences, is for the most part business oriented, the majority of stu-dents pursuing careers in accounting, finance, and computer science (preferably of the information systems variety so suited to today's banking houses), I did not expect indignation to greet Jack Conroy's novelistic accounts of the hellish stench of the Midwest rubber factory or management's attempts to plant spies or found a company union. What I did hope for was an increased awareness that, then as now, big business exploits the working stiff and causes economic suffering and that to care about the protagonist of a novel by a Conroy is in some way to care about a whole class of people.

Though my students could recite the latest rock tunes and speak volubly of cast changes in "Roseanne" (which they considered a "real-life blue-collar sitcom"), they hadn't heard about the thousands, some out of a job for a year or more, who stood in the predawn Chicago cold for some crummy hotel jobs a year or so ago. News to them too was the Southern chicken processing plant fire, a sad reprise of the Triangle Shirtwaist Factory debacle of 1911. Nor did they know that of the failed Midwest Caterpillar Strike, in which, despite a powerful international United Auto Workers (UAW), longtime workers had to watch scabs take their work, sometimes permanently. And when I asked what they thought the title of the 1930s song "Brother, Can You Spare a Dime?" meant, they laughed knowingly and said it was written by someone weary of being hassled in the subways.

To generate some enthusiasm about novels that challenge rather than celebrate upward mobility in a classroom filled with its devotees, I devised a three-stage syllabus. The first part of the semester was spent demystifying what turn-of-the-century tenement crusader Jacob Riis, with both telling accuracy and unconscious condescension, called "the other half": the working and workless poor, the homeless, and the vast criminal population of the stale beer dives and bottles-alleys of New York. Though not a worker-writer, Riis was a good choice, for the ideological transformation of the "poor" into the "working classes" was a recent one, and Riis was halfway between the two ideologies: on the one hand, castigating the immorality of the impoverished and, on the other, lauding honest toil.

To usher Riis in, we began with a recent *New York Times* piece on the city's roving hordes of transients, moved to the stunning Lower East Side poverty photos and somewhat elitist descriptive/reformist essays of the *How the Other Half Lives,* and generally dwelt in a climate receptive to what one student called the realization that the other half might be "equal to the half that I thought I lived in."

In stage 2 of the term's work a novel from the Depression era, when the largest number of literary texts on labor unrest were produced, was a crux for discussions about mass production, job site injustice, and the hero who can only, in Conroy's words, "rise with his class." In the course's final stage, the research component, students tied Conroy's realistic fiction to events such as the Akron Rubber Strike of 1936 or the use of black strikebreakers in the coal industry; surveyed other "proletarian authors" such as Meridel Le Sueur or Nelson Algren as well as what their period critics—and bitter foes—thought of them; or took more modern occasions such as the controversy raging about the mental stability of New York City's homeless or the place of women in the construction trades as their subjects of inquiry.

Because, whether in basic or advanced courses, virtually all of my students needed solid writing instruction, a brief sampling of a *Times* article, in this case a 1991 one on a derelict collecting return-deposit bottles, scrutinizing a homeless man combined well with reviewing the principles of essay construction. Had the bylined article advanced a thesis? Provided detailed support through idea and example? Moved logically from one part of the argument to the other? Concluded clearly and thoughtfully? And so on. After a few assignments to write their own descriptions of "subway people," neighborhood barflies, and some dissection of the *Times*'s brand of temperate muckraking— including discussion of "liberal" bias in reportage about the poor—it seemed proper to turn to a more complicated text and series of writing assignments: Riis's other half.

The Riis text is, of course, a compelling social document. But, as recent revisionists have pointed out, it is also a middle-class one. Given the tension between the egalitarian and elitist Riis, asking students to compare the poignant photos with the rather stiff essays damning female "dishonor" and freely using terms like *Jewtown* is a valuable exercise. It proved particularly useful to analyze the structure of a classic *Other Half* essay, "The Working Girls of New York," again from the dual perspective of structure and content.

After some prodding, students discovered that the celebrated news reporter delayed his thesis (which was confusing), offered a disorganized argument, and circled back needlessly to the obsessively reiterated idea of the working girl's need for purity. Riis's very emphases led to new insights. Why were working women judged on their virtue when the men were not? Why, if the women, as Riis pointed out, did the same garment trades jobs as men but were paid less, did he not voice moral outrage about that? And why, although he alluded to prostitution as an evil road for starving seamstresses, could he not bring himself to use the word?

Having analyzed the bourgeois Riis, we turned to his less moralistic, and more brilliant, side. In a series of comparison essays using Riis's photos, we came face to face—"as if you were there without looking at the pictures," as one student put it—with the emotional toll of poverty: sad-faced child-rearing girls, mothers to slightly younger brothers; shivering urchins, sleeping on top of grates; pinched sweatshop women, breathing the lint-filled air of the contractor's apartment-factory;

maddened-looking Police Lodging House alcoholics, female and male. All of these subjects produced a level of eloquence in my students' responses which I had never seen when I assigned a Shakespeare play or a William Carlos Williams poem. "In Jacob Riis's *How the Other Half Lives*," wrote one of my weakest students, "although the children in the pictures 'Prayer-time in the Nursery' and 'Street Arabs in Sleeping Quarters (Areaway, Mulberry Street)' are both young, the youngsters in the first photo have a place to sleep, unlike the boys in the second, who have none." She had not produced anything like this relative stylistic sophistication in responding to the department's rather dry placement test question regarding then–New York City Mayor Dinkins's fiscal management. With her (single) mother she had recently moved from one rather unsafe apartment in the Bronx to another, and most days she arrived late and flustered; I wondered to what extent she identified with the two sets of hapless children Riis had immortalized.

Other students, more emotionally and financially serene, began the semester freely using the word *bum* to describe the subway mendicant. They too produced sensitive descriptions of Riis's classic "Didn't Live Nowhere," a medium closeup of two barefoot street boys, who stare exhausted into the camera, otherwise disclosing nothing. In the best of the student papers subject and viewer seemed almost to fuse, as writers replaced Riis's emotionally distant narrative voice with their own newly gentle ones.

Riis's text was a "landmark in the annals of American social reform,"[6] and he was instrumental in the kind of tenement house reform which brought open spaces, parks, and playgrounds to a dangerously overcrowded Lower East Side. Nevertheless, his proselytizing brand of philanthropic benevolence placed him on the side of those who Jack Conroy, who incorporated his own experience as a factory hand and sometime hobo into his novel of the 1930s, satirized as do-gooder intruders. Conroy's newly reissued novel *The Disinherited*—like reprints of Meridel Le Sueur's *The Girl*, Daniel Fuchs's *Summer in Williamsburg*, Agnes Smedley's *Daughter of Earth*, and Tillie Olsen's *Yonnondio*—wrests verbal control of work from the bourgeois reformer. The Conroy text—an account of mining camp youth Larry Donovan's travels through the worlds of coal workers' families; railway car, steel, and rubber factory toil; strikes, organizing marches, and Hoovervilles—was, like the others, a text on which the working-class writer stamped his or her personality.

Used in stage 2 of my courses, sometimes in tandem with Farm Security Administration photographs or female writers of the 1930s,

The Disinherited contains scenes to which students, building on their own experiences, are particularly responsive. In one key chapter a Christian committee comes to take away the children of the newly widowed Mrs. Donovan to foster care. Her husband has just been killed in a mining accident, and the committee's presumption is that middle-class parents can give the Donovan brood the gentility they require to be civilized. The whole vignette, complete with comic references to the pretentious visitors, is written from the insider's perspective, albeit an insider who has taught himself to write a somewhat stilted prose: "One day a group of church workers came to see us. They sat decorously in the front room, their inquisitive eyes ferreting into every crevice."[7] Despite students' reluctance to read such ponderous stuff—much less look up the vocabulary used in such sentences— they liked the man who had written the description. Conroy, after all, had frequently redeemed himself with passages on young Larry's humiliations by the flaxen-haired farmer's daughter, who considered him "camp trash" (44). If they themselves had not endured quite such abuse, many of my students knew what it was to be humiliated in minimum-wage jobs or chance meetings with Ivy Leaguers.

Using my colleagues' but-is-it-art objections to the worker novel of the 1930s, I asked the students to consider why so many of the Conroy chapters seemed episodic, fragmented. A number of them, pressed to define why they considered that structure "realistic," pointed out that events are depicted as if they are happening, not recalled later. I asked why Larry (and his creator) was so earnest, humorless, intense, and why he/they needed to strew big words in front of the reader. Some students noted—admittedly, after many generous hints from the instructor—that he saw the lives of workers as deadly serious, that he was proving his ability to compete with the "educated" authors of classic fiction. I inquired, too, why Larry renounces their own white-collar ambitions, in a (beautiful) passage such as this:

> I no longer felt shame at being seen at such work as I would have once, and I knew that the only way for me to rise to something approximating the grandiose ambitions of my youth would be to rise with my class, with the disinherited: the brick-setters, the flivver tramps, boomers, and outcasts pounding their ears in flop-houses. (265)

There the responses were more negative. Students were skeptical whether a 1990s Larry would have to make such a decision. A few of them termed the novel's final passage—in which Larry rides off in a second-hand auto, cold wind in his face, to become an organizer—"corny."

Certainly, any teacher who employs the polemical novel favored by leftist writers from Conroy to Le Sueur, Gold to Olsen, early James T. Farrell to Smedley, will have to prepare careful responses to this kind of objection. For my part I asked my classes to consider what today's unemployed blue-collar man and woman, or the nation's vast homeless population, had to look forward to without a group allegiance. And I wondered aloud whether the class knew if companies they wished or planned to work for had any unions or, instead, trumpeted their "generosity" to employees.

Finally, in their thinking about Conroy, the more introspective not only found Larry's decision understandable but even made allowances for the racist language that cropped up so often in the text. In the semester's last phase, in which students prepared their research essays, some of the African-American students, justly angered at the racial ignorance of so many white workers in the Conroy novel, were sufficiently interested to hunt down information on blacks in actual 1930s unions and labor upheavals. Most of the students flinched at any mention of Larry's potential work as an organizer for the Communist Party and were soothed when told Conroy soon broke with the CP. Too, they saw the reasonableness of labor strikes, remembering the smallest details for an in-class essay on that theme. And several constructed admirable essays on the ideological contradictions between empowering all people and consigning women to being helpmeets rather than comrades in the 1930s worker novel, at least the masculine version—though with a generous push from a female instructor.

If there were time, some semesters I shifted to a reconsideration of classic American texts from a revisionist viewpoint. Conventionally considered on a loftily (and conveniently?) symbolic level, the 1853 Melville story of a lawyer who has a clerk who will not work carted off to the Tombs Prison raises crucial questions about the kind and quality of monotonous modern work. Why, I asked, are the clerical workers Turkey, Nippers, and Ginger Nut cast so comically? With whose interests do they identify, those of their marginally white-collar class or of the employer? Why are they so hostile to Bartleby? Is it solely the result of his refusal to shoulder his work burden? Or, given their loyalty to the narrator-lawyer, do they refuse to see their connection to another ill-paid member of clerkdom? When the worker-characters speak, are they permitted lengthy speeches? Do their voices sound real? Or does it seem that Melville and the narrator distort them? And so on.

In searching out the literary criticism of American work as depicted in canonical texts, most instructors are on their own. In researching a book on images of breadwinning women in late-nineteenth- and early-twentieth-century fiction, I was surprised at the dearth of studies on the work experience in American fiction. Still, in courses combining the literature survey and the composition requirement, a scrutiny of works such as James's *The Princess Casamassima* (1886)—with its lively, censoriously viewed shopgirl, Millicent Henning—from a labor-class perspective can illuminate how these texts exemplify period fears about social revolution and the dangerous classes, uncover the injustice in their creators' ideology of "the deserving poor," and locate idées fixes about the immorality of the female breadwinner. While such a perspective need not replace the traditional "masters of literature" one, it is essential for deepening it.

When it came to stage 3 of my courses, library research (a department mandate), as a springboard to further labor studies, it seemed to me that the Depression era cried out to be investigated. Students with a literary critical bent could scour *Writers in Revolt: The Anvil Anthology* (1973) to mine the rich field of short proletarian fiction. Those with historical interests could research the 1935 National Labor Relations (Wagner) Act, the Akron Rubber Strike of 1936–37, the Flint sit-down strike of 1937. Others, usually a minority, could compare the supposed solution to the social problem of the economically disenfranchised or exploited in our time with the New Deal's—or else the Communist Party's—programs. And students sophisticated enough to summarize literary critical controversies could chart the culture wars of the Left and take a stand on Conroy's merit, citing a Mike Gold or post-Party sympathizer James T. Farrell.[8] While many instructors wishing to introduce their classes to working-class studies may prefer more timely topics, it is well to remember that often-alienated students can feel as empowered rediscovering an obscured past as in mastering a modern social problem.

In these acts of resurrection a good number of my students came to care about long-dead labor organizers, the militant rank and file (presented, perhaps, as overly violent by their accounting or finance professors), the hostilities against black workers that constitute the underside of the labor movement. One wrote enthusiastically about Margaret Cowl and the Women's Commission. Another went to Schomburg Center, the New York Public Library's jewel in the black studies crown, to look at back issues of the Harlem-based journals *Crisis* and

Opportunity. And another secured a copy of the Wagner Act from the university's law library. All students had the opportunity to acquaint themselves with the new rich bibliographies on or with large sections concerning the working class: *American Working Class History: A Representative Bibliography* (1983); *American Women and the Labor Movement, 1825–1974* (1976); *Women and Sexuality in America: A Bibliography* (1984); *The Progress of Afro-American Women: A Select Bibliography* (1980). Significantly, none of these sources is listed among the standard handbooks of research technique, which pelt students with *The Reader's Guide to Periodical Literature* and *The Encyclopedia of Banking and Finance*, both certainly no less specialized than those about labor studies.[9]

In terms of dictionaries and encyclopedias all college students, whether fascinated by the Flint sit-down strike of 1937 or modern rulings on abortion which impact on lower-class and poor women, should know of *Labor in Conflict: An Encyclopedia* (1990); *Biographical Dictionary of American Labor Leaders* (1974); and the *Handbook of American Women's History* (1990). For students of labor literature surveys such as Fay M. Blake's *The Strike in the American Novel* (1972); Walter Rideout's *The Radical Novel in the United States, 1900–1954* (1956); and, in the women's studies category, Janet Zandy's anthology *Calling Home: Working-Class Women's Writings* (1990); and my own *Tales of the Working Girl: Wage-Earning Women in American Literature, 1890–1925* (1992) are contributions to a still under-researched field.

To conclude. A reexamination of a neglected classic of labor life such as Depression-era Jack Conroy's novel *The Disinherited* uncovers aspects of the human experience erased from or presented condescendingly by canonical texts and thereby provides excellent occasions for Composition and Literature assignments. Corollary texts from the social history of muckraking—Riis's *How the Other Half Lives*, to name a prime example—are rich sources of exercises in the classroom, stimulating students to challenge the trope of the American Dream, to make new connections between the arresting photography of Riis and their own immigrant backgrounds and/or experiences of economic dislocation. Students find they are able to forge their own eloquence about the miseries of the underclass, all the while practicing the traditional rhetorical forms of classification, definition, argument, and comparison. Above all, these new pedagogical strategies, by expanding the canon (or the black, ethnic, and feminist anticanons) to include texts by and about the working classes, enable students, particularly college entrants from modest circumstances, to revisit an idea that threatens to fade away entirely in our materialistic time: the dignity of labor.

NOTES

1. Although I avoid the term *proletarian fiction* for its too-rigid association with the 1930s—save for isolated exceptions, themselves largely the products of "undercover" eyewitness historians (Dorothy Richardson's *The Long Day*) or former workers ascended socially (Theresa Malkiel's *Diary of a Shirtwaist Striker*)—the worker-writer's literary visioning of labor under capitalism does not mark the American scene until the Depression. Precursors such as the muckraking factory fiction of Rebecca Harding Davis and Elizabeth Stuart Phelps, not to mention the rabidly antistrike novels of John Hay, were produced by solidly middle-class authors. Comments Nancy Armstrong in "Introduction: Literature as Women's History" (*Genre* 19 [Winter 1986]: 347–69), "Middle-class practitioners of the novel "located the cause of working-class misery in the improperly socialized working-class individual and not in the violent conflicts and crashing changes of a society that was undergoing rapid industrialization" (353). I agree with Paul Lauter that working-class literature may be about or by working-class people, but note that the former is more likely to include works "ignorant of or hostile to" workers. See Paul Lauter, "Working-Class Women's Literature—An Introduction to Study," *Radical Teacher* 15 (March 1980): 16.

2. Dan Georgakas and Ernie Brill, "Proletarian and Radical Writers—1930s and 1940s," in *The Encyclopedia of the American Left*, ed. Mari Jo Buhle, Paul Buhle, and Dan Georgakas (New York: Garland, 1990), 605.

3. See James D. Bloom, *Left Letters: The Culture Wars of Mike Gold and Joseph Freeman* (New York: Columbia University Press, 1992).

4. Janet Zandy, "Introduction," *Calling Home: Working-Class Women's Writings— An Anthology*, ed. Janet Zandy (New Brunswick, N.J.: Rutgers University Press, 1990), 10. This is not to contend that feminist or multicultural texts do not require an equally radical pedagogical shift, particularly to the extent that class intersects race, ethnicity, and gender. But it is to suggest that American working-class texts inevitably raise the issue of leftist orientation in a way that a lost suffrage novel or an African-American slave narrative need not.

5. Marc Miller, "Teaching the History of Work," *Radical Teacher* 12 (May 1979): 27.

6. Charles A. Madison, "Preface," *How the Other Half Lives*, by Jacob Riis, (1901; reprint, New York: Dover, 1971), vii. Less adulatory discussions occur in Carol Shloss, *In Visible Light: Photography and American Writers, 1840–1940* (New York: Oxford University Press, 1987), chap. 3; and Maren Stange, *Symbols of Ideal Life: Social Documentary Photography at the Turn of the Century* (Cambridge: Cambridge University Press, 1989), chap. 1. Stange points out that not only did Riis often "rehearse . . . imagery familiar to any reader of illustrated periodicals" but that his photographs often borrowed from his fellow Bowery watcher Richard Hoe Lawrence (11).

7. Jack Conroy, *The Disinherited: A Novel of the 1930s* (1933; reprint, Columbia: University of Missouri Press, 1991), 82; hereafter cited in text.

8. Mike Gold, "A Letter to the Author of a First Book," *New Masses* 9 (9 January 1934): 25; James T. Farrell, "A Working-Class Novel," *Nation* 137 (20 December 1933): 714.

9. See, for instance, *The Prentice-Hall Handbook for Writers* or *The Bedford Handbook for Writers*. Oh for the day that the handbooks also include rich sources such as Jayne Loader, "Women in the Left: A Bibliography of Primary Resources," *Michigan Papers in Women's Studies* 2 (September 1975): 9–82; *Women and Work, Paid and Unpaid: A Selected, Annotated Bibliography* (New York: Garland, 1987); Mari Jo Buhle's classic work *Women and the American Left* (Boston: G. K. Hall, 1983); and Virginia Prestridge, *The Worker in American Fiction: An Annotated Bibliography* (Champaign: University of Illinois Institute of Industrial and Labor Relations, 1954).

Laura Hapke, *Professor of English at Pace University in New York City, is the author of* Tales of the Working Girl: Wage-Earning Women in American Literature, 1890–1925 (1992) *and other books and articles on the working class in literature and pedagogy.*

A Community of Workers

Marilyn Anderson

The images and text on these pages are from an ongoing project to document and interpret the range and diversity of work performed in a single community—Rochester, New York. In 1990 Jon Garlock, a writer, historian, and active unionist, and I, as photographer, began to collaborate on this project. Thus far we have visited over fifty worksites, photographing and interviewing hundreds of industrial, building trades, service and public sector, and transportation and communications workers. To date we have shared extensively with the community images and texts edited from these photo shoots; through an exhibit we have traveled to schools, union halls, galleries, and public events.

Because our project is sponsored by the local labor council each shoot is initiated through calls to one of the affiliated unions. Whenever we go to a workplace we arrive under the auspices of a union and with the approval and cooperation of management. One simply can't gain access to many worksites without such support—which is probably one reason one finds so few pictures of workers.

Generally, the workers are pleased to see us. In some cases they have discussed the shoot and decided what operations should be documented. In other cases, especially at construction sites, the activities photographed and the workers interviewed are determined by what is happening at the moment. Workers like to tell us about what they do, whether it is giving a detailed description of work processes or expressing pride in their skill. Or they may note how younger workers lack skills or how new work processes require less skill. Or they may talk about how people don't understand or appreciate what they do:

> I've shown thousands and thousands of miles of film, enough to go from here to the moon and back; people who come to the movies don't even know we exist.

> I've tried to explain what I do and it's very hard. A friend of mine asked me, "So what is it you do there?" I go, "Oh, well, I run a lathe." He says, "Oh, a lathe. What does a lathe do?"

As we go around a worksite, we hand out printed brochures that have my photographs of workers, interview text, and information about the educational purpose of our documentation project. Most of the workers are positive about the project and want to participate, especially when they recognize that it will be used to help kids to understand what work is about.

We find that teachers appreciate being able to use the exhibit, often in conjunction with career education. Teachers and guidance counselors are able to show students a wide range of occupations within their own communities. Not infrequently, students recognize family or friends in the photographs or have family members who work at the job sites documented in the show. This immediacy helps them to relate to issues raised by the exhibit's images and text, especially workers' feelings about their jobs, working conditions and issues of job security, the social significance of their labor, and changes in work resulting from global competition or the introduction of new technology.

During "Career Exploration Night" at a local high school the exhibit provoked as much discussion with parents as with youth, including many parents who were as concerned with keeping their own jobs as finding work for their kids after graduation.

Because the exhibit touches on many aspects of work, it offers teachers an opportunity to discuss work-related issues with their students, rather than introducing the topic of work uncritically, as a range of employment opportunities. A workshop we did on "Teaching Work" revealed that some teachers were willing to have students examine the arrangements and question the assumptions underlying employment in capitalist society.

Because all the workers in the exhibit belong to unions (as do many of the teachers themselves), the exhibit can also be used to stimulate consideration of the role of unions in providing job protections through contracts.

Teachers of social studies, English, art and photography, business and economics, and other subjects have developed assignments and exercises based on the exhibit. Students have conducted research, interviewed family members about work, reflected on their own summer and part-time work experience, and even photographed and interviewed workers.

Doing the Community of Workers project, we have been privileged to enter factories, schools, garages, hospitals, construction sites (including a sewer tunnel being dug *beneath* the Genesee River), and other worksites rarely visited except by workers themselves. My partner and

I have been moved by the language people use to describe their work and by their insights into their situations. In our document we try to avoid romanticizing either workers or their labor: our project, like Studs Terkel's book *Working,* "being about work, is, by its very nature, about violence—to the spirit as well as to the body." At the same time, we cannot report only the casualties of class warfare as is is waged daily in the workplace. To do so would be to ignore the humor, to strip away the dignity, and to distort the humanity of these women and men.

It is our hope to extend this project to the point that it truly documents a community of workers. More than a collection of images and words from myriad distinct trades and occupations, more than an exhibit or curriculum supplement, such a document will connect these tasks and these workers, demonstrate their common unity, and corroborate Walt Whitman's insight:

> The hourly routine of your own or any man's life, the shop, yard, store, or factory,
>
> ....
>
> In them the development good—in them all themes, hints, possibilities.
>
> (A Song for Occupations)

Marilyn Anderson *is an activist artist-photographer, author of* Guatemalan Textiles Today *and co-author, with Jon Garlock, of* Granddaughters of Corn *(Curbstone Press). As a team, they collaborate in an ongoing project to document workers in Rochester, New York.*

IUE 509/Delco
It's a very essential part of the car,
    what we do.
The transmission for the wiper—
Every car's got to have a wiper
    transmission.

Laborers Local 435/Perini
I like working outdoors.
I did secretarial work before this
And that was a hard job, you know.
I worked in a real estate office—
You've got telephones, you've got
    people.
At least now I get fresh air and
    sunshine.
I really like it.

PEF Local 283/Rochester Psychiatric Center
We do have quite a few people
That are homeless,
That don't have relatives
And can't take care of themselves
And are actually walking around on
　the streets very ill.
They find their way here,
And it's very important
That they have something, someone,
To help take care of them.

We're here as that support for them.

ACTWU Local 14/Hickey Freeman
It's a tradition.
They don't want to sew the but-
　tonholes by machine.
It's very cheap.
All the buttonholes are done by
　hand.
But it's very hard to learn how to
　make a buttonhole.
It's one of the skilledest jobs in the
　building.

Here and Now Local 466/Rochester Convention Center

All right, listen up.

Tonight we're going to have cocktail
  servers at the tables.

They've got about five tables per
  server.

So if anyone turns to you and asks
  for a cocktail,

Just take a look at the board where
  your station is,

And they'll be able to handle the
  drinks.

Seven-fifteen are doors

And then they're going to have the
  welcome and the prayer.

About seven-forty we'll have the
  dinner.

NYSUT 2969

I check passes. I do so much. I show
    students to classes
If they don't know where they are. I
    do some study halls.
I run any kind of errands the school
    needs help with—
I might bring something to the main
    office for a teacher.
We work in the office, the library.
    Sometimes we put labels
on envelopes for large mailings.
    Break up fights.
We monitor in the lunchroom. We
    talk to students a lot.
They really confide in us a lot—their
    personal problems.
They borrow money when they for-
    get their lunch money.
It's just like being a housewife, you
    know:
Do everything but nobody pays any
    attention to you.

Here and Now Local 466/Wesley-on-East

I was a nurse here for thirty years.
Well, it went by fast. Left me in good
    shape.
So it didn't hurt me. They called me
    a couple of times,
Wanted to know if I could come back
And just help them out.
I come in and work a couple of days
And I'm happy—you know—
Because the most important thing is
    being happy.
I have to keep it in my mind that I'm
    retired.
Things now, nothing is going to
    come to me.
I've got to go to it,
I've got to go to things.

We have different levels of environ-
    mental service workers.
Level 1 is laundry—cleaning resident
    areas.
Level 2 is fresh linen:
They pull the carts back and forth
    with clean linen and so forth.
Level 3 is the heavy equipment level.
All of us in environmental services
    just say "Housekeeping."

"Women Have Always Sewed": The Production of Clothing and the Work of Women

Janet Zandy

One characteristic of working-class studies is an attentiveness to those seemingly mundane tasks and things that are either invisible or generally ignored. This attention to material existence is not from the ubiquitous business perspective of salable commodities, but, rather, it is with the intent of seeing the human labor relationships embedded inside finished products. This brief outline of clothing production is intended to historicize and localize textile work for students. This factual world of labor history can be expanded to include novels, photographs, music, films, oral history, and fieldwork. Foregrounded are the human hands—usually women's—which produce the jeans, shirts, and socks we buy today and the shirtwaists and overalls purchased by earlier generations.

As Alice Kessler-Harris and others have documented, women have always worked. They have also always sewed, providing their families with clothing and household linens, bedding and quilts. Technological change and the accumulation of capital shifted the site of clothing production from the home to the factory. The invention of the cotton gin heightened the efficiency of producing cotton, as it accelerated the technology of slavery. The Industrial Revolution produced huge quantities of material goods and a technology of work. But technology is not just hardware; it was and is also a technique or system of human labor. If we look at what's behind the shirt we buy, we see a confluence of gender and race ideologies embedded in textile production. Styles may change, but patterns of labor relationships have a stubborn continuity. From Lowell to the global assembly line, the women who make the garments worn by the consumers of the world are caught inside intersecting technologies of gender and capital. These are techniques that involve gender-specific systems of work production. The sites of clothing production have frequently been contested. Women workers have struggled for better wages, safe and sanitary working conditions, and more control over their own labor. They have asserted their humanity and refused to be turned into "its"—that is, "things"—mere adjuncts to their sewing machines. Perhaps it is in the recognition and development of that resistance that new trade union models can be forged in solidarity with other workers, political activists, and cultural workers.

> Needle, running in and out,
> In and out, in and out,
> Do you know what you're about,
> In and out, in and out?
> —Hazel Hall, "Puzzled Stitches," 1925

> I want you women up north to know
> how those dainty children's dresses you buy
> at macy's wannamakers, gimbels, marshall fields,
> are dyed in blood, are stitched in wasting flesh,
> down in San Antonio, "where sunshine spends the winter."
> —Tillie Olsen, "I Want You Women Up North to Know," 1934

I. "The Lowell Girls": New England mill women (1840–54)

A. Francis Cabot Lowell, the stolen power loom design, and the construction of Lowell, the first planned industrial city.
1. Starting in 1822, the mills expanded to nineteen five-story mills.
2. A departure from the family mills system
3. The expanding market for raw cotton in the North increased cotton production in the South, and expanded slavery.
B. The Lowell mill system employed New England farm girls: the intersection of economic and social systems.
1. Seventy-five percent of the Lowell employees were young, farm-raised, highly literate New England women.
2. Lowell perfected a form of corporate paternalism in its construction of boardinghouses for the factory workers; every aspect of daily life was regulated.
3. Despite the boardinghouse system of surveillance and moral policing, the "girls" resisted a degradation in their working conditions in the Ten-Hour movement in the 1840s and exercised a kind of literary release in the publication of their writing, collected in *The Lowell Offering*.
C. Of seven thousand operatives in 1836, fewer than 4 percent were immigrants; by 1860, 61.8 percent were immigrants, mostly Irish.

SOURCES AND PARALLEL READINGS:

Atwood, Margaret. *The Handmaid's Tale* (1987) (an interesting fictional contrast to Lowell).

Dublin, Thomas. *Women at Work: The Transformation of Work and Community in Lowell, Massachusetts, 1826–1860* (1979).

Eisler, Benita. *The Lowell Offering: Writings by New England Mill Women (1840–1845)* (1977).

II. The East: The sweatshop—from the loom to the finished goods

A. The Shirtwaist: The Gibson Girl and the labor of immigrants

B. The Uprising of the 20,000 (1909–10)

C. The Triangle fire, 25 March 1911—146 workers died because of locked doors and unsafe working conditions.

D. The movement of the clothing business

1. In the 1950s New York lost jobs to low-wage domestic areas in Pennsylvania, where wives of unemployed miners were eager for work.

2. Manufacturers moved to the antiunion South.

3. With further breakdowns of work into low-skill operations and improvements in cargo transport, garment manufacturers turned to Southeast Asia; as a result, imported clothes sold at wholesale prices 20 percent below domestic goods.

E. More recent sweatshops

Garment workers in New York City in the 1980s are frequently Chinese or Central or South American immigrants who face a two-tiered industry: a legitimate sector, in which workers earn about 5 dollars an hour (in the mid-1980s), and an illegitimate, under-the-table system, in which workers earn considerably less. In both cases female workers sew pieces of a garment, have no opportunities for advancement, and work long hours under stressful, unhealthy conditions.

1. Seventy percent of garment workers work in outside, contract shops. These jobs compare unfavorably to welfare and so are filled by undocumented immigrant women.

2. Men are still cutters, women sewers.

3. Unlike the Lowell girls, many of the female garment workers are mothers who must settle for piecework at home or bring their children to work if relatives cannot care for them.

4. The unions: Membership in the International Ladies' Garment Workers' Union (ILGWU) is 90 percent female, but the leadership is still all male.

SOURCES:

Jensen, Joan, and Sue Davidson, eds. *A Needle, Bobbin, Strike* (1984).

Llewellyn, Chris. *Fragments from the Fire: The Triangle Shirtwaist Company Fire of March 25, 1911* (1987).

Stein, Leon. *The Triangle Fire* (1962).

Weiner, Elizabeth, and Hardy Green. "A Stitch in Our Time: New York's Hispanic Garment Workers in the 1980s." In Jensen and Davidson, *A Needle, Bobbin, Strike.*

III. Textiles and the South

A. The South had industrial workers since the colonial period, but large-scale textile production did not develop until after the Civil War and the construction of textile mills in the 1880s.

1. Mills depended heavily on the labor of women and children.

2. Textile work served as the main conduit into industrial waged labor for families unable to make a living as tenant farmers.

3. The South had greater blending of farm and mill, with textile mills dotting the Piedmont region down to the Carolinas and into Georgia and Alabama.

4. The mills were racially segregated, and mill work was reserved for "whites"; women were supervised more closely than men.

5. As in Lowell, corporate paternalism declined as the numbers of desperate workers increased. In 1975 the average textile wage was only 61 percent of the national average, or $1.30 less.

B. The South frequently had absentee corporate owners living in the Northeast, producing what Herbert Gutman describes as a "colonial economy."

1. The Gastonia strike—the largest and most famous of a series of walkouts in textile mills across the Carolinas and Tennessee in 1929.

2. Oneita Knitting Mills—a runaway shop from Utica, New York, moved to Andrews, South Carolina. In 1963 the company decided to break the union (ILGWU). In 1964 the Civil Rights Act forced Oneita to hire black workers. The Textile Workers Union began organizing workers in 1971 and took advantage of the racial mix of workers. In 1973 Oneita workers walked off their jobs. The workers held the line

against the company in a bitter six-month strike and finally won a contract.

3. Greenville, South Carolina: the "most relentlessly anti-union city in the nation."

SOURCES:

Byerley, Victoria. *Hard Times Cotton Mill Girls* (1986).

Hall, Jacquelyn Dowd. "Disorderly Women: Gender and Labor Militancy in the Appalachian South." In *Unequal Sisters: A Multicultural Reader in U.S. Women's History.* Ed. Ellen Carol DuBois and Vicki L. Ruiz (1990).

Miller, Marc S. *Working Lives: The Southern Exposure History of Labor in the South* (1980).

IV. The Southwest border

El Paso and the two-year strike at Farah Manufacturing Company in El Paso, Texas.

A. A typical labor story: the owner, Willie Farah, claimed he'd rather be "dead than union." The workers had low wages, unsafe conditions, and, frequently, speedups. The local power structure harassed the strikers with police dogs and anti-picket ordinances. The strikers had the support of the Amalgamated Clothing Workers of America, which mustered a boycott of Farah pants. After two years the strike ended with a weak union contract.

B. The Farah strikers were virtually all Chicanas.

C. The Farah strike illustrates the difficulty of unionization in the garment trade and in the face of the mobility of capital and the abundance of needy workers.

D. Border cities like El Paso have been able to take advantage of documented and undocumented laborers from Mexico.

SOURCE:

Coyle, Laurie, Gail Hershatter, and Emily Honig. "Women at Farah: An Unfinished Story." In Jensen and Davidson, *A Needle, Bobbin, Strike.*

V. Global restructuring and female workers in transnational settings

A. The emergence of the global assembly line, in which research and management are controlled by the developed countries and assembly line work is relegated to peripheral nations.

1. Overlapping of the formal and informal sectors of women's work.

2. Growth in the informal sector.

3. The name of this old game is to move capital to the cheapest labor site.

B. Life for women workers in Transnational Corporations (TNCs).

1. The "assurance" of patriarchal stability—women move from the control of their families to industrial settings, with male managers and systems to ensure control.

2. Female garment workers (according to a 1984 study) earn 16 cents an hour in China, 57 cents an hour in Taiwan, and 1 dollar an hour in Hong Kong. Many women remit most of their earnings to their families. In some cases (e.g., a case study of female workers in Java), families subsidize their female workers.

3. In the short run TNCs offer some new economic opportunities; in the long run female workers face lack of mobility, hazardous working conditions, and low wages.

C. The informal sector of the global assembly line, in which women do both production and domestic work at home, is a highly problematic "solution" to the contradictions between women's patriarchally defined domestic roles and the demand for cheap female labor.

D. Situated along the Mexico-U.S. border, more than one hundred assembly plants, or *maquiladoras,* have sprung up in Ciudad Juarez, across the border from El Paso, Texas.

1. Eighty-five percent of the workers are women.

2. As in Lowell, plant managers like to employ women who have been recommended by current, reliable workers.

3. Sexual harassment is especially blatant. Women are blamed; fears of loss of female virtue blend with fears of female independence.

4. The mobility of capital, the competition for available jobs, and the fragmentation of work make organizing workers on the global assembly line a formidable task.

E. Resistance of female workers: in addition to forming unions and striking, women have used innovative strategies to resist their work exploitation. Some of these "oblique strategies" include "hormone breaks," baby showers, and possession by religious spirits.

1. Noncapitalist imaginations speaks to alienating class relationships (Ong).

2. The social construction of work is comparable to earlier patterns—absentee (Japanese) corporate owners, families dependent on young women's wages, segregated work sites, frequent turnover, no mobility, gender hierarchy, paternalistic

mystification; moral concerns translate into economic and social control.

F. Transnational worker solidarity: In March 1992 sixty demon-
strators picketed the Van Heusen Factory Outlet store in Pen-
field, New York (a suburb of Rochester), owned by Phillips–Van
Heusen (PVH), this country's leading seller of men's shirts, in
support of shirt workers employed by PVH in Guatemala, who
earn only two to three dollars a day and are trying to form their
own union in the face of frequent physical abuse and even
death threats.

SOURCES:

Fernandez-Kelly, Maria Patricia. "Maquiladoras: The View from the Inside." In
   *My Troubles Are Going to Have Trouble with Me: Everyday Trials and Triumphs of
   Women Workers*. Ed. Karen Brodkin Sacks and Dorothy Remy (1984).
Ong, Aihwa. "Japanese Factories, Malay Workers: Class and Sexual Metaphors
   in West Malaysia." In *Power and Difference: Gender in Island Southeast Asia*. Ed.
   Jane Monnig Atkinson and Shelly Errington (1990).
Ward, Kathryn, ed. *Women Workers and Global Restructuring* (1990).

For information about **Janet Zandy**, *please see page 6 in this issue.*

The Fire Poems

On 25 March 1911 a fire at the Triangle Shirtwaist Company took the lives of 146 workers, mostly young Jewish and Italian immigrant women. Located near Washington Square Park in New York City, Triangle Company was of the largest manufacturers of the sheer blouse known as a shirtwaist—emblem of a freer, more independent, and, of course, class-privileged American woman. Triangle employed hundreds of female workers under an "insider contracting system." The workers were hired by a factory middle man, who negotiated with the boss. The payroll listed only the contractors and not the female workers. The women who produced the shirtwaists were both figuratively and literally invisible to the owners who profited from them.

The famous strike of 1909–10, called the Uprising of the 20,000 (some historians estimate 30,000), actually began at the Triangle factory. The strike lasted five months, as one by one factory owners settled, but the workers at the Triangle factory had to return to work without a union contract. They lost their fight for a shorter workweek and safer and more sanitary working conditions. Rose Safran, one of the Triangle strikers, said, "If the union had won, we would have been safe, but the bosses defeated us . . . and so our friends are dead."

It was spring, a late Saturday afternoon. The workers had already received their pay. The Triangle factory occupied the eighth, ninth, and tenth floors of a building that was considered technically fireproof. There was no sprinkler system, heavy metal doors opened inward and one was kept locked, and the one narrow fire escape reached only to the second floor and collapsed under the weight of escaping workers. The fire spread rapidly; workers on the ninth floor had no warning and were trapped. It was spring. People along busy Washington Place heard the muffled explosion. Someone noticed "a bale of dark dress goods" come out of a window. He thought it was an attempt to save expensive cloth. Then another bale came down and another. One caught the wind and opened. It was not a bale of goods; it was a young woman (Leon Stein, *The Triangle Fire* 1962; reprint, New York: Carrol and Graf / Quicksilver, 1986).

I have always felt a visceral reaction to the knowledge of this fire—a deep sense of injustice. I thought this feeling was just my own until I began researching and collecting material for an anthology of working-class women's writings and I received a number of poems about the fire from contemporary writers. One writer said, "I know that everybody writes about this fire, here's my version." I realized that I am not alone in my private interest in this fire. Others have taken it personally, too. Others have been compelled to read the old newspaper accounts, look at the photographs, actually go to the site of the fire and imagine that terrible moment of choice—fire or sky.

Working-class writers have historical and literary references that come out of lived experiences, handed-down accounts of bad and risky jobs, old newspapers, songs, family lore. They often draw on these as a set of literary antecedents, noncanonical texts that trace a history that is rarely learned in school. The Triangle fire seems to tap a collective memory of class oppression and injustice—especially for women. What is distinctive about the "fire poetry" is that most of the contemporary writers do not work in the garment trade, nor are they from New York City nor of the same race or ethnicity as the workers. What the writers have in common is gender and class, a connection to other female workers, and a call to tell the story so that it won't be forgotten. The subject of these poems is not the personal angst of the poet but, rather, the muted and silenced voices of the 146 women who died. This event—because it was a profound tragedy inflicted on common people—becomes through memory and language and history a catalyst for breaking silence and recovering working-class identity. The communal quality of the Triangle fire poetry allows the reader and the writer to engage in a ceremony of mourning, remembrance, and continual struggle.

Carol Tarlen's "Sisters in the Flames" and Safiya Henderson-Holmes's "Rituals of Spring" are fine examples of this fire poetry.

Janet Zandy

Sisters in the Flames

Carol Tarlen

for Leah
Spectators saw again and again pitiable companionships formed in the instant to death—girls who placed their arms
around each other as they leaped. In many cases their clothing
was flaming or their hair flaring as they fell.
        —"The Triangle Fire," *New York World*, 26 March 1911

Greenhorn
bent over the machine
your hair a mess of red curls
like flames I said
my words extinguished
by the wailing motors
we never spoke
together we sewed
fine linen shirtwaists
for fine ladies we worked
in our coarse gowns and
muslin aprons 12 hours
in the dank rooms
nine floors above the street
our fingers worked
the soft cloth
our coarse hands
fed the machines

Stranger
I saw you once in the elevator
going down going home
your eyes laughed
when I whispered too loud
strands of red hair falling
over your cheek and neck I
touched your red rough hand
my shoulders ached

my pay envelope tucked
in my coat pocket
for Papa for Mama
for the rent I need
a new skirt I need
a day in the sun
I need to unlock the doors
of this factory
I'm still young
I whispered and you laughed
because of course
we all were young

Sister
of the flames
take my hand
I will hold you in the cradle
of my billowing skirt
in the ache of my shoulders
the center of my palm
our sisters already dance
on the sidewalk nine
floors below the fire
is leaping through my hair
Sister I will hold you
the air will lick our thighs
grab my hand
together now fly
the sky is an unlocked door
and the machines are burning

Carol Tarlen *is a clerical worker and a member of two unions: The National Writers Union (UAW) and AFSCME. Her writing has appeared in* Hurricane Alice, Berkeley Poetry Review, Rain City Review, Exquisite Corpse, *and* Calling Home: Working Class Women's Writing *(Janet Zandy, editor, Rutgers University Press).*

rituals of spring

(for the 78th anniversary of the shirtwaist factory fire)

Safiya Henderson-Holmes

from bareness to fullness flowers do bloom
whenever, however spring enters a room
oh, whenever, however spring enters a room

march 25th, 1911
at the triangle shirtwaist factory
a fire claimed the lives of 146 people, mostly women,
mostly children in the plume of their lives,
in the room of their lives
begging for spring, toiling and begging for spring

and in my head
as i read the history, afraid to touch the pictures
i imagine the room, i imagine the women
dressed in pale blues and pinks,
some without heads or arms—sitting
some without legs or waist—hovering
hundreds of flowering girls tucking spring into sleeves,
tucking and tugging at spring to stay alive

and so a shirtwaist for spring
a dress with a manish collar, blousing over breast,
blousing over sweat, tapering to fit a female waist,
tapering to fit a female breath
sheer silk, cotton, linen
hand-done pleats, hands done in by pleats
hands done in by darts and lace

colors of spring
pale blues, pale pinks, yellows, magentas, lavender, peach,

secret thoughts of spring
falling in love under a full moon, forever young
with money enough to buy a flower or two,
time enough to smell it

yes, from bareness to fullness a flower will bloom
anytime, everytime spring enters a room
and here, near these machines, hundreds of flowering
girls

shirtwaist factory room 1911
crowded, hard, fast, too fast, closed windows,
locked doors, smell of piss, of sweat,
of wishes being cut to bits,
needle stabs, electric shocks, miscarriages over silk,
fading paisley, fading magenta,
falling in love will get you fired, forever old,
never fast enough, buying flowers is wasteful
so hurry, hurry, grind your teeth and soul
six dollars a week send to grandfather,
four dollars a week send to aunt ruth, sleep over the
machine and you're done for, way before you open your
eyes ma'm, madam, miss, mrs. mother, girlie
hundreds of flowering green spring girls in rows
waiting with needles in hands for spring to show

women workers
from ireland, poland, germany, france,
england, grenada, mississippi
thin clothes, thinner hopes, months full of why,
of how, of when
answers always less than their pay
but the sewing machines grew like weeds,
thick snake roots strangling the flowers everyday
strangling the roses, daises, lilies everyday
hundreds of blooming girls
hundreds of blooming, spring girls

the shirtwaist building 1911
135-feet-high, wooden, cold, three floors,
not enough stairs,
one fire escape ending in midair,
ending in the spring midair
a tender room of hundreds of blooming bright girls
hundreds of daisy bud girls who pray for spring
to enter their world,
who pray and sweat for spring to enter their world

the strike the year before
and they shouted; open the doors,
unwire the windows, more air,
more stairs, more quiet time, more fire escapes
and to the ground damn you,
and more toilets, more time to be sick,
more time to be well,
and remove the fear and slow it down,
for god's sake, slow it all time, it's spring

they shouted
hundreds of flowering girls,
hundreds of flowering girls shouted
for spring to hurry, hurry and enter their world

and
triangle won a half-day
but the doors remained locked,
windows remained wired, no extra air,
no extra quiet time, or sick time, the fear stayed,
nothing slowed
and god watched hundreds of flowering girls twirl
hundreds of flowering girls willow and twirl

march 25th 1911 at triangle
a worker is expendable
a sewing needle is not
a worker is bendable
a sewing needle is not
a worker can be sent straight to hell
a sewing needle is heaven sent
and must be protected well
a sewing needle is the finger of god
and must be protected well
over hundreds of flowering girls,
hundreds of flowering sweet dandelion girls

march 25th, smoke
smoke, stopping the machines
run to wired windows, run to locked doors,
run to the one and only fire escape,
everyone run to the air
hundreds of flowering girls

smoke
stopping eyes, stopping hearts, stopping worlds
elevator move faster, elevator you are a machine
managed by a human being move faster, c'mon faster
carry all the flowering girls, carry all the sweet,
sweet orchid girls

fire
catching bouquets of girls in a corner, tall, long
stemmed lilies on fire in a corner,
from bloom to ashes in a corner, smell
them in the rain hundreds of tulip girls

on a window ledge
pelees for life, on a window ledge lovely, ribboned young
ladies on their tiptoes twirling, twirling
an arabesque for life
hundreds of flowering girls
smell them in the rain
hundreds of jasmine girls

the ladders were too short
the hoses were too short
the men holding the nets were not gods, only men
who were never trained to catch falling bodies, or
falling stars, or hundreds of flowering girls, hundreds
of carnation bud girls

and the girls
were girls not angels jumping,
not goddesses flying or hovering
they smashed, they broke into
large pieces, smell them in the rain

and the sidewalks
opened in shame to meet the flowering girls
the sidewalks opened in such horrible shame to cradle
the remains of violets
and the gutters
bled for hours, choking on bones, shoes, buttons,
ribbons, holy sewing needles
the gutters bled for hours all the colors of spring
the cool magenta of delicate spring

and the fire ate
the locked doors and the wired windows,
ate the fast machines
in their narrow rooms, ate the lace and hand-done pleats,
the silk, the cotton, the linen,
the crisp six dollars a week, the
eternal buzz of someone else's dreams
nightmares and screams of quiet girls,
loud skull-cracking noises from shy girls
smell them in the rain, the lilacs, daffodils
in the rain

spring, 78 years later
triangle is now part of a university, with offices
and polished intellect, arched unwired windows,
hydraulically controlled and unlocked doors,
air conditioning, swivel chairs, marble walls and fire
alarms

but oh, hundreds of flowering girls still roam
hundreds of blushing spring girls still roam
78 years later in the paint, in the chrome
in the swivel of the chairs
hundreds of blossoms twirling in the air
daring to descend if ever, oh ever the fire comes again

yes, like lead they will drop
if ever, oh ever the fire comes again
to hundreds of flowering girls
smell them in the rain, iris, peonies, magnolias,
bending for the rain

Safiya Henderson-Holmes *is currently Assistant Professor at the Graduate Creative Writing Program at Syracuse University. She has published two collections of poetry,* Daily Bread *and* Madness and a Bit of Hope, *which won the Poetry Society of America's William Carlos Williams Award. Her work has appeared in numerous newsletters, magazines, and anthologies.*

Readerly/Writerly Relations and Social Change:
The Maimie Papers as Literature

Carole Anne Taylor

A symposium on race and ethnicity in the United States views the documentary film *Who Killed Vincent Chin?* and watches spellbound as violence by General Motors autoworkers toward Japanese cars spills over to the beating death of Vincent Chin, himself Chinese but mistaken as Japanese in a Detroit bar. Afterward the discussion does not center on who gains from scapegoating the Japanese as being responsible for local unemployment or on the corporate encouragement for anti-Japanese sentiment. Rather, it focuses on the shocking brutality of the workers and their terrible ignorance of racist stereotypes. Or student discussions of Frank Norris's *The Octopus* or Rebecca Harding Davis's *Life in the Iron Mills* acknowledge the pathos of poor characters, but focus primarily on the problematics of art depicting "deprived" social conditions. Or students reading *The Maimie Papers* foreground her self-repudiating anti-Semitism and her "manipulation" of her benefactors, even as they sentimentalize how the correspondence with the patrician Fanny Howe "allowed her to grow." All such instances attest to a trying pedagogical problem in teaching working-class materials to either largely middle-class students or students who have internalized middle-class values (and therefore, to at least some degree, perhaps most students): the sensibilities they find in the voices of those talking about lived experience often seem less insightful, less artful, less complex in their understanding of social relations than do the writerly sensibilities of more privileged writers, theorists, or observers who analyze or portray the experiences of both working and nonworking poor.

Here I describe experience in teaching and understanding *The Maimie Papers* as a work of literature, one with provocative relation-indifference to the genre of autobiography and the modes of realism and naturalism. I want to suggest that finely argued positions about who is or is not a working-class writer, or exactly what the parameters of definition for a working-class might be, may matter less to pedagogy than does close attention to the positioning of both readers and writers in relation to what a writer describes. Rather than pursuing some calculus with which to determine the class positioning of readers, writers, or texts, one might more fruitfully ask about how the world of writing relates to lived experience and why it matters. Although classes specifically on working-class literature or traditions of dissent might well use more self-consciously theoretical approaches to how class intersects with other social categories, my approach presumes a survey class that reads Jacobs's slave narrative alongside Melville's "Benito Cereno," Pinzer alongside Howells or James or Norris, and Le Sueur alongside Dos Passos or Steinbeck. Here the primary task involves framing work with texts in ways that provoke seeing a writer's representation of life struggles as part of a specifically literary complexity, different from that they recognize in the overt "literariness" of James or Faulkner, but no less interesting or artful. Insisting that students engage Maimie Pinzer *as a writer*, rather than as victim or anomaly, can provoke engaged discussion about the character of writerly lives that are not synonymous with social privilege. Concomitantly, focusing on how *The Maimie Papers* engages its readers in readerly/writerly relations intersects several important theoretical discussions about class and resistance, most notably, the contemporary idea that resistance always participates to some degree in what it resists (an idea applicable to both readers and writers).[1]

Maimie Pinzer's letters represent for readers problems of editing and evaluation not conventional to most literature classes. Yet, because she wrote outside her own understanding of received literary genres, she provides a provocative enactment of writing that becomes literary in the act of negotiating tensions between real and written experience. Although it makes pedagogical sense for my students of twentieth-century American literature to read *The Octopus* (1900) first and then refer comparatively back to this earlier text when reading *The Maimie Papers* (written 1910–22), I want here to foreground work on Maimie Pinzer's lifestory in letters, referring back to *The Octopus*—as we do in class—when its relation-in-difference as a privileged, canonical text helps to differentiate how texts may embody conflicts they do not overtly represent. Such a reading under the influence of pedagogy intends to address many concerns common to anyone reading or teaching working-class literature, but readers should understand my narrative past tense as putting a great deal of pedagogical trial and error under happy erasure, emerging instead with a combinatory, idealized version of how the teaching works when it does, yet not losing sight entirely, I hope, of what it costs to teach in ways that chafe away at students' habitual ways of thinking about texts and about themselves.[2]

My primarily middle-class students tend to take at face value the implied readerly/writerly relations of Maimie's letters, as though eavesdropping on a private correspondence that has no very sustained or artful development.[3] Because so many of her letters serve clearly instrumental purposes—justifying money spent or choices made and rehearsing the hardships of her daily struggle for subsistence—they may seem "unliterary," especially when they overtly plead for approval from her addressee-benefactors. When asked about what characterizes artful or literary texts, students generally respond that literary texts show complex developments in theme, structure, and style, developments that reach some kind of climax in which all the parts, usually through indirection, in some way show forth their connections. This, they often argue, implies that the writer has explicit aesthetic control over the genre or genres in which she writes, a kind of aesthetic self-consciousness they see nowhere in *The Maimie Papers*. Thus, the sequential tasks I ask them to work on with the text address both the nature of developmental complexity in the letters and the relation-in-difference to the representation of social change in a writer such as Norris, with both realist and naturalist novels before him as fictional models. If presented before close reading, classes tend to resist the argument that, though Maimie's letters may embody tensions not explicitly resolved by her, this does not differentiate her from those writers writing firmly within specifically literary modes or generic conventions. The resistance resembles, I think, that experienced by those in social science disciplines trying to teach that those with power and privilege also possess ideologies, that white folks also have race, heterosexuals a stylized self-presentation, and so on.

Among initial responses many complain that the chronic suffering recounted in *The Maimie Papers* wears them down as readers and that the verisimilitude of daily, recurrent hardship has a relentless sameness rather than cumulative power. Classes as a whole may fall into a felt superiority to Maimie's anti-Semitic repudiation of her own Jewishness, her manipulations of her benefactors, and her own class consciousness. And they may chide her for a cloying subservience, even while acknowledging the conditions that produce it. Over the years I have tried (often unsuccessfully, when acts of repression are at stake) to respond to aesthetic judgments grounded in social distance not with contrary judgments, but, rather, with specific analytical tasks designed to lead to revisionary reading—and, if not to that, then at least to framing responses in ways more aware of the social tensions implicit within aesthetic judgments. After initial responses I ask students to form groups in which they look for evidence of changes in

Maimie's concerns or departures from the terms of these early self-repudiations. Depending on prior discussion, they may choose to divide the tasks according to Maimie's developing social views on class, Jewishness, education, prostitution, and philanthropy or according to literary categories (developments in theme, structure, style, tonality). In either case what the groups discover tends toward mutual and overlapping insights about precisely the correspondences and interrelations they have formerly designated as artful.

In describing developmental changes, students sometimes initially presume that changes in Maimie's ideas and self-representations occur because of the good influence of Fanny Howe, and in this case their explanations of those changes range from "Mrs. Howe gave her self-esteem" to "the correspondence with Mrs. Howe allows Maimie to develop." But when asked to find passages in which Maimie herself either identifies changes in her own frame of reference or evinces such change, Mrs. Howe fades from the center of discussion. Without diminishing the value of Mrs. Howe's encouragement and material support, the focus on Maimie's changes—both in her concerns and in her self-representations—show little evidence that Maimie moves beyond either her anti-Semitism or her social pride because of contact with Fanny Howe. Rather, her own experience of discrimination and sexism in trying to make a living in business and her engagements in the lives of needy young women spur her to more intense personal reflection on social conditioning and injustice, reflection that shapes her relation to her correspondence.

Students variously trace how Maimie's early self-repudiations alter as her social vision develops. They note that Maimie, like any of us, cannot entirely reject the constructions that mold her early values, and yet she progressively supplants judgments based on those values with judgments based on social action. In the value she places on Bennie, her loyal and socially progressive husband, Mr. and Mrs. Goldstein, and others, she largely overcomes earlier stereotypical associations of Jewishness with loudness, fatness, acrimoniousness, and so on, even though her descriptions may still betray vestiges of those associations. Similarly, early emphasis on the lack of manners and crudity in language or gesture gives way to concern for the exigencies and constraints of others' lives, even though she may still note who appears clean or neat or well-spoken. Students work out that, as her social vision of a home for "unfortunates" matures into fruition, she increasingly treats character as shaped by possibility—i.e., as nurtured or distorted by social conditioning rather than somehow deserved or earned. They note, too, that just as she much less often refers to bad character or habits as essential traits, so she tends increasingly to identify her own life with the lives of those she helps. Stories from her own past once told to illustrate her mother's or brother's failures in sympathy becomes stories told to illustrate the commonality of young girls' desires. She even comes full circle: whereas she once differentiated herself because of superior education or manners from other women fallen into prostitution, she now identifies fully:

> And somehow—Stella is Maimie. Do you get the idea?
> I am afraid I am not able enough to describe how I mean this. But I know every heartache and longing "Maimie" had. And instead of running true to form—which is, that being older and not desiring the same pleasures, one must condemn them in a younger person—I foresee what will make this girl's lot easier and relieve that terrible pressure that everyone condemns her—and love her instead. (274)

The "pleasures," of course, refer to material and not bodily pleasures (sometimes misread), but the issue of prostitution itself represents a significant pedagogical quagmire, since one could devote a full semester to dealing with many students' feelings that only starvation could force *them* to such a thing; they often have little sense of prostitution as a necessary consequence of differentials in gender and power relations and even less of the way in which, by an extension that is not just figurative, constructions of sexuality imply an economic or market context as present in marriage contracts as on streetcorners. They do engage readily, however, in thinking about how "who pays for what" affects all gender relations, and, having at least introduced the terms of an argument that none of us escape those connections, I try to get students to focus, instead, on how what Maimie feels she can and cannot write about her life matters to the writing. How does the process of writing for an audience change as the letters progress, and how does she conceive of literary genres and her own relation to them?

Perceptive students note that passages some formerly described as "manipulative" seem to struggle to accord with the unacknowledged rules of what her correspondents expect from her and what she might expect from them. (Judith Butler puts this well when she describes how "the production of the *un*symbolizable, the unspeakable, the illegible is also always a strategy of social abjection" [1993, 190].) The early letters talk much of the financial hardship of a "clean" life, and adopt the locutions of the society in referring to her attempts to "live right." Thus, forays into the temptations beyond the "life of prayer" recommended by Mr. Welsh usually acknowledge that their articulation belongs to a forbidden realm. Even with Fanny Howe, Maimie resorts to frequent circumlocution and makes frequent reference to the impossibility of total honesty, as in: "Now I believe I told you all, and it is off my conscience; for I believe though I try to be absolutely honest with you, I can't help but let some deceit creep out. I know I wrote you that I did not need anything—and it is because it is galling that I do. I don't mind the sordidness of it all as much as the thought that I can't help myself" (15). That this letter ends with an appeal for information of a very different kind marks the felt assymetry of the correspondents' roles: "Will you write me something about your home? If you have a dog and what kind—or something I can place around you, as I only can think of you now in that chair with your hat on, and that sort of awes me" (18). In fact, Maimie's early repudiations of other prostitutes and the pains she takes to differentiate herself from them occur frequently in defensive assurances to Fanny Howe that she would never embarrass her, as in her protestation that "you need never fear that I would get into some public place; I don't have to do that. I never did that before, never did anything even one-tenth as low, and consider that the last gasp. I never associated with low women—I don't think I ever met, to talk to the second time, a woman who was publicly known to live other than she should. I shun such people" (77).

In Maimie's early epistolary personae, students find all kinds of textual evidence that she understands as such both her acts of self-justification and even the contrition her correspondent's role demands, and that she makes fine distinctions between how she writes to Mr. Welsh and how she writes to Fanny Howe. She explains to the latter, for example, the self-consciously "therapeutic" role adopted by the "father" in Mr. Welsh, when even in writing about a time of severe depression, she begins with an extrapolation on his role as evaluator:

> Mr. Welch . . . when I first began to correspond with him, would send back my letters if there were any grammatical errors in them: he made just three corrections altogether, and then ceased. I never forgot the corrections, and never made the mistake again. So lately, in a recent letter, I asked him if he would not do as he did in the beginning—that is, tell me of my errors. And he answered that he certainly should have corrected errors had there been any, but there had not been *one*. But—he would suggest that I adopt "brevity of style"! (121)

Above all, she senses a need to reinforce her correspondents by showing improvement or at least being hopeful, often putting off writing because "I have no excuse except that I hated to write to complain— and I have wanted to do nothing else" (125).

Structurally, students begin to relate self-repudiating tonalities to felt abjection, and they begin to understand the logic of why Maimie does not tell the story of her own prison experience or describe bodily suffering from venereal disease until much later. Later tonalities have more assertive resonance, as when, at the end of a paragraph pleading with Fanny Howe not to continue to suggest that she perform her social work in an institutional setting, she insists that "prisons and institutions for reform should not be tolerated by Christian people" (257). A self-referential layering attends her description of the difference in Stella's voice on her return from a horrific experience in a public ward for venereal disease: "Though her appearance has changed considerably, her general mental condition has changed more. I mean by that, that she asserts herself. Prior to this, since the time I first knew her, she was absolutely without opinion or desire, and it would be hard to imagine any one more acquiescent and 'ductile' (I just learned this word). While she is not aggressive now, nor disputatious, still there is a change; and it is one for the better" (300).

As Maimie's stories of others acquire more self-referential layering, they also undertake acts of transformation as she herself moves from subservience to passionate explication and from viewing her own life as exceptional to viewing it as representative. Such transformation mitigates against mere chronology because, far from depending on editorial selection or the letters' dates for coherence, the only kinds of "made" coherence initially felt relevant, they cumulatively order personal experience in designs that develop self-reflective themes, weave others' stories into her own, and use flashbacks, foreshadowings, and levels of irony to elaborate a more and more replete social vision. True, the letters present a loosely episodic structure in which links between events and moods have an often brutal chronicity. But students speculate that, as she works out for herself what unpatronizing and noncondescending forms of help to others might be, she also revises how she thinks about writing and what she values in storytelling. They find accumulating evidence of resistance to the "insincerity" the writing demands, especially that of the later accounting to benefactors beyond the former inner circle.

Increasingly, Maimie establishes the habit of writing letters that go beyond obligatory reportage, and, increasingly, she testifies to being drawn into narrative art even when describing incidents in her own life. Understandably, such narration may lose its sense of a specific epistolary address: "I did not think to tell you this story so thoroughly;

but I felt, when I began, I just wanted you to know: then, as I wrote, it seemed to be as though I was writing the story of that particularly ugly part of my life as though it was a narrative. Somehow, I feel now as though perhaps I wrote you this before" (197). Students find changes evinced in style as well as narrative tonality, as Maimie moves from that vaguely artificial, even occasionally sickly-sweet style of the Brownie and Poke episodes to the much more colloquial, earthy, assertive mode in which she describes her social work with "errant" young women. In 1912, after hearing of a pet by the name of Brownie in the Howe household, Maimie tells a story about the "tragic" end of a different Brownie, framing it formally with, "Perhaps you could tell the children about this little Brownie," at the beginning and closing with: "I hope I haven't bored you with this tale about Brownie. I feel you and the children might sometimes think of your Brownie as our Brownie on earth again for another lease of life" (120). What might have been a pithy story about battling a neighbor who poisoned dogs becomes a somewhat cloyingly sentimental one about dogs who eat with refinement, press noses against the glass "crying to get in," and end in pathos. Framed as though in a genteel tradition highlighting fine feminine feeling, as though a set-piece for a "literary" magazine of the kind sent to her by Fanny Howe, the story has little of the stark expressivity of later stories about her own life and those of her "girls." Increasingly concerned more with agency than with pathos, she confines sentimentality to tales of her dog Poke, who gradually diminishes in importance as her emotional engagements turn to young women in need and danger. With an imaginative range that draws from her own past, from the pasts of those whose stories she tells, and from her own social and philosophical reflections, she increasingly moves toward narration and storytelling with not one whit of sentimentality (such as the story about her being imprisoned on the evidence of her mother and sexually abusive uncle as a punishment for running away from home). And in so many episodes, what she has always prized as a well-educated, literary life reveals itself as limited in its social vision (as in her meeting with Mary Antin, for example, whose "conceited" self-promotion and rudely insensitive treatment of those who have come to admire her convinces Maimie of the social boorishness that may accompany a genteel, writerly existence).[4]

Toward the end of the letters students discover that Maimie evinces much more overt resistance to matching epistolary tonalities to rhetorical goals; by the time she observes to Fanny Howe that she has had to tell her mother, "I am obliged to write in fine detail of my expenses," the observation has a critical edge. She makes almost purposefully dry, formal reports on what Mr. Welch has insisted on calling "The Montreal Christ's Mission for Friendless Girls," despite her conviction that coming to a "mission for friendless girls" would be tantamount to admitting defeat. After nearly two pages on the harmful implications of calling her home "a mission for friendless girls," Maimie only *seems* to follow Mr. Welch's request that she ask Fanny Howe for her advice, making even the question part of the explanation: "Mr. Welch . . . thinks you far more capable of knowing what is better than he does, and in this matter *and in all matters* . . . [writes that] I should follow any advice you'd be kind enough to give. Therefore I ask you what you think of making this mission a 'different kind' in more ways than one—as, for instance, leaving it nameless?" (344). Still conscious of Howe or Welch as audience, she nevertheless prioritizes her understanding that the girls need relationship, stories to tell, in order to enhance their own changes. With the impossibility of interactive relationship across the correspondences she undertakes before her, she questions Mrs. Howe about how to write another donor:

> Shall I disillusion her and lose the possible benefits? Shall I write as if to compel her attention, and thus reap the benefits? . . . I am capable of doing either but is it sincere?
>
> What shall I do? I hate to write knowing it isn't sincere. I hate to accept her benefits knowing they are given under false pretenses. And yet, aren't most charitable things fostered under the same conditions—and should I sit down my personal feelings and be insincere for the girls, who are at present in greater need than ever . . . ? (385)

Maimie's increasing emphasis on the therapeutic intimacy of exchanged lifestories gradually eclipses any mention of autobiography, and students find particularly remarkable the correspondences between changes in personal aspiration and the function of storytelling. Throughout Fanny Howe has encouraged Maimie to work on an autobiography, but neither she nor Maimie herself conceived of her letter writing as relevant to the project. Even at the height of her epistolary output, Maimie bemoans having no time to write anything of literary value:

> I had wanted to write about the possibility of writing my autobiography, as you suggested, but as I couldn't seem to feel sure of my own opinions on the subject, I didn't write. There seems so many reasons why I could not do it. For instance, the little time—even if it only took fifteen minutes a day—is so hard to spare. There are so many tasks—

stockings always to be darned, letters to write, sometimes work for the
office—that I don't feel I could accomplish much, if I did start. I really
feel I could write it—if I could only write a bit at a time. And maybe I
will try it; and if it goes easy, keep on with it. (199)

"Letters to write" takes its place among darning and office work as a
duty keeping her from autobiography, even the kind that might be done
"a bit at a time"! Later, with a replete social philosophy intact, Maimie
uses her own lifestory to make others at ease and to encourage their own
tellings, wearing down their resistance to her status as "social worker"
with frank and empathic self-revelation. Now she tells the stories of her
"girls" as they themselves tell it, if not directly quoting them, then as a
second-order telling imitating their own narrations. The work she seeks
for her charges prioritizes self-worth and cooperative context and thus
corresponds to the value of a storytelling outside the context of writing
as production. An interactive intimacy foregrounds the human context
and function of storytelling art rather than demonstrating the virtuosity
of a writerly art. Quite opposite to a cult of individual genius, Maimie
regards this storytelling as belonging not just to herself but to many; its
place in her own development, cultural and otherwise, stands available
to any of those entering her home.

Relatedly, Maimie's social philosophy informs a literary criticism
able to contrast the sincerity and self-revelatory quality of Wilde's
writing in prison with the letters and poems of an anonymous pris-
oner published in *Harper's Monthly* under the name of X107. Earlier
she has remarked on qualities of the books and articles sent to her by
Mrs. Howe with self-deprecating appreciation, as when she asks for
explanations of meanings "beyond my powers of comprehension," yet
now she sees that the protective timidity of X107 covers for unacknowledged privilege: home as a clean and lovely place that she
abandoned, regular meals, and presumably schooling. Some students
felt that Maimie showed a lack of sympathy for mental illness (not
seeing how Maimie refers it to dominant definitions), but most of them
focused on the primacy of the value placed on a self-revelation that
works through to a common humanity rather than merely inducing
pity. They note how Maimie moves from the superficial symptom of
the pseudonym to more writerly complaints about originality and
authenticity which contrast markedly with her earlier, clearly derivative critical judgments:

I don't share her viewpoint. (I don't like to even think that "X107," so
I've got her fixed as Ruth Ramsey, and that because she reminds me

of Ruth who was an associate of mine at one time, and who wasn't unlike X107 in her utterances—so X107 is now Ruth Ramsey to me.) The viewpoint about people knowing about her past and the prison term, etc. . . . I'd have liked her to be original enough to want to live now in the open. *I am what I am.* It sticks in one's throat at first to admit it, but it gets easier. . . .

I am afraid you will think I take a great deal on myself to criticise anything which has so much in it to excite pity and not criticism. . . . I warn you that I am practicing a code now that admits of no cheap sentimentality, for I find that is as bad—perhaps worse—than cold indifference. (373–74)

Maimie's supposed "failure" to produce an autobiography has clear relevance to students' frequent opinion that *The Maimie Papers* "just ends," as opposed to the artful pulling together of textual elements in more literary works. The opinion asks that the class pay attention to what gives nonfictional works the "sense of an ending." Does the fact that the letters stop so suddenly deprive the reader of that sense? What themes does the final silence bring to an end? How does this ending reflect Maimie Pinzer's final view of the human purpose of storytelling? Maimie's coming to self-confidence about her own perceptions of "errant" girls (her quotation marks, by this point) and what they need coincides with her rejection of benefactors' patronizing and judgmental interference, that of the "Rescue Band," Mrs. Yerkes, and the woman dubbed "Creeping Jesus," who tries to persuade girls to leave houses of prostitution though she herself "never speaks ten words without religious references" (345). But she also more subtly suggests, despite the ritual incantations of goodness, that certainly Mr. Welch and even Mrs. Howe do not understand about her as much as they think nor as much as do the girls whom she is committed to helping. Describing how a first girl inducts a second into her home by telling stories about the photographs, the books, Maimie herself, and other household lore, she writes to Howe, "This second girl generally comes in knowing more about me and my affairs than you do—really."

With self-referential insight Maimie demonstrates how the development of taste accompanies the development of intimacy and the capacity to tell stories about "our little circle," so that the best therapy attends the girl's conviction that she can "be one of us."[5] Students speculate, initially, that, if not dead, then Maimie might well have slipped back into a life of prostitution, perhaps at her age and condition of life more degrading than she could admit to her correspondents. But I like to suggest a different but related possibility, that having discovered the importance of ongoing engagements with those whom she sought to help through to a sense of their own agency and worth—not as a benefactress but, rather, as a kindred spirit who understood because she had been there—she sensed something of the barriers keeping even Mrs. Howe from understanding her as she tried to understand others. In the penultimate letter of 1918 she describes nursing others through the influenza epidemic, along with the loss of her sister-in-law and her own unborn baby. She works at raising her deceased sister-in-law's children and has not "the remotest idea as to plans for the future." Over four years later the last letter refers to uneven correspondence (including her having failed to write for over a year after receipt of a letter), and she reports living in a resident hotel and teaching English to a Filipino student. Significantly, the end of the letter begins, "You haven't any idea of what I am thinking of these days." The rhetorical need to ask for advice has receded to an empty convention, here only a promise to do so at some time in the future because "just now I can't go into it." Instead, a final paragraph circumscribes both an intellectual aspiration very much intact and a skepticism about formal education appropriate to such formidable self-education: "I want to go to school—i.e., I want to take up the study of something. I am fearful lest my equipment is inadequate. I haven't any ida of what I should aim for, and above it all, I am so afraid that I overestimate the worthwhileness of it. I haven't discussed this with Ira, mainly because in his estimation I know now more than anyone alive! However, I know what I have yet to know" (416). The line "I am so afraid that I overestimate the worthwhileness of it" followed by "I know what I have yet to know" suggests a revisionary view of her own educative agency and a revision, too, in how to read this sense of an ending.

Whether or not Maimie could have written and chose not to or simply succumbed to her life's exigencies, her progress justifies a story that becomes entirely oral, with the social interactions it thrives on replacing the formal correspondence to her benefactors. In response to a question about what kind of genre the letters as a whole represent, students distinguish the work not only from autobiography, realism, and naturalism but also from an oral history more like a written tradition in its recording of a lifestory told in a narrative past tense and overviewing the whole of a life lived up to the point at which narration begins. Part essay, part lifestory, part social philosophy, now a nongenre and now an outlaw genre, some agree that what at first seemed a disappointing nonending in fact approaches a kind of metarealism. Life changes have a recursive effect on prior telling and the writer evinces the ultimate control of leaving the writing. Pinzer's relation to the real bears only tangential relation to what literary critics have called "realism" in the writing of fiction; no *-ism* applies well here because she conceives no difference between her relationship with those to whom she writes and the writing itself: her poses, confessions, pleas, and, finally, her self-reflective explanation of her own differences and allegiances. Yet in its unraveling of the connections between economic need and the writing itself lies a critique of the social relations on which the correspondence relies. And all agree, too, that Maimie has rearticulated the terms of her own legitimacy and, in so doing, has called into question the basis of the correspondence's intimacy and purpose.

Now students refer back to *The Octopus* in order to take up more global issues about how writing relates to social injustice and social change. In creating the character of Presley, a participant-observer desirous of "capturing" the struggle of ranchers against the railroad and banks in California's San Joaquin Valley, Norris's fiction also poses complex autobiographical self-reference.[6] The literary forms to which Presley most often refers, romance and epic—the heroic genres—not coincidentally inform Norris's own description. The obvious difference in the fictional and nonfictional status of novel and letters notwithstanding, both writers reveal understandings about literature and genre which have self-referential relevance to how they think about the literary qualities of their own work in relation to the lives of what Norris conceives as "the masses" and what Pinzer regards as "unfortunates" like herself. Norris's writer-observer Presley aspires to a great epic poem about the ranchers' struggle with the railroad, and Norris comes to California to research that same struggle and write about it in extremely lyrical prose. Both maintain their distance from social turmoil, but Presley becomes ridiculous the moment he tries to resolve felt tensions between writing and acting. It would be hard not to see some correspondence between Presley's coming to terms with a necessary impotence and Norris's turning Presley toward the shepherd Vanamee's mystically optimistic romanticism. The writer's conflicted will to expression and to action climaxes in a scene in which Presley frightens himself into hysteria by throwing a silly, impotent bomb, only to feel prostrate with relief when the bomb fails to kill S. Behrman, the railroad magnate. Later he "discovers," in direct confrontation with the banker Shelgrim, that he has misconceived problems and misdirected his energies; that is, he feels himself pitifully outargued by the authoritative overview of corporate power. It occurs neither to Presley nor, presumably, to Norris that an actual participant in the struggle might also tell its story; both imagine a heroic tale that must be produced by the outsider-observer.

Because the class's consideration of *The Octopus* has understood both narrative discussion of genre and the character of Presley as self-referential, it now mitigates against the critical fashion to take a fiction as *only* a fiction, suspending disbelief in any writer's agency or responsibility. Even without the pressure from his publisher to make the moral dilemma of the contest between ranchers and railroad more "equal-handed," the choice of a figural consciousness so much more detached from the working-class characters than from the potentially "heroic" or "tragic" ranchers mediates any portrait of their suffering, a suffering depicted primarily in sentimental vignettes. Where does the story of Mrs. Hooven's gradual starvation and her daughter Minna's inevitable prostitution—partly sentimental realism and partly naturalistic melodrama—fit into the self-referential discussions of the epic, the heroic, and the romantic? Although Norris does not heroize his own relation to his characters' supposedly "real" experience, yet—as so often in American fiction—when he gets closest to addressing what writing may or may not have to do with social action, he thrusts his alter ego into fits of self-abnegation and the intellectual's ultimately passive cynicism about social change, retreating, in the end, to the latent romance that has hovered behind much of the prose. Yet neither the plight of workers nor the idyll of Vanamee and the two Angeles (lacking the symbolic authority of fully conceived romance) has strong structural ties to the battle between commercial and ranching interests. Though narration has at regular intervals distanced itself from the effete, browbeating, even effeminate side of Presley, Norris ends with narrative encomiums to a kind of generative fatalism that couples an almost perfect cynicism with a romantic paean to necessary cycles. The "WHEAT," capitalized like an earlier inchoate "FORCE," becomes the only agency in a book that comes down on the side of an inevitable distance between social action and writing, with the writer's attempts to portray social turmoil always already doomed. Despite the triumph of corporate capital, the ruin of the ranchers, and the total destruction of all the book's working poor, the "WHEAT" moves onto ships "to feed thousands of starving scarecrows on the barren plains of India," and, wondrously, "the individual suffers but the race goes on" (whose suffering and whose race?): "The larger view always and through all shams, all wickednesses, discovers the truth that will, in the end, prevail, and all things surely, inevitably, resistlessly work together for good" (458).

A class's comparative invocation of an earlier reading of *The Octopus* works to suggest that Norris's writing, incorporating much of a romantic realist's representation into a naturalist's design, should demonstrate that Norris has no more "control" over his ideological framework than does Maimie Pinzer over that of her letters. Rather, each in some way exemplifies the conflicts represented, conflicts that may or may not be articulated in the texts as such. Although the fictive world and the naturalist's premise may seem to endow Norris with more self-consciously artful "distance" from his subject, such distance becomes itself part of conflicted fictional representation. In Norris's case narration has increasingly conflicted relation to Presley as figural consciousness, both mocking his effete detachment yet simulating his insights and social judgments. In Pinzer's case the immediacy of the letters address, their presentation as self-validation and justification, initially make Maimie's motivations vulnerable to charges that self-serving overcomes the formal or "aesthetic" values associated with art.[7] Yet an overall logic orders a development that increasingly displaces the values of genres received as literary with those of an oral storytelling inseparable from both social solidarity and social change.

Both Pinzer and Norris face the problems of taking real-life experience as subject matter for writing. That Norris retreats to a romantic idealization of stable order without moral demands for social action should interest us no more than that Pinzer wrote beyond her audience's conception of the reasons for writing and, therefore, disappeared into a world more characterized by oral stories told for therapeutic or salvational ends (the felt validation for most orature, after all) than by stories meant to publish and sell as literature.[8] In the experiential present tense of a perennially fraught immediacy, the letters unfold a growth toward a storytelling self-sufficiency unnoticed by either Mrs. Howe or Mr. Welsh, though moved forward by wide reading in any number of genres. In review students remember that they initially complained that Maimie's letters repetitively document her daily circumstances, seemingly important to her but for them subject to a tedious verisimilitude. When asked questions about an implied audience, they easily named Fanny Howe and Mr. Welch as Maimie's straightforward addressees, talking about Maimie's narration as though this audience mandated a unitary persona. Now they find evidence of multiple and developing personae, double consciousness, irony, and complex negotiations of her correspondents' roles at every turn. In contrast, the students remember immediately understanding as literary Norris's overt encomiums to Presley's—and presumably his own—attempts to understand his own role as "a poet of the people." Having engaged the text *as literature*, they no longer experience it primarily as an activity of social distancing but, instead, as an interpretive activity.

The theoretical issues emerging in teaching *The Maimie Papers* help distinguish the work as literature from works that necessarily describe the suffering of the poor from above, as characters whose suffering represents some aesthetic dilemma for the writer even though their subjectivity has no representation in writing. In addition to arguing for the explicit relation of *The Maimie Papers* to aesthetic traditions and problems (as opposed to its conventional status as a social or historical "document"), I want to recommend a paradigm for encouraging all students to take their own readerly assumptions as part of intellectual difficulty and then to move forward to consider how writerly positioning might also affect how to read. Especially when interpreting works embedded in experience not one's own, in an environment in which issues of class may differ, conflict, or overlap with issues of gender, race, ethnicity, sexuality, and other social categories, it seems especially important for teachers of working-class materials to work with and through, rather than simply acknowledge, the importance of relational social positions. The distance between *The Octopus* and *The Maimie Papers* is not only that between what critics have considered literature or not but also between very differently situated conflicts regarding writing and social action.

Pedagogically, the sequence of tasks and discussion has moved readerly concerns closer to writerly ones, with "What does it mean?" at least temporarily displaced by "How does the writing represent the life?" Even without Bakhtin (1981) or concepts of heteroglossia or the dialogical, such discussion encourages students to reflect on how taking Maimie Pinzer seriously as a "writer" of "literature" means changing our conceptions of both.[9] For writers, one's own experience does not necessarily disallow imaginative creation of very differently placed social experience; nevertheless, writing always in some way embodies felt social tensions of which writers are more or less aware, and perhaps especially those distances they understand as simply natural, a part of the way the world is. For readers, critical understanding that writing embodies social tensions very differently for those writing from different social positions need not imply an essentialism that sees some straightforward relation between a writer's social class and the interests served by that writing.[10] Rather than an autobiography conceived retrospectively and ordered according to an overview of development that fits some received paradigm of knowledge and value, Maimie Pinzer's letters develop in form, structure, style, and theme even while in some ways still participating in what they resist.[11] The analytical tasks performed by groups of students ideally help them see the degree to which they associate the literary with the privilege of control over one's own life and, by extension, with control over one's own life-as-text.

Read relationally, *The Maimie Papers* and *The Octopus* suggest alternative and differently complex cases of writers representing social changes contemporary to their own lives—cases suggesting that writing about experience one vicariously witnesses or imagines has as conflicted relation to social experience as has writing about experience as it happens—in the conflicted realm of a present only just become a narrated past. And if, as Barthes suggested in *S/Z* (1974), literature has as its goal the conversion of the reader into the writer, then the ultimate accolade to reading is that it encourages us to become writers, to undertake new projects. Thus, I am pleased when a student moves from thinking about her own positioning to thinking about the writer's positioning to suggesting excitedly that she would not be able to judge the explicitly literary value of Maimie's letters until she had read them all with an eye to just that, editing with different criteria than those steering Rosen and Davidson. (And is there any greater testimony to editorial work than inspiring one to imagine a new edition based on one's own interpretive logic?) Other students criticize the representation of the letters on the book's back cover, which identifies its relevance to women's studies, history, and Jewish studies but not to literary studies. They find the mirror figure cited in the *New York Times*'s blurb inadequate to Maimie's development ("Fanny Howe became a mirror in which Maimie could know, speak and feel her thoughts, unacceptable though many of them were to polite society and, often, to Maimie herself,") and they reject as condescending the domestic verb *spicing*, the trivializing "tale of woe," and the devaluative adjectives and genres in the *Atlantic Monthly*'s "Maimie wrote vividly and well, spicing her tale of woe with sharp little vignettes, conversations, and quirky reflections."

Considering readerly/writerly relations not only necessitates self-reflective analyses of social positioning, but it also discourages the tendency to take as givens the generic parameters of literary tradition (so that, e.g., only novels illuminate other). Students have familiarity with criticism that takes as formally irrelevant any consideration of an author's lived relation to the social worlds she or he creates, and they take classes in literature which proceed as though the meanings of texts reside somehow "in" the texts themselves. Any activities or tasks that involve locating the desire to read and to write also involve negotiating conscious and unconscious personae, complex relations among desire, knowledge, fantasy, and the real which make all representations to some degree conflicted. Yet coming to an understanding that nongenres, mixed genres, and outlaw genres may effectively and artfully resist the differentials of power which characterize dominant genres means coming to an understanding that Norris (or James or Faulkner or other any writer of privilege) does not necessarily have more aesthetic control over his work than do writers such as Maimie Pinzer who stand outside dominant genres and traditions. The art of writing against the grain of received notions of the literary—while still admiring Montaigne, Dickens, and Wilde, among others—may merge with the art of forging a writing at all, a writing that needs to both learn from and yet resist dominant constructions of knowledge and power in order to assert its own value.

The point, after all, is not simply that Maimie Pinzer understands more about chronic hardship than either Norris or ourselves, as readers, though a respect for the experiential wisdom of her social philosophy should follow from discussion. Rather, when students complain that she lacks conscious control or design of the kind they associate with autobiography or literature, they measure her against some misconstrued idea of literary art as fundamentally intentional, monological, controlled, and, perhaps most important, formally related to the literary genres familiar to them. Critical and comparative reading should illustrate that both those with little power or privilege and those with much bring their social baggage with them to understanding readerly/writerly relations. Because the weight of pedagogy has for so long been behind the formal, aesthetic training in genres and traditions felt necessary to read the great canonical books, students may express understandable dismay when confronted with a very different, experiential kind of readerly disability. So that, when they initially see only a singular, flat, descriptive prose in Maimie Pinzer's letters or complain of a "politically correct reading list," they show the felt threat of values that their own lives have not embodied or, in some cases, even engaged. And when a resisting commitment to social action and interaction overtakes the status of writing itself, the privileged classroom faces its own ultimate critique.

NOTES

1. I adapt here the readerly/writerly distinction made by Roland Barthes in *S/Z* (1974) to distinguish practices that consume the text (a readerly naming of signifieds) from practices that produce the text (a writerly extension of the play of signifiers), where I intend *readerly* to suggest "reading while

thinking about our own position as readers" and *writerly* to signify "reading while thinking about the writer's positioning." I do not, unlike Barthes, extend this distinction to texts.

Part of the pedagogical problem becomes engaging students in the theoretical questions that inform criticism in classes with literary texts as primary sources. Though not always in agreement with students' evaluations, many resent taking literature classes they view as "theory heavy" or "top-loaded with theory," even though they may willingly engage in theoretical arguments in the context of discussing literary texts. Here I try to represent how I negotiate theoretical issues in classes devoted primarily to working with texts read as literature.

2. Although my classes have predominantly middle-class students and teachers at Bates are like those elsewhere, and like myself, predominantly middle-class, working-class students and students with self-identifications that otherwise marginalize them may also participate in the responses I describe here as belonging to simply "students." Whether internalizations of dominant values and censored self-presentations produce conformity or whether the subservient tonalities of especially the early letters discourage sympathetic readings, resistance to thinking of Maimie's letters as artful easily dominates initial responses to reading.

3. In describing classroom tasks and discussion, I follow the lead of my students in calling Maimie Pinzer "Maimie" throughout, even though it would no more occur to them to call Norris "Frank" than to call Shakespeare "William." Calling attention to this asymmetry of naming often leads to discussion about both the power relations affecting who calls whom by their first names and the conflictual sense in which "Maimie" both responds to the implied intimacy of the letters and at the same time might subconsciously diminish her status as a writer.

4. Usefully, some students here relate how their own sense of Mrs. Howe's status as benefactress and Maimie's as the needy victim shaped their initial presumption that if Maimie grows, it must be because of contact with the better-educated, more genteel woman. They may even consider the implications and consequences of formal versus informal education, admitting to a presumption that Maimie's efforts to educate herself must necessarily fall short of a "real" education.

5. If ever there were a temptation to introduce external argument, this kind of discussion seems to ask for reference to key passages in Pierre Bourdieu's *Distinction: A Social Critique of the Judgement of Taste* (1984).

6. I capitalize "Other" as an unrepresentable category that resists the objectification the naming implies. Homi Bhabha explicates it in this sense in "Interrogating Identity: The Postcolonial Prerogative" (1990).

7. In previous classes discussion has noted the asymmetry of which writers' works have stood as self-explanatory and which have had their motivations and characters always under a skeptical scrutiny.

8. My interpretive emphasis here differs from Rosen's hypothesis that Maimie may have stopped writing simply because, "with her husband available to provide the support, intimacy, and friendship which she had shared with Mrs. Howe, Maimie found less urgency to write as frequently" (1977, Intro., xix–xx).

9. For an example of dialogical analysis of writerly desire, I refer interested students to the explications in Peter Hitchcock's *Dialogics of the Oppressed* (1993).

10. This argument usefully coincides with Walter Benn Michaels's insight that the logic of naturalism in general "served the interests not of any individual or any group of individuals but of the money economy itself" (1987, 178), such that the personification of the economy and the dehumanization of characters propels a kind of category mistake. This figurative mistake provides "a singularly compelling image of the naturalist distinction between material and identity. Failing to be a person, it images by the way it isn't a person the condition in naturalism of the possibility of persons" (180).

11. Perhaps those explicating colonial and postcolonial/postindependence literary resistance have argued most strongly for the idea that resistance is always in some way complicit with what it resists. Jenny Sharpe's "Figures of Colonial Resistance" (1989) finds an emphasis on the partial, complicit nature of literary resistance common to such theorists as Gayatri Spivak, Homi Bhabha, Abdul JanMohamad, and Benita Parry; and Stephen Slemon (1990) uses the "double, necessarily mediated" location of literary resistance to argue for the inclusion of "second world" texts by white Australian, New Zealander, Southern African, and Canadian writers in "postcolonial literary studies."

REFERENCES

Bakhtin, Mikhail. *The Dialogical Imagination: Four Essays by M. M. Bakhtin.* Trans. Caryl Emerson and Michael Holquist. Austin: University of Texas Press, 1981.

Barthes, Roland. *S/Z.* Trans. Richard Miller, with preface by Richard Howard. New York: Hill and Wang, 1974.

Bhabha, Homi K. "Interrogating Identity: The Postcolonial Prerogative." In *Anatomy of Racism,* ed. David Theo Goldberg, 183–209. Minneapolis: University of Minnesota Press, 1990.

Bourdeiu, Pierre. *Distinction: A Social Critique of the Judgement of Taste.* Trans. Richard Nice. Cambridge: Harvard University Press, 1984.

Butler, Judith. *Bodies That Matter: On the Discursive Limits of "Sex."* New York and London: Routledge, 1993.

Hitchcock, Peter. *Dialogics of the Oppressed.* Minneapolis and London: University of Minnesota Press, 1993.

Kaplan, Caren. "Resisting Autobiography: Out-Law Genres and Transnational Feminist Subjects." In *De/Colonizing the Subject: The Politics of Gender in*

Women's Autobiography, ed. Sidonie Smith and Julia Watson, 115–38. Minneapolis: University of Minnesota Press, 1992.

Michaels, Walter Benn. *The Gold Standard and the Logic of Naturalism*. Berkeley, Los Angeles, and London: University of California Press, 1987.

Norris, Frank. *The Octopus*. New York and Scarborough: New American Library, 1964.

Rosen, Ruth and Sue Davidson, eds. *The Maimie Papers*. Intro. Ruth Rosen. New York: The Feminist Press and Indiana University Press in cooperation with the Schlesinger Library of Radcliffe College, 1977.

Sharpe, Jenny. "Figures of Colonial Resistance." *Modern Fiction Studies* 35.1 (1989): 137–55.

Slemon, Stephen. "Unsettling the Empire: Resistance Theory for the Second World." *World Literature Written in English* 2(1990): 30–41.

Carole Anne Taylor *teaches literature and American cultural studies at Bates College. Books on Roland Barthes (1983) and visual poetics (1985) as well as recent articles on resistance and subjectivity represent her sustained interest in the ideology of literary forms. Her work-in-progress interrelates tragic and comic forms of resistance as they appear in women's lifestories.*

Between Theories and Anti-Theories: Moving toward Marginal Women's Subjectivities

Roxanne Rimstead

Paulo Freire has urged that shifts in theory be grounded in human narratives. Since these narratives are a location in which the oppressed may imagine liberation in the context of their own experiences, Freire notes, they yield knowledge about the particularities of people's suffering and the multiple possibilities for their emancipation (xi–xii). Especially in the context of a postmodern world in which subjectivities have become unmoored from previous narratives of social justice, Freire encourages academics to listen to and ground our own educational praxis in the language of everyday experiences (Freire and Giroux, ix–xi). Yet, within the context of current literary discourse, for feminist critics to turn their attention to the narratives of marginal women is as problematic as it is challenging. Tony Bennett has noted in *Outside Literature* that there is a struggle, a "wresting" of discourse materials needed in order even to begin to speak from or about a place outside "Literature": "There is no ready-made theoretical position outside aesthetic discourse which can simply be taken up and occupied. Such a space requires a degree of fashioning; it must be organized and above all won . . ." (10). Whereas Bennett would suggest we win that place by scientifically analyzing and exposing a heirarchy of discourses within the academy, Freire's concept of cultural struggle urges academics to look beyond the limits of academic perception and actively engage with oppressed groups to help them achieve subjecthood and to learn from them. But, given the demands of established literary discourse, of which mainstream feminist criticism is now a part, populist feminist critics cannot move directly beyond theoretical exclusions toward marginal subjects; we must learn to move consciously between the theoretical positions we inherit and sometimes oppose and those I call, for the purposes of this discussion, anti-Theory.

Anti-What?

By "anti-Theories" I do not mean anti-theoretical discourse that mistrusts all theoretical formulations or anti-intellectual discourse or even the resistance to poststructuralist theory described by Paul de

Man as generalized "resistance to theory." Anti-Theories, as I see them, question the exclusions of Theory when it assumes its own primacy above other theories or other ways of knowing culture and marginality—for example, through scientific, homogenizing, or totalizing abstractions. By anti-Theories of marginal women's subjectivities, I mean those discussions about reading and interpreting marginal voices, often quite theoretical themselves, which steadily work toward political agency in the form of populist goals or coalition politics. They constitute an oppositional force within academic feminist criticism by trying to bring feminist literary criticism back to a more direct interest in community and everyday life—or, in political terms, back to praxis. While some anti-Theories reach beyond theory into the area of experiences and particularities of concrete subjects, others scrutinize Theory to expose its own subjective blindspots, which sometimes reduce the complexity of the marginal subjects or eclipse them altogether. Finally, these critical gestures toward greater community alliance are not simply acts of faith and often include, as part of their own political self-reflexivity, questions about the nature of political coalition and the claim to know and access marginal subjectivities as an alternative form of knowledge. (For examples of such self-questioning, see Linda Alcoff's "The Problem of Speaking for Others"; and John McGuigan's *Cultural Populism*.)

In the early days of "authentic realism" in American feminist criticism (1970s), the problematic of moving back and forth between androcentric Theory and women's everyday experience was resolved by a veering away from theory and toward a direct assertion of the preeminent truth value of experience and subjectivity. As Sara Mills has observed in *Feminist Readings / Feminists Reading*, at that stage in experientially based criticism, the claims on the text were unabashedly prescriptive, privileging authenticity as a measure of the social effect of the text to challenge the status quo by correcting misrepresentations. Authentic realism implied an anti-theoretical stance because, as it sought to make literary texts accessible to more women, it also encouraged a more plain-speaking, less jargon-ridden form of critical inquiry and the received values enshrined in that discourse. In "unacademic" language grassroots discussion groups probed the transformational power of autobiographical and confessional texts in respect to the lives and experiences of ordinary women readers, an act that by its very existence raised important questions about knowledge claims in critical discourse and the social effect of literature (Mills et al. 51–82). But current poststructuralist debates on knowledge claims and experience across the disciplines have developed more complex

attitudes about accessing knowledge, attitudes that mistrust the representationist assumptions of accessing a concrete reality assumed to be
out there waiting for a purer, truer form of representation. (See, e.g.,
Joan W. Scott's "Experience"; and Mary E. Hawkesworth's "Knowers,
Knowing, Known: Feminist Theory and Claims of Truth".)

Chris Weedon has critiqued the earlier strains of anti-theoretical
and experiential criticism in *Feminist Practice and Poststructuralist Theory* through a deconstruction of the fiction-reality dichotomy and a
more complex understanding of the relation between texts and everyday reality. But, while more complex representationist theories have
emerged, it has sometimes been at the expense of neglecting realist
texts altogether and privileging only those texts that consciously experiment with postmodernist forms and playfully deferred subjects.
Rita Felski, among others, has expressed a concern with this neglect
and has argued for reinstating the value of realist texts in the shadow
of a postmodernist feminist canon. In *Beyond Feminist Aesthetics: Feminist Literature and Social Change* she argues at length for the political
need and theoretical efficacy to reinstate the value of realist literature
as a vital part of an oppositional feminist discourse. Felski has observed that certain types of feminist literary theory, especially those
influenced by poststructuralism, have carried the implicit assumption
that a concern for subjectivity based in lived reality is anachronistic
and naive. She concludes that there is, consequently, a need to defend
the theoretical validity of a culturally based feminist criticism:

> . . . it becomes possible to see the debate between "experiential" and
> "poststructuralist" feminism does not lend itself to simple resolution
> by adjudicating their respective validity as theories, but springs from
> conflicting ideological interests: on the one hand a populist position
> which seeks to link texts to everyday life practices in the hope of
> affecting direct social change, on the other the emergence of an
> academic feminism with often quite different affiliations and profes-
> sional commitment to more rigorous and intellectually sophisti-
> cated, and hence necessarily more esoteric, forms of analysis. (11)

Bella Brodzki and Celeste Schenck have also noted that the complex theorizing practiced by feminist deconstructionists may have
served to legitimate feminist discourse professionally but that it may
be time to "uncouple" feminism and deconstruction in order to look
at other forms of feminist theorizing and the politics of theory itself. As another critic has so succinctly put it, once again linking
theoretical schools to subject positions grounded in power relations:

"Whereas the dominant position requires acts of self deconstruction, the subordinant position entails collective self-construction" (Radhakrishnan 277). Yet those of us who prefer the ideological positioning of collective self-construction and populist feminism—and I use the term *populist* here, as Felski does, in an affirmative sense (see Jim McGuigan's discussion of the complex etymology of the term in *Cultural Populism*)—are still in need of more wide-ranging theories and reading practices to help us make these links between art and everyday life.

Subjectivities

A plural form of "subjectivities" is now fashionable within the context of postcolonial and poststructuralist debates because it invokes, paradoxically, both a sense of inclusiveness of other identities and a sense of playfully deferred identities. One notable exception to this generally blurred invocation of the term is Regenia Gagnier's astute theoretical introduction to a recent study by this title, *Subjectivities: A History of Self-Representation in Britain (1832–1920)*, which begins by stating that "subjectivity," according to cultural studies, is broader than that previously known within the realm of literary studies. Not only did literary studies tend to limit the choice of texts to those reflecting bourgeois subjectivities, Gagnier observes, but the questions asked of those subjectivities were not broad enough or probing enough to reveal the full cultural role of subjectivity. She reviews a wide range of definitions now circulating actively in academic discourse: first, "the subject is a subject to itself, an 'I' "; second, and simultaneously, it is a subject to others appearing as the "Other," which often leads it to construct itself, especially in the case of groups, communities, classes, and nations, in opposition to others; third, the subject is one of knowledge, especially in terms of "the discourse of social institutions which circumscribe its terms of being"; fourth, the subject is a body separate from others (except in the case of a pregnant woman) and dependent upon its concrete environment; fifth, the subject is often identified, despite challenges by deconstructionists, as the site of subjective knowledge as opposed to objective knowledge, in other words with the partial and particular view of the world rather than the Cartesian and hypothetical universal view; and, finally, the subject is also a textual convention, or, as Gagnier describes it: "The 'I' is the self-present subject of the sentence as well as the subject 'subjected' to the symbolic order of the language in which one is writing" (8–9).

Gagnier's is not an exhaustive list, but it is complete enough to hint at the complex theorizing of subjectivity in the context of current academic discourse and to show how precisely defined the use of the term should be to avoid blurring and slippage among these applications. For example, marginal women's subjectivities are represented in current academic discourse, more often than not, in terms of the second definition—how the working-class and poor women are defined as Other in terms of both class and gender. Yet, increasingly, some of the more radical critics aligned with these women are willing to ask, like the proponents of a Marxist history-from-below tradition, how working-class and poor women experience themselves as I as well as Other and also according to any of the other applications (e.g., according to Gagnier's fourth definition, we might also ask how the working-class or poor subject might experience her body differently because it is classed as well as gendered). As Patrick Brantlinger notes, however, rendering the subject more theoretically complex is not in and of itself an oppositional act, and, therefore, the cultural critic who claims to be critiquing dominant culture, must posit more than increasingly complex ways of representing the subject or exposing hegemonic misrepresentation; she must also posit through her critique alternative social orders (145).

Interestingly enough, populist feminist critics seldom spend publication time rigorously defining their precise theoretical application of the term; they usually focus, instead, on the importance of listening more closely to the heterogeneous and complex composition of classed and gendered subjectivities as it is represented by the voices of marginal subjects themselves and the problematics of listening to and speaking for others. For example, populist critics such as Barbara Christian, bell hooks, and Janet Zandy, whose anti-Theories I will discuss shortly, urge the study of utterances by marginal women as the first and primary step in accessing their subjectivities and look to the voices and the concrete subjects in their communities as more than objects of study but, foremost, as subjects capable of imparting knowledge about their own meanings and imaginings. That is not to assume that we can access these subjectivities purely and simply through good faith and solidarity but rather that we listen closely to the idiom, the texture, and the testimonial function of the stories in which subjectivities are expressed.

Understanding marginalized subjectivities in terms of class, race, and gender should involve a radical critique of our own categories of analysis, the context of our inquiry as well, and how and why we invoke marginalized subjects from our relatively privileged positions as academics. For example, it is important to remember that current inquiries about class and gender come after an embattled era, when Marxists and feminists vied for the primacy of their respective categories of analysis: class and gender—with socialist feminists caught in between. The following excerpt from "The Very Last Feminist Poem" by the little-known Canadian writer and propagandist for Marxism, Sharon Stevenson, dramatizes a socialist feminist's struggle with conflicting subjectivities: on the one hand, a feminist subjectivity she fears is less politically potent than a man's and bourgeois in its self-absorbed nature and, on the other hand, a Marxist subjectivity that will not make room for a woman's private concerns and yet cannot resist the concreteness and emotional texture of those experiences either:

> if I were, for instance, Chris Marlowe
> (dead soon after)
> I might be thinking a great deal of the future
> of possibility
> of how to affect change
> if only I were a man.
> instead my mind runs in argument
> over & over again
> with the husband
> the lovers
> the absence of child
> held small in the womb
> seeming lack of purpose
> chaos in day-to-day life
>
> & subjectivity
> rushes soft & clinging
> along the thighs
> before nestling in the brain
> as the strongest weapon
> of the bourgeoisie.
>   (ll. 9–20)

The speaker's sensuous diction reveals ambivalence over her womanly subjectivity, which she rejects as alien and invasive on the surface but "clinging" and "nestling" in a softly, sensual way. As a Marxist, she despairs of her lack of focus on the public sphere and her distraction from a historical mission, a distraction that leaves her wanting beside Marlowe, a man remembered by history as both artist and political agent. Yet her guiltily confessional moment does invoke a different scene of historical struggle: the early stage of socialist feminism, when highly politicized women experienced their subjectivities (and their political souls for that matter) as contested territory. (For a good overview of the theoretical dilemmas of socialist feminists, see Louise C. Johnson's summary "Socialist Feminisms.")

This historic tug-of-war with the fundamentally conflicting notions of public and private subjectivity in Marxism and feminism warrants more careful study because the assertion of the primacy of one category over the other was more than theoretical "nitpicking," as Josephine Donovan noted in *Feminist Theory: The Intellectual Traditions of American Feminism*. The conflict implied questions of loyalties to various communities and different "revolutionary strateg[ies]" (87). In the early days of socialist feminism in U.S. academia, revolutionary strategy depended not only on where one's primary loyalties lay in terms of theory, Donovan notes, but also on how theory extended into strategy—especially, how one perceived the formation of revolutionary consciousness in oneself and others as subjects of history—for example, whether working-class women would be brought to class consciousness through the efforts of an educated elite or through their own insights into oppression.

Theories of the Classed and Gendered Subject

> It is equally necessary for feminist theory to acknowledge that gender is only one of the many determining influences upon subjectivity, ranging from macrostructures such as class, nationality, and race down to microstructures such as the accidents of personal history, which do not simply exist alongside gender distinctions, but actively influence and are influenced by them. To define gender as the primary explanation of all social relations, to speak of the male and female subject in abstract and ahistorical terms, is in fact ultimately counterproductive for feminism, in that such an account can offer no explanation of how existing forms of gender inequality can be changed. (Felski 59)

Most schools of feminist theory are now demanding that the theoretical basis of feminist coalition has to be more historically and socially informed than an idealized category of gender. And the inclusion of marginal subjectivities is central to this project of informed coalition among women. But the great majority of academic feminists are still theorizing from a position of privileged status (of several types: economic, racial, ethnic, educational, social, professional, and cultural), which tends to idealize the relation of a pluralist feminist discourse to lived marginality. An idealist feminist discourse claims to transcend elitism and unfold truths about female subjectivity which apply to all women no matter how different their stories may be. For example, Elaine Showalter's pioneering essay "Feminist Criticism in the Wilderness" (1981) posited a theory of culture whereby all women were represented as culturally marginalized and thus part of a binding reality. Furthermore, Showalter claimed, "It is in the emphasis on the binding force of women's culture that this approach differs from Marxist theories of cultural hegemony" (27). Showalter may be seen as having posited, first, an idealized concept of collective female culture as a rallying cry to theory and, second, a theory that by its very nature would not make a significant place for the knowledge that marginalized women have of difference and hegemony in their everyday lives. As evidenced by Donna Perry's more recent overview of the discipline in "Procne's Song: The Task of Feminist Literary Criticism," mainstream, academic feminist criticism still posits the concept of a community of female readers and writers which ultimately transcends class and race. Through the rather optimistic notion that the feminist critic is one consciously "writing to and for the converted," Perry claims that dissenting voices and differences among feminists are able to emerge and challenge what those shared concerns are (302–3). As anyone knows from looking at the class and racial makeup of student and faculty populations and attendance at academic conferences, however, women do not all speak with one transcendent and homogeneous voice: we are not all being heard through "the voice" of academic feminism.

High theorists as well as populists are increasingly arguing that the assumptions behind gender-specific categories of analysis may detract from theoretical rigor by failing to recognize women's different group and individual social locations and subject positions. For example, Jean Costello's "Taking the 'Woman' out of Women's Autobiography: The Perils and Potentials of Theorizing Female Subjectivities" calls into question not only the homogenizing of the female subject through disregard for social forces such as class, gender, and sexual orientation but also the whole strategy of still creating gender-specific categories of texts at this point in feminist criticism. Costello criticizes recent theories of women's life writing, in particular those based on the application of psychological gender theories such as Chodorow's and Gilligan's, showing how essentialism often creeps into feminist practices of reading and questioning women's texts. Judith Butler's *Gender Trouble* also suggests dismantling the gender paradigm as a gesture toward greater theoretical rigor. As an antidote to the homogenizing aspect of heterosexual feminist identity politics in high theory, Butler prescribes even higher theory: "a critical genealogy of [feminism's] own legitimating practices" (5). But her own genealogy is historically lopsided on the side of academic feminism, leaving out the dissenting voices, the anti-Theorists among feminism's populist critics and activists who have traditionally exceeded Theory in their capacity to embrace heterogeneity by going outside the academy among those very women whom Theory has excluded. Consider, for example, Sheila Baxter, activist and welfare mother, who compiled a collection of interviews with poor women in 1988 in Vancouver, *No Way to Live: Poor Women Speak Out,* and included women of diverse racial and ethnic groups, lesbian women, elderly women, single women, married women, handicapped women, and so on. (For further critiques of gender as a category of analysis, see Joan Wallach Scott, "Gender: A Useful Category for Historical Analysis"; Rita Felski, "Subjectivity and Feminism"; and Sandra Harding, "The Instability of the Analytical Categories of Feminist Theory.")

Although populist critics may be as falsely idealistic about a common community of women as practitioners of high theory by invoking unproblematized claims of identity and macropolitical goals, populists do not need to rely exclusively on increasingly complex theory to invoke the heterogeneity of subjects in their community because the very practice of their cultural critique is linked to recovering and exploring the particular and heterogeneous voices of concrete subjects. With our eyes on the complexity of everyday life, we are more likely to see that alliances between a given individual and various communities and subcultures, with their accompanying constructions of identity, are tentative because they shift with material circumstances, age, sexual orientation, race, ethnicity, and so on. (For more detailed theoretical discussion about coalition politics and reading practices, see Caren Kaplan, "Resisting Autobiography: Outlaw Genres and Transnational Feminist Subjects"; and Radhakrishnan, "Negotiating Subject Positions in an Uneven World.")

In the last two decades, in particular, feminists have advanced beyond the dispute over the primary identity designation (class or gender?) and refined the discussion by asking how class, race, and gender work as interacting contexts that construct the subject. This challenge has arisen partly from anti-Theories such as Janet Zandy's, when she asserts empirically the importance of women's gendered difference within the working class: "The boundaries and texture of working-class women's lives are not the same as men's. Not separate, but not the same" (7). And the relation between class and gender has also been problematized by theorizing class differently. For example, Christine Delphy in *Close to Home: A Materialist Analysis of Women's Oppression* (1984) has challenged the Marxist conception of class identity with an alternative theoretical formulation; instead of class identity based solely in market modes of production (the public sphere), she posits the construction of working-class identity within the domestic mode of production (the private sphere). Of particular interest in Delphy's challenge is the method of bringing her own empirical observations of rural women in everyday life to bear on intellectual Marxism—yet not in a scientific or even a methodologically systematic way but, rather, in a descriptive way that shows the complexity of lives that exceed Theory (ix, 43–46).

Materialist feminists, especially in British feminist theory, have also called for greater rigor in theorizing the classed and gendered subject through consideration of a more psychologically complex subject. For example, Carolyn Steedman has described how necessary it is to allow an unconscious life to working-class childhoods in order to understand the individual formations of class consciousness and the different textures of classed and gendered experiences. She attributes the devaluation of the unconscious in class theory to gender bias. What Steedman terms the "refusal of a complicated psychology to those living in material distress" has come about, she suggests, not only because of the privileging of experiences of working-class men as a source of knowledge about class identity but also because of the generally debased position of mental life in Marxist philosophy and the fact that the theory of emotional and psychological selfhood was executed by people in a central class relationship to the dominant culture (285).

Materialist feminists have been discussing subjectivities recently in two significantly different ways: while some generate what I call anti-Theories to explain the utterances of working-class and poor women as subjects of oppositional culture, others have approached class and gender through "high theory," as inscriptions that need to be decoded by engaged critics applying oppositional reading practices to texts. In other words, while some feminists write anti-Theories to locate the agentive potential for cultural opposition in marginal women's voices themselves as subjects of knowledge, others are working on new theories to refine how we read class and gender in these voices and more traditional canonical texts as objects of knowledge, thus locating the agentive potential with intellectuals in the act of critical analysis itself. The purpose of the discussion here is not to valorize one method over the other but, instead, to show how anti-Theories often function to balance theories and bring them back to political praxis and a more concretely inclusive sense of community and culture.

In "Pandora's Box: Subjectivity, Class and Sexuality in Socialist-Feminist Criticism" Cora Kaplan suggests that we reframe the theoretical debate about one social construct—class or gender—containing or taking precedence over the other by studying texts in terms of how the speaking subject is constructed by class and gender, given that they interact reciprocally and in a complex way upon the speaking subject (346, 364). Class and gender work upon the subject as reciprocal processes, she argues, rather than fixed contents or static territories that can be located in and around the subject definitively. Kaplan suggests that fiction, in general, can reveal subjectivities if we study it as "the ordering of the imagination," as the site of expressions of "hidden" or taken-for-granted ideological beliefs about the self and other classes of women, especially in respect to a history of conventional formulations of femininity: "Literary texts give these simultaneous inscriptions narrative form, pointing towards and opening up the fragmentary nature of social and psychic identity, drawing out the ways in which social meaning is psychically represented. It is this symbolic shaping of class that we should examine in fiction" (359). In addition to identifying the "construction of dominant definitions of the inner lives of working-class women," Kaplan suggests, therefore, that we learn "how dominant definitions of both class and gender are lived by these women" (361). She implies that taking class and gender into account in "a more complex way" would mean, in addition to the appropriation of semiotic and psychoanalytical methodologies by materialist feminists, turning to "non-literary sources, to the discourses in which [working-class women] themselves [speak]" (361). But she adds that the integration of these voices falls beyond the theoretical scope of her own essay, perhaps because at this point her theory necessarily heads into the uncharted area of anti-Theory.

Catherine Belsey, on the other hand, does not discuss the possibility of counterhegemonic knowledge coming from the utterances of ordinary women in her essay "Constructing the Subject: Deconstructing the Text." Belsey implies that the power to challenge ideology lies in the hands of a reader/critic, who can discover contradictory subjectivities by deconstructing the canonized text: "Having created a canon of acceptable texts, criticism then provides them with acceptable interpretations, thus effectively censoring any elements in them which come into collision with the dominant ideology. To deconstruct the text, on the other hand, is to open it, to release the possible positions of its intelligibility, including those that reveal the partiality (in both senses) of the ideology inscribed in the text" (58, 51). Belsey's use of the term *subjectivity* may be partly explained by the concept of ideology to which she subscribes, that of the Althusserian school, which defines ideology as a determinate and dominant force of misrepresentation acting upon all subjects to create false and partial consciousness. Given this context, Belsey refers to subjectivity as though it were an ideologically determined location that is knowable or partially know-able through discourse analysis, historical analysis, psychoanalysis, and deconstruction—in short, through scientific or objective means. This implies that a woman's own narratives about herself and her lived realities are not potent enough to challenge the misrepresentations (and thus hegemony) which ideology imposes—unless, perhaps, the subject herself is capable of applying a method of deconstruction to open her own utterance and see how ideology is operating within it.

By comparing Kaplan's and Belsey's theorization of the subject, we can see that Kaplan's discussion of subjectivity implies more faith in individual agency and in personal formulations of lived experience as an additional source of knowledge in challenging oppressive ideologies. Kaplan's use of the term valorizes subjectivity as a way of knowing, as politically grounded perspectives and sensibilities through which we can know and feel, rather than merely deconstruct and map, the female subject. Thus, as noted earlier, Kaplan invites emergent voices into the process of oppositional analysis as epis-temologically valid subjects, though she stops short of theorizing how this might be done. The nuances between the two theorists' concepts of subjectivity illustrate how materialist feminists must struggle with residual and somewhat divergent Marxist theories about ideology and subjectivity while striking out with new feminist theory to explore subjects that have previously been off the map. (On accessing women's subjectivities through fiction, see also Weedon 74–113; Felski 51–85; and Rabinowitz 97–136.)

I would agree that it is useful to be vigilant about the dangers of mystifying subjectivity and prioritizing it above other forms of knowl-edge, practices that Chris Weedon links with assumptions in humanist discourse of the free, self-determining individual and those of certain radical and essentialist theories of gender (78–79) and which Cath-erine Belsey also links with assumptions of autonomous agency ("Lit-erature," 51–52). But the fact remains that theories that are not informed by these subjectivities, even when acknowledging the voices of working-class women as worthy *objects* of study, have tended to be too abstract or too idealist to bring us much closer to any "inside" knowledge of what Zandy referred to as "the boundaries and textures of working-class women's lives." It seems that the mundane and messy sphere of material struggle, class identification, complicity, and the complexity of life in the concrete world have not been able to emerge through highly abstract language and theory of literary discourse— whereas these subjectivities are palpable in testimonies about the lived experiences of class and poverty.

Accessing Subjectivities

Among the theories and anti-Theories of materialist feminism there emerge nuanced but significant differences between projects to map marginal women's subjectivities and those that claim to access them as knowledge and cultural exchange. These projects are not necessarily separate, and sometimes one critic will attempt both in the course of a particular work—but it is interesting how the choice to "map" subjec-tivities often signals that the critic is about to write a theory from a more distanced bird's-eye view, so to speak, rather than from the more closely identified position of coalition with the marginalized commu-nity itself. Although both of these projects are invaluable to feminist criticism and cultural studies, anti-Theories are the more devalued of the two. Critics who place greater value on the power of marginal voices to inform reading and writing practices are often seen by the literary establishment, at worst, as anti-intellectual and, at best, as less academically rigorous than those who confine their methods to archival research or abstract theorizing about these voices as objects of study.

I have already mentioned that Janet Zandy's introduction to *Calling Home: Working Class Women—An Anthology* constitutes what I would call an anti-Theory based on accessing working-class women's voices and reading them "from the inside out." Zandy has suggested that working-class women in late capitalism in the United States experi-ence a special kind of cultural exclusion which is so pervasive that it denies us a "cultural home." This severe experience of muting re-quires, more than the academic mapping of difference, the cultural accessing of stories, memory, and subjectivities specific to this com-munity of women. Cultural accessing comes with assumptions that the phenomenological potential of reading will allow it to play a role in social therapy and in identity construction. For example, Zandy calls for an intertextual rather than theory-oriented cultural criticism which would allow us to bypass complexly exclusionary Theory and claim access to a cultural home through a process of recognition and retrieval, a collaborative process between reader and writer.

Zandy is pragmatic and respectful in her discussion of working-class women's utterances, expressing a great faith in the internal coherence of these voices and their potential to inform the oppositional reader: "To try to fit this literature into the neat academic categories of genre or period is like squeezing a wilderness into a cultivated park. Despite its diversity and unconventional literary forms, working-class literature is not a mass of dangling parts but a collective body of work. To see these connections, one has to look from the inside out, that is, through the impulses and intentions of the literature itself" (9). While affirming the coherence of working-class texts as a body, Zandy also affirms the uncontainable nature of these utterances in the image of the wilderness. This motif recalls Showalter's paradigm of cultural muting in "Feminist Criticism in the Wilderness" but stresses heterogeneity, class differences, and lack of cultural access as realities within a nonidealized cultural wilderness. Furthermore, Zandy implies that accessing the inside of working-class women's experience of cultural wilderness is possible by assembling voices that come from the inside of these experiences not in terms of essence but, rather, in terms of point of view: "I looked for pieces from the inside of working-class experience either by virtue of the author having been born into the working class or through close political and cultural identification with working-class life" (8). Thus, the inside of this community is determined by a sense of coalition-based empathy, political analysis, or an insider's knowledge of experience, rather than essence.

In her brief discussion of "intentionality" Zandy gives the impression that she has been selective in drawing together narratives that express subjectivities based on collectivity and struggle. This selectivity makes the project of reading "from the inside out" one partly dependent on the inside of a consciously idealist (vs. idealized) category of narratives which has been fashioned by the critic for, by, or about a particular group of working-class women or women who empathize with this position—all who have achieved an awareness of the importance of struggle (10). What I am saying here is that the claim to read from the inside, in this case, is more a politically demarcated space than a theoretical one; it comes to mean reading from the inside of a community of women writers and readers who are brought together through political coalition. To use Zandy's own distinction, then, she implies that we strive not only to read from inside a space (a cultural home) of class knowledge but also, more specifically, inside a space of willed class solidarity: "Class knowledge comes from experience and story, history and memory, and from the urgency of witnessing. Class solidarity is born from perception of common struggles and common enemies" (8). By distinguishing between the search for class knowledge, which tolerates heterogeneity, and that of class solidarity, which wills commonalty, Zandy avoids having to idealize the stories of working-class women, as earlier categories of proletarian literature did.

Although avoiding the word *populist,* probably because of its negative political implications under Reagonomics, Zandy's populist goals are overt; they outweigh any merely ethnographic concerns for broader representation and are the clearest aspect of her anti-Theory. When she gives priority to a reading practice and a form of critical discourse which "would not alienate working-class people from their own texts and would not privilege the critic at the expense of the writer," her commitment to make her own theory more accessible, relevant, and serviceable to a community of readers and writers among working-class women represents a stronger bond with the concerns and sensibilities of this community than with the abstract notions of class and gender (10). This bond is perhaps one reason why her concept of reading from the inside out remains inadequately theorized for academic consumption (especially on the point of intentionality)—inadequate, that is, given the bourgeois tradition of literary discourse to speak an academic insiders' language.

The exclusionary aspect of theoretical language and theoretical practice has been eloquently challenged by Barbara Christian in "The Race for Theory." For example, Christian maintains that African-Americans have always had to theorize as a strategy for survival. Although their theories have not been academically sanctioned, they have always been a race whose members theorized their own oppression to make sense of their world. In the present academic climate, however, Christian argues that African-American critics and other radical critics often feel pressured by the institutional exigency of creating and prescribing one Theory that will contain or homogenize the voices under study: "Some of us are continually harassed to invent wholesale theories, regardless of the complexity of the literature we study. . . . I consider it presumptuous of me to invent a theory of how we ought to read. Instead, I think we need to read the works of our writers in our various ways and remain open to the intricacies of the intersection of language, class, race, and gender in the literature" (570). Christian's solution to the race for theory, which she sees taking place at the expense of recognizing difference, is twofold: first, to valorize theoretical formulations other than those of "high" criticism by learning to listen to the theory couched in the ordinary or the poetic language of the people themselves; and, second, to ground theory constantly in the practice of reading the literature of people who are not usually heard, because, Christain notes, "theorizing is of necessity based on our multiplicity of experiences" (577). The bottom line she sees for engaged critics from oppressed groups is to always interrogate our own praxis ethically by asking, "For whom are we doing what we are doing when we do literary criticism?" Grounding our inquiry in feelings of coalition and our own subjective experiences of class and gender—as well as our concepts of these forces—will bind us more faithfully to the community about whom we write and help us to resist acculturation in an academic community that often pressures us to deal in the currency of theories and authorities that are alien to our subjective experiences.

Though the current fashion is to engage in critical discourse about marginal subjectivities, we may still devalue those same subjectivities through institutional discourse and reading practices. In *Yearning: Race, Gender, and Cultural Politics* bell hooks has noted: "Too often, it seems, the point is to promote the appearance of difference within intellectual discourse, a 'celebration' that fails to ask who is sponsoring the party and who is extending the invitations. For who is controlling this new discourse? Who is getting hired to teach it, and where? Who's getting paid to write about it?" (54). hooks suggests that white academics refuse to perceive the existence of a special psychosocial/ cultural space based on black sensibilities and experiences: "The tendency to overvalue work by white scholars, coupled with the suggestion that such work constitutes the only relevant discourse, evades the issue of potential inaccessible locations—spaces white theorists cannot occupy. Without reinscribing an essentialist standpoint, it is crucial that we neither ignore nor deny that such locations exist" (55; see also Steedman; and Mukherjee, on the topic of informed and subjective reading by insiders in marginalized groups). Yet stepping forward and signifying difference subjectively in the academy provokes negative feedback, according to hooks, as long as it occurs within a feminist movement in which well-intentioned, but nonetheless privileged, white women impose a transcendent and idealized "notion of friendship and sisterly bonding . . . based on principles of seamless harmony" and an unacknowledged code for "nice, nice behavior" (89).

Without making subjectivity the exclusive or even the preeminent source of knowledge about life and culture on the margins, populist critics such as Zandy, Christian, and hooks are beginning to present us with a clearer image of how the academic world pushes marginal voices to the outside via theories and institutional practices that actively, though often unintentionally, assert a hierarchy of subjectivities. Anti-Theories show feminists how the wilderness of female culture has already been colonized by classist and racist values and that the way back to a history of that colonization should include, as well as a collection of muted voices inscribed in narratives, the critic's own subjective knowledge and even her or his own oppositional idiom. For example, Christian has described how accessing knowledge through texts is a way of feeling connected with her own community of women and men and a means of cultural survival: "What I write and how I write is done in order to save my life. And I mean that literally. For me, literature is a way of knowing that I am not hallucinating, that whatever I feel/know is. It is an affirmation that sensuality is intelligence, that sensual language is language that makes sense" (578). And bell hooks recalls that her attempts to use language from the vernacular invariably met with editors' corrections, which she herself accepted until she realized how "disempowering it was for people from underprivileged backgrounds to consciously censor our speech so as to 'fit better' in settings where we are perceived as not belonging" (90). Similarly, writing about the politics of representation in Canadian native women's writing, Barbara Godard has noted that the literary institution has asserted "its authority monologically by refusing to engage in dialogue with these alternate discourses" (186). Godard explains that so few subject positions are left open to native writers, given the literary institution's enforcement of a limited author position, that their subjectivities and idiom are sometimes rejected by publishers—in Lenore Keeshig-Tobias's words, for sounding "too Indian" or "not Indian enough" (186). As an English literature professor of East Asian origin in Canada, Arun Mukherjee has reported that students may also participate in discouraging a discourse of cultural difference by reasserting a dominant apolitical and ahistorical humanist discourse. Mukherjee explains how students may resist oppositional readings of texts and embrace, instead, a "prophylactic view of literature," described by Richard Ohmann as filtering subversive content from even the most provocative texts (27–28). Important steps in oppositional criticism are, therefore, not only the recovery of marginal subjectivities but also the exposure of a hierarchy of subjectivities within theoretical discourse and the exposure of academic discourse as an insider discourse subjectively formed in the interests of that reigning group. For, as Terry Eagleton noted in *Literary Theory: An Introduction,* you may speak a "regional dialect" of critical discourse, "but you must not sound as though you are speaking another language altogether" for "to do so is to recognize in the sharpest way that critical discourse is power": "To be on the inside of the discourse itself is to be blind to this power, for what is more natural and non-dominative than to speak one's own tongue?" (210). There is a terrible irony here. Pronouncing difference within a tightly policed formal discourse risks pushing populist critics further toward the margins, yet in order to move closer to marginal women's subjectivities we must speak different critical languages through which we can construct a more radical subjecthood. And so we move between theory and anti-Theory, not so much playfully as critically—not celebrating detachment but, rather, looking for a home.

NOTE

I am grateful to Chin Bannerjee for his comments on an early draft of this essay. He helped me see that I was indeed reaching for a theory of anti-Theory.

REFERENCES

Alcoff, Linda. "The Problem of Speaking for Others." *Cultural Critique* 16 (Winter 1991–92): 5–32.

Baxter, Sheila. *No Way to Live: Poor Women Speak Out*. Vancouver: New Star Books, 1988.

Belsey, Catherine. "Constructing the Subject: Deconstructing the Text." In *Feminist Criticism and Social Change*, ed. Judith Newton and Deborah Rosenfelt, 45–64. New York and London: Methuen, 1985.

———. "Literature, History, Politics." *Literature and History* (1983). Rpt. in *Modern Criticism and Theory: A Reader*, ed. David Lodge, 400–10. London and New York: Longman, 1988.

Bennett, Tony. *Outside Literature*. London and New York: Routledge, 1990.

Brantlinger, Patrick. *Crusoes Footprints: Cultural Studies in Britain and America*. New York and London: Routledge, 1990.

Brodzki, Bella, and Celeste Schenck. "Criticus Interruptus: Uncoupling Feminism and Deconstruction." In *Feminism and Institutions: Dialogues on Feminist Theory*, ed. Linda Kaufman, 194–208. Cambridge and Oxford: Basil Blackwell, 1989.

Butler, Judith. *Gender Trouble*. New York and London: Routledge, 1990.

Christian, Barbara. "The Race for Theory." In *Women, Class, and the Feminist Imagination*, ed. Karen V. Hansen and Illene J. Philipson, 568–79. Philadelphia: Temple University Press, 1990.

Costello, Jeanne. "Taking the 'Woman' out of Women's Autobiography: The Perils and Potentials of Theorizing Female Subjectivities," *Diacritics: Feminist Miscellanies*. 21, nos. 2–3 (Summer–Fall 1991).

Delphy, Christin. *Close to Home: A Materialist Analysis of Women's Oppression*. ed. and trans. Diana Leonard. Amherst: University Press of Massachusetts, 1984.

Donovan, Josephine. *Feminist Theory: The Intellectual Traditions of American Feminism*. New York: Ungar, 1987.

Eagleton, Terry. *Literary Theory: An Introduction*. Oxford: Basil Blackwell, 1983.

Felski, Rita. *Beyond Feminist Aesthetics: Feminist Literature and Social Change.* Cambridge, Mass.: Harvard University Press, 1989.

Freire, Paulo. Foreword. *Paulo Freire: A Critical Encounter.* Ed. Peter McLaren and Peter Leonard, ix–xii. London and New York: Routledge, 1993.

Freire, Paulo, and Henry A. Giroux. "Pedagogy, Popular Culture, and Public Life: An Introduction." In *Popular Culture: Schooling and Everyday Life,* ed. Henry A. Giroux and Roger Simon, vii–xii. New York, Westport, and London: Bergin and Garvey, 1989.

Gagnier, Regenia. *Subjectivities: A History of Self-Representation in Britain (1832–1920).* New York and London: Oxford University Press, 1989.

Godard, Barbara. "The Politics of Representation: Some Native Canadian Women Writers." *Native Writers and Canadian Writing,* ed. W. H. New, 183–228. *Canadian Literature,* special issue. Vancouver: University Press of British Columbia, 1990.

Harding, Sandra. "The Instability of the Analytical Categories of Feminist Theory." In *Feminist Theory in Practice and Process,* ed. Micheline R. Malson, Jean F. O'Barr, Sara Westphal-Wihl, and Mary Wyer, 15–34. Chicago and London: Chicago University Press, 1986.

Hawkesworth, Mary E. "Knowers, Knowing, Known: Feminist Theory and Claims of Truth." In *Feminist Theory in Practice and Process,* ed. Micheline R. Malson, Jean F. O'Barr, Sara Westphal-Wihl, and Mary Wyer, 327–51. Chicago and London: Chicago University Press, 1986.

hooks, bell. *Yearning: Race, Gender, and Cultural Politics.* Toronto: Between the Lines, 1990.

Johnson, Louise C. "Socialist Feminisms." In *Feminist Knowledge: Critique and Construct,* ed. Sneja Gunew, 304–31. New York and London: Routledge, 1990.

Kaplan, Caren. "Resisting Autobiography: Outlaw Genres and Transnational Feminist Subjects." In *De/Colonizing the Subject: The Politics of Gender in Women's Autobiography,* ed. Sidonie Smith and Julia Watson, 115–38. Minneapolis: University Press Minnesota, 1992.

Kaplan, Cora. "Pandora's Box: Subjectivity, Class and Sexuality in Socialist-Feminist Criticism." In *British Feminist Thought: A Reader,* ed. Terry Lovell, 345–66. London and Cambridge: Basil Blackwell, 1990.

McGuigan, John. *Cultural Populism.* London and New York: Routledge, 1992.

Man, Paul de. "The Resistance to Theory." *Yale French Studies* 63 (1982). Rpt. in *Modern Criticism and Theory: A Reader,* ed. David Lodge, 355–71. London and New York: Longman, 1988.

Mills, Sara. "Authentic Realism." In *Feminist Readings / Feminists Reading,* ed. Sara Mills, Lynne Pearce, Sue Spaull, and Elaine Millard, 51–82. Charlottesville, Virginia: University Press Virginia, 1989.

Mukherjee, Arun. *Towards an Aesthetics of Opposition: Essays on Literature, Criticism, and Cultural Imperialism.* Ontario: Williams-Wallace, 1988.

Perry, Donna. "Procne's Song: The Task of Feminist Literary Criticism." In *Gender/Body/Knowledge: Feminist Reconstructions of Being and Knowing,* ed.

Alison Jaggar and Susan Bordo, 293–308. New Brunswick and London: Rutgers University Press, 1989.

Rabinowitz, Paula. "The Great Mother: Female Working-Class Subjectivity." *Labour and Desire: Women's Revolutionary Fiction in Depression America*, 97–136. Chapel Hill and London: North Carolina University Press, 1991.

Radhakrishnan, R. "Negotiating Subject Positions in an Uneven World." In *Feminism and Institutions: Dialogues on Feminist Theory*, ed. Linda Kaufman, 276–91. Cambridge, Oxford: Basil Blackwell, 1989.

Scott, Joan Wallach. "Experience." In *Feminists Theorize the Political*, ed. Judith Butler and Joan W. Scott, 22–40. New York and London: Routledge, 1992.

———. "Gender: A Useful Category for Historical Analysis." *Gender and the Politics of History*. New York: Columbia University Press, 1988.

Showalter, Elaine. "Feminist Criticism in the Wilderness." In *Writing and Sexual Difference*, ed. Elizabeth Abel, 9–35. Chicago: Chicago University Press, 1982.

Steedman, Carolyn. *Landscape for a Good Woman*. London: Virago, 1986.

Stevenson, Sharon. *Gold Earrings: Selected Poetry*. Vancouver: Pulp Press, 1984.

Weedon, Chris. *Feminist Practice and Poststructuralist Theory*. Oxford and New York: Basil Blackwell, 1987.

Zandy, Janet, ed. and intro. *Calling Home: Working Class Women's Writing—An Anthology*. New Brunswick and London: Rutgers University Press, 1990.

Roxanne Rimstead *teaches language and literature at l'Université de Montréal, where she is about to complete her doctorat in Littérature comparée. Her dissertation explores how to read "poverty narratives" by Canadian women oppositionally. She has published feminist critical articles in* Canadian Literature, Michigan Feminist Studies Journal, Textual Studies in Canada, *and elsewhere.*

"People Who Might Have Been You": Agency and the Damaged Self in Tillie Olsen's *Yonnondio*

Lisa Orr

Reading Tillie Olsen's *Yonnondio* makes me tired and unhappy. In my mind, I am back in the neighborhood where I grew up. Surrounded by corner bars and turn-of-the-century factories, we lived our lives by the rhythms of the unemployment rate. When times were good, we tried to pay off our bills: five dollars a month to the dentist, more money down on the credit cards. When times were bad, we juggled who got paid that month by how nasty their demands for payment sounded: who would turn off service first, the phone company or the gas and electric? With each layoff we sank deeper into debt. With each plant closing my parents found fewer jobs that paid more than minimum wage. There was no money to move, and there certainly wasn't enough to stay. For us, living constantly in the red, escape seemed impossible.

I got out on other people's money—economic opportunity grants and scholarships. Reading *Yonnondio* renewed the guilt I feel at the others left behind, because *Yonnondio* is stunningly accurate in the oppressive, hopeless feelings it reproduces. The sense of "horror . . . on everything," which critic Annie Gottlieb unfortunately character- izes as melodramatic, is actually one of the most authentically repro- duced aspects of working-class life in the book.[1]

I have spent years hiding that part of my life. Finding a book that proved that literature could include the lives of working-class people was wonderful. But the fact remains that reading this book does not feel empowering to me. If anything, it makes me want to start taking the rungs two at a time on my way to the bourgeoisie. I don't want to identify with the working class in this book—it is just too painful.

The reader experiences what the characters feel: hopes collapse with the knowledge that life will continually beat one down. I have watched this sense that nothing can change prevent fellow workers from voting, participating in a union, turning in companies that violate safety codes—in short, from attempting anything that might improve their living conditions. The possibility of a person's having any effect on the system appears nil.

Disturbed by this hopelessness reflected in *Yonnondio* and in my own experience, I turned to Ernesto Laclau's *New Reflections on the Revolution of Our Time* to examine the question of agency. Writing in the late 1980s, in the midst of the transformations of various "socialist" countries into free-market economies, Laclau observes that classical Marxism cannot account for the survival of capitalist states. This leads him to re-examine Marx's argument that the proletariat will inevitably overthrow capitalism.[2]

What Marx could not foresee was the extent to which capitalism could create an efficient, nondisruptive worker who would readily produce and consume products. Capitalism's longevity has led Neo-Marxists such as Louis Althusser to posit that ideology creates the subjects necessary to perpetuate capitalism.[3] But if workers are entirely determined by outside forces, they will, according to Laclau, be incapable of overthrowing capitalism.[4]

Rather than accept this conclusion, Laclau notes that the belief that the worker is constructed by the system does not account for all the historical effects of capitalism. As he points out, capitalism has disrupted the lives of workers, but it has also generated unions and strikes, as well as worker-organized destruction of machinery.[5] The system has defined groups of people who are linked by economic circumstances. Eventually this group will disband, the individual members dispersing to join other groups defined by different circumstances, such as race or gender. In this way, Laclau believes, the voices of opposition become stronger, as they can rally against numerous points.[6]

Thus, for Laclau, the distinction between subjects who are completely inscribed by social forces and free agents who create their own society is an artificial one. The reality is constantly sliding between these two extremes. It is in this sense that Laclau sees a possibility of agency.

Olsen too sees capitalism as damaging people who nonetheless retain some sense of human agency. Olsen, however, does not pass over the "ravages of circumstance" inflicted on workers by capitalism as easily as Laclau does.[7] Her novel shows us the human cost of the system he so optimistically views as generating its own downfall. For example, *Yonnondio* demonstrates how economic status has a direct effect on behavior. When times are good—such as when the Holbrooks begin their life on the farm—Jim and Anna are happier together and kinder to their children. When money is tight, Jim cuffs them all around, and Anna strikes the children. She realizes, " 'Twasn't them I was beatin up on. Somethin just seems to get into me when I have something to hit."[8] The text takes a forgiving attitude toward Jim and Anna. The constant money worries, Jim's crippling, dangerous work, and Anna's struggle to care for her children without even the basics create tension and anger which cannot always be contained.

Significantly, we don't learn what Jim and Anna look like until they leave the mining town. Jim on the way to the farm wears "a look of being intoxicated, his heavy brown hair blowing back, his blue eyes glittering" (25). Later, at the barn dance, we see Anna with her "black eyes laughing, her black hair smooth and shiny to purple" (31). This is the most personal description the two will receive at any point in the novel. By the time they are described again, in Omaha, their personal traits are subsumed by the suffering or sullen appearance of most of their class. Anna's "great dark eyes" are lost "down a terrace of sunken flesh," and all that remains familiar of Jim is the strange blue of his eyes (48). In this sense capitalism does appear to be turning human beings into anonymous, identity-less workers.

The belief that the system cannot be changed is, as Laclau points out, paralyzing. Even the reader is conditioned to feel hopeless in this novel: we learn from experience to dread the bad times sure to follow any respite. Thus, when Olsen writes, "In everyone's heart coiled the fear of a blowup," when describing the family's final days at the mining town, she does more than create suspense (17). Suspense is only possible when there is a possibility that an incident may be averted. But Olsen's reference to a facile company statement on the "unavoidable catastrophe" indicates that this is an oft-repeated tragedy (20). The incompetence of the bosses, the gas-filled caves, the untimbered roofs make an "accident" not only difficult to avoid, but inevitable.

Outside forces collude to keep the Holbrooks down. Once at the farm, their neighbor Benson warns them, "You cant make a go of it . . . bad or good year, the bank swallows everything up and keeps you owin 'em" (31). Anna's "cumulating vision of hostile, overwhelming forces" is based on fact: the banks, the bosses, and the landlords all have a stake in extracting profit from the Holbrooks (93). No wonder Mazie cannot enjoy her family's fireworks. "O it's us again," she rejoices for a moment, but then realizes, "Now something bad's going to have to happen. Again" (107).

Jim's misguided optimism at getting work at the packinghouse— "Didn't I tell you we'd manage? Good times comin, honey, good times"—is no antidote (104). His failure to analyze the forces that shape his life leads him to believe that a few more pennies a day will make a difference. The reader, like Jim's friend Kryckszi, knows better.

These ominous passages must not be read simply as foreshadowing. Olsen clearly is not interested in aesthetic effects alone, as her comments during the blowup scene at the mine illustrate: "And could you not make a cameo of this and pin it onto your aesthetic hearts? . . . Surely it is classical enough for you—the Greek marble of the women, the simple, flowing lines of sorrow . . ." (20). Olsen's foreshadowing carries a political message: "hostile forces" attempt to convince working people that they are helpless, that nothing will ever get better, that resistance is useless.

With this knowledge, we can understand why Mazie is afraid to hope any longer. At one point she allows herself to pretend she is back on the farm, but then harshly chastises herself: the grief, the mourning is too hard to bear (100). This is how a working-class child is forced to cripple her own imagination. With even imaginative escape a cause of pain, the future for Mazie appears unalterably bleak.

According to many critics, what *Yonnondio* offers as a source of hope is the transcendence of the individual, such as the survival of "Anna's remarkable character."[9] The final scene, in which baby Bess discovers her ability to affect the world around her, has also been read as an illustration of that fundamental optimism (132). But to read this novel as only a story of the "rebirth of the spirit," as a Village Voice critic rhapsodizes on my edition's back cover, is to gloss over what it has to tell us about the destruction that capitalism causes, the destruction that Laclau so easily passes over. These critics are ignoring what actually occurs in the novel: while Olsen imagines children born with a self intact, their circumstances crush it out of them. No workers survive undamaged. At best they manage to retain something of their identity. This is why Olsen's novel focuses on retaining a sense of self, while at the same time she has been quoted as saying, "It is irrelevant to even talk of a core of Self when circumstances do not sustain its expression or development, when life has tampered with it and harmed it."[10] Worrying about having a self, she suggests, is a luxury. But it is also a form of resistance.

Anna knows the value of keeping one's inner self alive, and tries to pass this knowledge on to her children. On the one day when Anna is free of her daily routine—the day she and the children pick dandelion greens—Anna repieces the parts of herself that have been scattered by the various demands on her.

At first it seems that Anna's escape comes at the expense of her children. She wears a "remote, shining look . . . on her face, as if she had forgotten them, as if she . . . was not their mother any more" (100). Later, "Mazie felt the strange happiness in her mother's body, happiness that had nothing to do with them, with her; happiness and farness and selfness" (101). Her mother's distance is profoundly disturbing to Mazie, who longs to snap her fingers under her mother's nose.

But having momentarily recovered a selfhood, Anna can offer her children the kind of mothering that gets lost in caring for everyday needs. Her fingers stroke Mazie "into happiness and intactness and selfness" (102). In this mood Anna can heal the "hurt and fear and want and shame" that she ordinarily cannot redress (102).

The interlude does not last long. A whiff of the packing house brings back "the mother alertness, attunement, in her bounded body" (102). But even after her return to boundedness, she uses a phrase the children have never heard her say before: "Holy Meroly" (102). Something of the Anna who is more than clothes-washer, cook, or cleaning lady survives.

In interviews, Olsen insists that "her involvement in a 'full extended family life' did not fracture her selfhood."[11] Anna cannot be conflated with Olsen, but Olsen's insistence suggests we should read this scene carefully. The fact that the packing house smell brings Anna back to motherhood is significant. It is not motherhood that limits women, it is motherhood in these economic circumstances. While Anna has been ill, "a separation, a distance—something broken and new and tremulous—ha[s] been born in her" (93). It is free to develop because the house is neglected, a neighbor tends the baby, someone else prepares the meals—for a while she is free of her deadening routine.

In Laclau's terms, the Anna who sits under a tree stroking Mazie's hair is not the same Anna who hits her children. Olsen optimistically sees the Anna who sings to her children as Anna's "real self" who can bring out the "selves" within her children; to Laclau this very fragmentation precludes any essential self, which, to use his terms, is both "blocked" and "affirmed" by the forces arrayed against it.[12] But Laclau would agree that Anna is not reducible to the sum of capitalism's effects on a working-class wife. The Anna who stubbornly insists, "Better . . . to be a cripple and alive than dead, not able to feel anything," is a source of resistance in the novel (37).

Mazie, too, resists the "inevitable . . . reduction of iron-willed humans to scrap."[13] Repeatedly she seeks confirmation from those around her that she is a human being. In the first chapter she seeks out her father in order "to force him into some recognition of her existence, her desire, her emotions" (8). When the family moves to Omaha, Mazie feels most threatened by the anonymous faces passing her on the street, "faces that knew her not, that saw her not" (69).

Yonnondio demonstrates repeatedly how ugliness can crush the
spirit. For Mazie the shock of the city is so great that she wanders in a
dream until a drunken passerby knocks her down. Later, she suddenly
notices the morbid, depressing stories Ben has been telling Jimmie,
and realizes they are destructive. As the narrator explains, "The
conjurer is working spells on Anna's children. Subtly into waking and
dreaming, into imagination and everyday doings and play, shaping,
altering them" (108). The poems Ben recites are part of the spell,
hardening them, numbing their senses. Mazie seeks out happier children's stories from her parents, but her father can no longer tell them:
"The day at Cudahy's has thieved Pop's text" (101). Anna might remember some, but by the time she finishes her household chores, "it is too
late for texts" (110).

Thus Anna, dreaming of a future on the farm and beautiful things
to keep, is not succumbing to bourgeois brainwashing. She is not a
materialist dreaming of acquiring objects for the sake of status. She
simply knows the price of raising children in such surroundings. An
ugly world is as deadening to the senses as meaningless, monotonous
work. Locating beauty is not an empty aesthetic exercise but a tool
for survival.

In the struggle to maintain selfhood, Mazie has an advantage that
Anna and perhaps Ben share. She has a gift for finding beauty in
surprising places, and she uses this gift to resist the numbing effects of
her circumstances.

Beauty is what helps Mazie survive. In the mining town she finds
release from pain in the "purty tongues" on the burning culm (10).
When horrible memories of her abduction by McEvoy haunt her, she
pushes them away by finding beauty wherever she can: "Butterflies live
behind your eyes, Will. . . . Go ahead and try it—push your finger in
your eye and you'll see 'em, butterfly wings" (43). The entire family
can enjoy obvious beauty when it presents itself, as when they sing
together at Else and Alex's house, or when they are watching the
fireworks. It provides a saner release than damaging each other, or
feeding nail-filled meat to dogs, as the men in the neighborhood do.
But Mazie's gift for discovering hidden beauty is a rare one, and even
more surprising considering her surroundings. For this reason Old
Man Caldwell is amazed when Mazie speculates on whether stars are
"lamps in houses up there, or flowers growin in the night" (32).
"Children have marvelous minds. I hate to see what life does to 'em,"
he tells Anna (34).

Not all of Mazie's attempts succeed. The corn silk she treasures turns
brown; her homemade perfume smells, but not pleasantly. That she

continues to try is thanks to Anna, who uses precious energy scrubbing out an ink bottle to catch sunlight in the window.

Ultimately, this sense of self and sensitivity to beauty will be politically useful. In Olsen's original plan for the book, "Mazie was to grow
up to become an artist, a writer who could tell the experiences of
her people, her mother especially living in her memory. In Mazie's
achievement, political consciousness and personal creativity were
to coalesce."[14]

The world the Holbrooks live in is not sympathetic to creativity—
next to everyday needs, it appears trivial. When Anna dreamily suggests that the mist on the river looks like "soft laundry blowin on a
line," Jim responds, "You fixin to get sick on me again?" (93). Minutes
later, Anna squelches Ben in a similar way. Ben admires the way she
folds the clean laundry, and asks, "Are you making it a sunflower? Can
I try trees and branches?" Anna responds fiercely, "You touch that
wash with your dirty hands, and you'll never touch another thing"
(94). Maintaining creativity in spite of such rebuffs is an everyday
challenge for Anna's children.

A later passage, in which Anna begins speaking, is even more
revealing:

> "Jim, a man came by today and for a quarter a week if we start now,
> a kid gets three hundred dollars when he's sixteen. For a sure ed-
> jication."
>
> Jim jabbed at Ben's arm, shadow-punched at his face. "Don't you
> know how to duck yet?"
>
> Holding his father's hand to stay it: "Guess what, Poppa? We
> blewed soap bubbles today with green onions" (94).

Anna wants to educate her children out of the working class, but Jim
is more concerned with teaching them the skills they will need to
survive within it. Ben's answer is something altogether different. His
answer indicates he shares Mazie's gift for finding beauty in the
humblest things. With such a gift, he can survive without giving up his
working-class roots. Of the three, only Ben's view has the potential to
create change.

Deborah Rosenfelt has written that Olsen "has not wanted to be
misread as encouraging a withdrawal from political activism for the
sake of 'art' or self-fulfillment."[15] Rather, her stated purpose has been
paraphrased as the responsibility to " 'voice the unvoiced,' to speak
for all those millions like us whose lives are such that they can never
come to writing. . . . In our brutal and inhuman society we injure each

other, she reminds us, and any person who achieves recognition does so at the expense of others; this fact we must always remember, not with guilt but with a sense of responsibility to articulate the realities we come from."[16]

Mazie is suited to be the voice of her people by the fact that she feels a connectedness between herself and others, even when she would rather not. Her meeting with the deformed Erina at first seems like a repeat of the McEvoy incident, but Mazie is older now and part of her understands that private suffering is not necessarily a sign of private fault. Still, this connectedness is frightening; at first it seems merely like a doubling of one's own pain. Mazie shudders over a dream she had of being Erina: "Last night I was your body. Go away" (119). Erina would understand Mazie's dream of drinking from the Big Dipper; Erina finds happiness watching a bird play in a saucer of water. Olsen is aware, and probably Mazie is, too, that Erina is what Mazie would have been had she been even less fortunate. Erina reflects Olsen's knowledge that "there is so much more to people than their lives permit them to be. It almost kills you how much is lost and wasted in people who might have been you."[17]

Mazie's sense of connectedness prevents *Yonnondio* from being a story of individual success. All of Olsen's characters are individuals, but they are not isolated. Jim's lament that he has no way to buy the foods the doctor says Anna needs is echoed by a "million swollen throats" (78). When Anna goes to the clinic, she is surrounded by "distorted faces of pain," all with their private griefs, which, however, they experience as a result of their shared economic circumstances (82). As Laclau would argue, that part of the self which is shaped by capitalism forms a common link among these people.

If Mazie does appear to have a special gift, it is one preserved by what Olsen in *Silences* calls "chancy luck" as much as by her own effort.[18] *Yonnondio* does not imply that Mazie deserves special credit. Some critics find this disturbing. "If 'circumstances' are to be blamed for one's failure or 'silences,' " writes Abigail Martin, "then is one free to take credit for any successes achieved?"[19] The answer, I feel, must be no. Anyone who has escaped from that life knows that equally deserving people are left behind. Circumstances account as much for successes as failures.

If Mazie became a writer only to pat herself on the back for her success, she would be implying that all those she left behind had somehow not worked hard enough to escape. The Holbrooks work hard and still have nothing to show for it because outside forces, as I have demonstrated above, work against them.

Mazie as a self-absorbed artist would not be a voice for her silenced class. The fact that Mazie has been damaged, that even the "terrible lands of dream" offer no escape to her, makes her the better activist (112). When Caldwell tells Mazie, "Whatever happens, remember, everything, the nourishment, the roots you need, are where you are now," he is pushing her to remain loyal to her class (38). But he is also reminding her of the source of her political usefulness. The conditions that make her life too horrible to escape even in dreams are the very conditions which make her a potential agent for revolutionary change.

Mazie can interact with and change the structure because the structure has partially created in her a person capable of undermining it. As Laclau explains, human beings create their own identities in the decisions they make, decisions that are made possible by the gaps in the structure. Thus "the constitution of a social identity is an act of power and . . . identity as such is power."[20]

As we have seen, this leaves us with a subject who is divided and unpredictable. But Laclau sees this fragmented subject as a source of optimism. In his words, "One of the consequences of fragmentation is that the issues, which are the rallying point for the various social struggles, acquire greater autonomy and face the political system with growing demands. They thus become more difficult to manipulate and disregard."[21]

Tillie Olsen's work demonstrates the importance of this divided self, even though she is also obviously advocating a communist revolution. Rosenfelt has written that Olsen "found herself unable to document the political vision of social revolution as authentically and nonrhetorically as she was able to portray the ravages of circumstance on families and individuals and the redeeming moments between them."[22] But the two subjects are not necessarily exclusive. In portraying individuals in moments when they are something more than products of the system, something more than victims, Olsen can also be writing subversive prose. In doing so, she prefigures Laclau by almost sixty years.

Laclau's optimism about the fragmented self is then justified. As he predicted, the system has produced an individual who has the potential to overthrow it. Rereading *Yonnondio* with Laclau in mind helps me see room for hope in it. *Yonnondio* does not merely reproduce that despair which can be so crippling and antirevolutionary. Ultimately, Laclau helped me understand what originally seemed like a contradiction in Olsen. Olsen can say in the same interview, "I am a destroyed person" and "I am a survivor," because they are both true at once.[23]

NOTES

1. Annie Gottlieb, "A Writer's Sounds and Silences," rev. of *Yonnondio*, by Tillie Olsen, *New York Times Book Review* (31 March 1974), 5.
2. Ernesto Laclau, *New Reflections on the Revolution of Our Time* (New York: Verso, 1990).
3. Louis Althusser, "Ideology and Ideological State Apparatuses," *Lenin and Philosophy* (New York: Monthly Review Press, 1971).
4. Laclau, 51.
5. Laclau, 39.
6. Laclau, 32.
7. Deborah Rosenfelt, "From the Thirties: Tillie Olsen and the Radical Tradition," *Feminist Criticism and Social Change*, eds. Judith Newton and Deborah Rosenfelt (New York: Methuen, 1985), 236.
8. Tillie Olsen, *Yonnondio: From the Thirties* (1974; New York: Delta-Bantam Doubleday Dell, 1989), 7. Citations are from this edition.
9. Michael Staub, "The Struggle for 'Selfness' Through Speech in Olsen's *Yonnondio: From the Thirties*," *Studies in American Fiction* 16 (1988), 137.
10. Erika Duncan, "Coming of Age in the Thirties: A Portrait of Tillie Olsen," *Book Forum* 6 (1982): 211.
11. Selma Burkom and Margaret Williams, "De-Riddling Tillie Olsen's Writings," *San Jose Studies* 2 (1976): 78.
12. Laclau, 21.
13. Rose Kamel, "Literary Foremothers and Writers' Silences": Tillie Olsen's Autobiographical Fiction," *MELUS* 12 (1985): 59.
14. Rosenfelt, 233.
15. Rosenfelt, 225.
16. Sandy Boucher, "Tillie Olsen Is a Survivor," *California Living Magazine* (10 Feb. 1974), 23.
17. Kenneth Turan, "Breaking Silence," *New West* (28 Aug. 1978), 59.
18. Tillie Olsen, *Silences* (1978; New York: Delta-Bantam Doubleday Dell, 1989) 39.
19. Abigail Martin, *Tillie Olsen*, Boise State University Western Writers Series 65, eds. Wayne Chatterton and James H. Maguire (Boise, ID: Boise State UP, 1984), 17.
20. Laclau, 31.
21. Laclau, 82.
22. Rosenfelt, 236.
23. Boucher, 24.

*For information about **Lisa Orr**, please see page 18 in this issue.*

Industrial Music: Contemporary American Working-Class Poetry and Modernism

Julia Stein

Tom Wayman, a Canadian poet living in Vancouver, has labored to create a movement of North American work writers for the last twenty years. After he earned his M.F.A. degree from the University of California–Irvine he published *Beaton Abbot's Got the Contract* (1974), his first anthology of work poetry. Two more anthologies of work poetry followed—*A Government Job at Last* (1975) and *Going for Coffee* (1981)—plus a book of essays, *Inside Job: Essays on the New Work Writing* (1983). His own poetry, published in over nine books, includes many poems about his job assembling trucks in a factory. Wayman's essays, poetry, and anthologies began a new dialogue throughout North America on work writing. Many small presses and literary magazines in both Canada and the United States have published working-class literature from 1970 through 1994.

In 1990 university presses published two anthologies of proletarian literature: Janet Zandy's *Calling Home,* the first American anthology of working-class women's writing (Rutgers University Press); and Peter Oresick and Nicholas Coles's *Working Classics: Poems on Industrial Life* (University of Illinois Press). Zandy includes over sixty poets, fiction writers, and nonfiction writers; the poets range from Tillie Olsen, who began writing in the 1930s, to Chris Llewellyn, who first published in the 1980s. Oresick and Coles, in their introduction, say they included "169 poems by 74 poets," all written after 1945 (xxii). Zandy includes many categories of writing derived from the feminist movement—home, sex, marriage, birth—but makes no mention of Wayman's anthologies. Oresick's and Cole's anthology is about industrial work. They only quote from one living poet, Tom Wayman, calling his work poetry anthologies "pioneering collections" (xxiv), and their editorial criteria are in reaction to Wayman's ideas in *Inside Job*.

In *Inside Job* Wayman puts forth a literary history in which Romantic poetry has a negative influence on contemporary literature. He offers three criteria for work poetry: it should use "internal realism"; it should play down such traditional subjects as love, nature, and death and, instead, describe work; and it should avoid nonrealistic modernism and experimental poetry. In the rest of this essay I would like to discuss Wayman's four criteria. I would like to look at a few outstanding working-class writers to see how well their work reflects Wayman's theories. Since a large body of contemporary working-class poetry has been produced in the last twenty-four years, it seems an appropriate time for an assessment both of Wayman's theory and of this poetry.

I would like to begin with Wayman's comments on literary history. He argues that European Romantic poetry—with love, death, and nature as its main subjects—has been an important, but negative, influence on North American poetry. He thinks that Romantic poetry causes many readers to lose interest in poetry while they attend school: "To most people, thanks in large part to high school English curriculums, the words 'poetic' and 'romantic' are synonymous. And Romantic poetry as introduced to us in school is an archetype of escape from reality in art." He thinks most poets continue to write about irrelevancies. In industrial society, he says, love, nature, and death are not central to our lives. He argues that work is the governing factor in our lives and, thus, work writing should be central to literature. He says that work poetry "leads in breaking the remaining shackles of Romanticism in art—obscurity, escape—in order to help us learn more about the everyday world we inhabit" (26).

Wayman's characterization of Romanticism and its relationship to the working class is not accurate. There was a working-class audience that once eagerly read Romantic poets. E. P. Thompson, in his book *The Making of the English Working Classes*, has shown how a British workers' audience was created by 1830. Hawkers "went round the working-class districts, hawking chapbooks, almanacs, dying speeches, and . . . Radical periodicals" (788). The working-class autodidacts created group reading circles in taverns and coffeehouses as well as reading rooms. From 1810 to 1830 the radical presses aimed at this working-class audience led an assault on government libel laws and stamp taxes. This radical assault forced the government to finally give the working class free speech by 1830. Thompson says, "This was the culture—with its eager disputations around the booksellers' stalls, in the taverns, work-shops, and coffeehouses—which Shelley saluted in his 'Song to the Men of England' and within which the genius of Dickens matured" (790). E. P. Thompson argues that this working class was part of the national British literary audience by 1819. Working people read middle-class radicals: Shelley, Byron, and, later, Elizabeth Barrett Browning. Browning's "Song of the Children" was an immensely popular poem protesting against the brutal abuse of children working in mines and factories. They read worker-writers such as Ebenezer Eliot, the corntax rhymer, and Thomas Hood.

Anglo-Americans brought this radical popular culture with them to the Americas by the 1830s. Barbara Wertheimer, in *We Were There: The Story of Working Women in America*, discusses the New England mill women at Lowell, Massachusetts, who during the 1830s and 1840s "read the protest journals of the day and followed accounts of strikes on the docks and in the cities" (65). After work they attended lectures, sewing circles, and literary "improvement circles." Wertheimer said that "out of one of these circles grew the *Lowell Offering,* the first journal ever written by and for mill women," which printed their poetry (65). Mill women began a new work literature in which workers wrote about their jobs.

Besides occupational groups such as mill workers and, later, miners, immigrants created work literature. Beginning in the 1840s, German immigrants arrived in the United States, bringing with them "the German dream of a working class Socialist culture separate from and opposed to the evolving mass culture" (Buhle 9). Carol Poore, in her article "German-American Socialist Culture" writes, "Not only did they produce a large body of original literature (poetry, drama, fiction) but they also established a flourishing network of newspapers, theaters, and other organizations aimed at large numbers of German-speaking workers" (in Buhle, 14). This poetry, influenced by such Romantic poets as Heine "expressed the sufferings of the proletarians and their utopian mission in a hortatory, often moralistic way" (15). German-American workers' culture and its institutions were widely copied by later-arriving immigrants such as the Finns, Ukrainians, South Slavs, and Eastern European Jews.

By the first decade of the twentieth century the working-class reading audience was massive. In his book *The Radical Novel in the United States* Rideout writes about the radical press in 1912: ". . . in that year alone 323 papers and periodicals with various shades of red were devoted to Socialism. The important periodicals by virtue of the size of their distribution were the monthly *Wilshire's Magazine* (400,000) and the two weeklies, *The Rip-Saw* (200,000) and *The Appeal to Reason . . .* over 500,000" (99). One of these periodicals was a literary magazine. In 1901 young New York intellectuals put out the *Comrade,* the first socialist literary magazine in the United States. Literature critics writing in the *Comrade* were highly critical of genres favored by socialist fiction writers—the moral-sentimental tale, the Utopian novel, and the romance—and they called for realism (24). Thus, the socialist critique of Romanticism began seven decades ago.

After 1900 English-language poets emerged out of the International Workers of the World (IWW, or Wobblies). The IWW encouraged working people to write songs and poems, printing these pieces in Wobbly newspapers. Cary Nelson, in *Recovery and Cultural Memory*, mentions three Wobbly poets—Covington Hall (1871–1951), Arturo Giovannitti (1884–1959), and Ralph Chaplin (1887–1961)—who "built strong popular reputations, and have remained important to those interested in labor history and culture" (62).

Like the Wobblies, Wayman wants to encourage working people to create their own culture. He applauds the Wobblies' efforts to organize U.S. workers from 1900 until the early 1920s. Though Marxists, the IWW's members differed sharply from those of the Socialist Party. The Wobblies promoted direct action through strikes, free speech fights, boycotts, and demonstrations. They distrusted the Socialist's emphasis on political elections, distrusted any person who "represented" the workers in politics or permanent trade unions. The IWW had its own definition of working class. This definition included industrial workers—longshoremen and garment workers—as well as loggers in logging camps, migrant workers on the farms, miners, fishermen, and homeless in the hobo camps. Their inclusion of migrant labor, the unemployed, and the hoboes made them different from East Coast Marxist groups, which only wanted to organize the industrial proletariat. Traditional Marxists ignored what Marx called the lumpenproletariat, the homeless or unemployed, because Marx thought the lumpenproletariat was irrelevant to the class struggle.

When I speak of contemporary working-class poets, I will use the Wobbly definition, including both those who write about eastern or midwestern factory work as well as those who write about migrant work and class struggle in other parts of the country. I will refer to such contemporary poets of the working class such as Philip Levine and Jim Daniels, who write about auto work in Detroit, the industrial heartland; Jimmy Santiago Baca from New Mexico, who describes how Chicano small farmers lost their land to the government; Tom McGrath from North Dakota and Wilma McDaniel from Oklahoma, both of whom deal with the conflicts between migrant farm laborers and large farmers.

Wayman developed his critical ideas while collecting poems for his anthologies. In *Inside Job* he says he was dissatisfied with his first anthology, *Beaton Abbot's Got the Contract,* because he feels that the poems written by outsiders, people observing other people work, were not as good as those written by insiders, people doing the jobs. Unfortunately, he neglects to include examples of these flawed poems in *Inside Job*. While thinking over these problems, he says that he presented some poems by insiders to a working-class audience:

> The enthusiastic reception the new work poems have received from those working at the jobs depicted—irrespective of the poet's background, or how long the poet has been employed, or whether the poet still works there—is testimony to the truth and power of these poems, I feel (21).

Wayman thinks that poetry by insiders is "more honest, deeper, richer . . . with an immense strengthening of the art both in complexity and aesthetics" than poetry by outsiders (48). When Wayman argues for insiders creating poetry, he carries on the Wobbly tradition of distrusting "professionals" and "representatives" who claim to represent workers, insisting that the workers "must act ourselves" (49).

Wayman argues that contemporary work poets write a "lyric as documentary," which uses anecdotal accounts of work events. He refers to John Lent, another Canadian poet and critic, who says that work poets document many different worlds of work. Wayman says Lent recognized that this lyrical documentary is "an extension of William Carlos Williams' poetics" (23). He says that, as working-class people read contemporary poetry, they discover that:

> Modern poems can be short, concise, unrhymed, anecdotal—exactly like the conversations in which the industrial culture itself is transmitted: People whose daily work leaves them without time, energy, or self-confidence for longer forms find contemporary poetry a handy vehicle to express what they feel is important to their lives (71).

Work poets, he thinks, are influenced by Williams's poetry, especially his short, unrhymed lyrics based on the "raw facts of ordinary life" (23).

When Wayman insists that work writing is primary, and then anthologizes work writers, he acts within a historical tradition of Marxism. Earlier I mentioned how the IWW encouraged work literature. Granville Hicks and Michael Gold, two Socialist Realist critics in the 1920s and 1930s who were close to the Communist Party, also used Marxist theory to argue that production was central to human existence and that work writing was central to literature. Wayman and the Social Realist critics are interested in writing about blue-collar work; both want this writing to have technical precision and to use a work vocabulary.

Though Wayman shares many ideas with 1930s critics, he calls contemporary work poetry "internal realism," claiming it is quite different from 1930s socialist realism, which he calls "external realism." He defines external realism as literature dominated by a vision of the great day when socialism would arrive; he adds that most external realist writing was created by outsiders observing other people work. He gives examples of external realism as Russian socialist realism and Diego Rivera's 1930s murals of the auto industry at the Detroit Institute of Art. Wayman even faults 1930s work writing by "participants inside the industrial process" (47). This future-oriented work poetry, Wayman feels, does not accurately describe daily work because "the poet uses an external ideological framework to try to bend or alter what is happening to fit a preconceived pattern" (47).

Wayman fails to see how 1930s poetry is connected both to modernism and to previous radical traditions. Cary Nelson, who has carefully reread proletarian poetry of the 1920s and 1930s, comments that proletarian poets were writing modernist lyrics from 1914 on:

> Indeed one of the more striking things about the gradual emergence of modernist forms in American protest poetry—from Arturo Giovannitti's prose poems of 1914 to Anna Louise Strong's free verse of 1919 to Lola Ridge's and Charles Reznikoff's imagist poems about immigrants in America, on through the poets of *We Gather Strength* (1933) is the lack of sense of radical break with the past. (25)

Proletarian poets did have a strong sense of the past. Nelson comments that Marcus Graham's *Anthology of Revolutionary Poetry* (1929) included "The Forerunners," such as Blake, Shelley, Whitman, William Morris, and poets who published in *The Comrade* as well as the "the moderns." Both the forerunners—Blake, Shelley, and the IWW poets—as well as the 1930s work writers had utopian dreams. The 1930s poets were the latest in a long history of writers who had utopian visions, stretching back to Shelley, Heine, and other Romantics.

Nelson thinks that 1930s proletarian poetry was *not* dominated by the Communist Party's theories of socialist realism:

> Yet, unlike proletarian fiction, poetry was rarely pressed to abandon all marks of stylistic and political idiosyncrasy. Indeed, even writers who generally had little patience with what they considered to be the bourgeois cult of individualism left considerable space for poetry to register individual experience, conflicts about political

commitment, and linguistic effects that suggested the peculiarity of an individual landscape. (150)

Nelson argues that the Communist Party asks merely "clear sympathy for the working class," and Communist-dominated journals "often settled quite happily for revealing portrayals of working-class life" (163). He discusses various 1930s labor poets: Mike Gold's found poems were taken from workers' letters to the *Daily Worker;* Joseph Kalar was a mystic poet who worked in paper mills; Sol Funaroff, influenced by Eliot, combined "abstract manifesto and personal lyricism"; Edwin Rolfe's complex lyrics are clearly influenced by Pound, Eliot, and William Carlos Williams (Nelson 150–51). Kenneth Patchen was most influenced by Auden, Hart Crane, and Whitman.

Furthermore, the Communist-influenced proletarian arts movement did have some real accomplishments. The *New Masses* and the magazine put out by the John Reed Clubs published many new (and old) working-class writers: Michael Gold, James Farrell, Richard Wright, Langston Hughes, Erskine Caldwell, Tillie Olsen, and others. These magazines, the critics who wrote for them, and the John Reed clubs created a support system crucial for working-class writers, encouraging them to write about lives that had been dismissed as trash, as garbage unfit for literature. Nelson argues that the myth of Party domination was started by Philip Rahv's "polemical 1939 *Southern Review* essay 'Proletarian Literature: A Political Autopsy.' " In discussing Philip Rahv's essay, Nelson argues that "the poetry is too diverse to fit any simple model of party influence" (163–64). The myths Rahv created about 1930s poetry have remained with us until the 1990s.

Wayman argues that contemporary work writers use internal realism, which is characterized by "the abandonment of heaven" (40). He thinks that internal realism accurately reflects the experiences of the postwar working class, which has abandoned any faith that "participation in the work force will lead to any particular future, let alone a glorious socialist one" (40). Instead, internal realism concentrates on the here and now, the minutiae of daily life. New working-class writers who give nitty-gritty descriptions of worklife as they experience it on their jobs are, he thinks, a reflection of working-class consciousness in this period.

Philip Levine's poetry illustrates internal realism. The white and black male factory workers in Levine's poems lack hope for a socialist heaven-on-earth. The poems describe working in a bleak factory. In 1948 the brother curses his job, angrily saying, "You can have it" in a poem with that title. In "Sweet Will" the narrator's coworker gets drunk on the job every Friday night, falls to the oily shop floor, and sleeps in his own blood. During the late 1940s the young man in "The Everlasting Sunday" loses his youth in the numb loneliness of his awful job:

> Bowed my head
> into the cold grey
> soup of the wash trough,
> talked with men
> who couldn't talk.
>
> (*Working Classics,* 138).

Twenty years later the narrator in "Coming Home, Detroit, 1968," finds the city burning up, the people with

> charred faces, the eyes
> boarded up, the rubble of innards, the cry
> of wet smoke hanging in your throat
>   (Levine, *Selected Poems,* 75)

A sense of hopelessness pervades Levine's factory poems.

Like the people in Philip Levine's poems, Jim Daniels's Detroit white factory workers have no belief in a socialist future. In "Recycled Lunchbucket" Daniels writes:

> I wiped it clean, sprayed black paint
> over the farm animals, the barn.
> Then it looked like the others in the factory:
> small black houses, our little coffins.
>   (69)

Daniels's internal realism is very much like the minimalism, or "new realism," of such writers as Raymond Carver and Bobby Anne Mason, two working-class fiction writers. The auto workers in Daniels's poem don't try to escape their "little coffins," just as the characters in Carver's and Mason's stories usually accept their small coffins. The inhabitants of Internal Realist poems or minimalist fiction make minimal demands on reality, certainly no utopian demands. This realism of the late twentieth century is quite different from Balzac's nineteenth-century bourgeois realism.

Wayman's concept of internal realism aptly characterizes a mood of many labor poets, yet this concept poses problems. Bruce Robbins, in *The Servant's Hand,* refers to Kenneth Burke's critique of proletarian realism in the 1930s: "Burke is afraid that a 'discourse weighted with symbols of proletarian life and exploitation might succeed only in isolating workers' agony,' " if that discourse is dissociated from utopian visions that "effectively mobilize allegiance and action" (5). Burke argues:

> To mobilize those whom the image of the alienated worker leaves unmoved, what is needed is to replace the usual realism of the present with a rhetoric . . . projecting images of the desirable (future) while it also reaches back to engage with the compromised values of the unconverted (5).

Robbins argues that realism must be altered to make room for "unrealistic visions or fictions of shared fate" (6). During the 1930s writers usually combined utopian visions and images of workers' agony, while by the 1980s the alternative visions had nearly vanished. Robbins's argument is probably even more crucial to the 1990s than to the 1930s. Furthur, Robbins analyzes in *The Servants Hand* the servants in literature, a job dominated by women, as he looks at work literature taking place in the boudoir and kitchen rather than factory floor.

While Kenneth Burke and Bruce Robbins developed one critique of proletarian realism, feminist critics in the 1980s began a second critique. Wayman (as well as 1930s Socialist Realists) encouraged labor poets to write primarily about the job rather than about love or reproduction. Two feminist critics, Alice Kessler-Harris and Paul Lauter, mention that "less than a quarter of all women . . . worked outside the home during most of the 1930s" (x). These critics say that in the 1930s "women writers of the Left chose to flout male convention and to write about themes that fell outside the frameworks of their male peers. . . . [In] her novella, *That Girl,* Meridel Le Sueur focuses on the regenerative power of pregnancy" (xiii–xiv). The two critics also quote Deborah Rosenfelt's discussion of Tillie Olsen's novel, *Yonnondio:* "The major transformation is based on . . . the regenerative life cycle of which mother and daughter are a part . . . and nurturing that creative capacity in the young is shown in *Yonnondio* to be an essential precondition to social change" (xiv). Feminist critics think women's "work" includes work within the home and the reproduction of life in the family. These critics do not see production as central to working-class writing but, rather, only as one facet of it. Contemporary female working-class poets continue to write powerfully about reproduction while also raising new feminist issues. African-American poet Audre Lorde broke new ground by writing about her breast cancer.

Another feminist critic, Janet Zandy, in her anthology *Calling Home,* includes literature that points to differences in the domestic labor of working-class and middle-class women. Marge Piercy, in "Out of the Rubbish," describes how her mother labored to fix up their shabby house:

> If we make curtains
> of the rose-bedecked table
> cloth, the stain won't show
> and it will be cheerful.
>   (123)

Piercy's poem points out that a working-class woman is a laborer who has to make her own curtains, while a middle-class woman is a consumer who buys her drapes. In the introduction to her book Zandy also contrasts working-class with middle-class women when she discusses "home":

> Working-class women have not found a home in middle-class America. Not really. Recalling the struggle against the dirt and filth of poverty, they try to make of their small and modest homes, safe, clean places. The curtains are changed; the glass doors polished with vinegar, the front stoop swept.... These homes ... can blow over with the slight shift in economic winds. (1–2)

Many female working-class writers from the 1930s to the 1990s write about how economic forces destroyed poor people's homes and families. Grace Lumpkin's 1930s novel about the Gastonia strike, *To Make My Bread,* describes the evictions of the strikers' families from their company-owned homes (in Salzman, 127). During the 1980s Wilma McDaniel published *Primer for Buford.* Many poems deal with how the Dust Bowl catastrophe, both economic and environmental, affected the "Okie" family: "Green Grape Pie" talks of how children coped with starvation; "Aunt Sula's Quilt" tells how the neighbors gave Aunt Sula a going-away gift before she left for California; "Via Dolorosa" recounts how Okie mothers suffered on the migration westward. As an old woman, McDaniel realizes that Okie history and customs are not transmitted to the younger generation in California. She then writes *Primer for Buford* for Uncle Claudie Windham's grandson Buford who

> don't know nothing
> his daddy done
> when he was boy in Oklahoma.   (15)

Wilma McDaniel writes an epic story of an Okie family.

Men as well as women write about how political or economic forces push people from their homes. Jimmy Santiago Baca, in his poem "Roots" from *Black Mesa Poems*, describes how his father lost his land, his family's home for generations, to the government; his family wound up as immigrants and exiles in their own land. In *Martin and Meditations on South Valley* Baca describes how his narrator, Martin, builds his family a home and also has a fine piece about Martin's wife giving birth. Both McDaniel and Baca create their own working-class visions of domestic labor. From the Wobbly hoboes to McDaniels's Okies in their jalopies to Baca's Chicanos, homelessness has been central to this poetry.

Wayman does make one very cogent point when he argues that our economic position influences our relationship to nature, love, and death. There are great differences between those, like Wordsworth, who have the income leisurely to contemplate a landscape versus those, like Tom McGrath, who work on the land as a farm laborer. Jim Daniels's does not describe a lovely landscape in "Still Lives in Detroit #2, Parking Lot, Ford Sterling Plant." Instead he writes of "a barren landscape decaying under the grey sky" (*Working Classics,* 54). In the 1930s Muriel Rukeyser published her long epic, "The Book of the Dead," about hundreds of silica miners in West Virginia who were dying from work-induced lung disease. *Working Classics* also includes two of many poems written in the 1980s about the Triangle Shirtwaist Company fire: Mary Fell's "The Triangle Fire" and a section from Chris Llewellyn's book, *Fragments from the Fire.* From the 1930s through the 1980s labor poets have created a poetry of industrial disasters and polluted landscapes.

Wayman proposes both a subject matter, work, and a method, the lyric as documentary. At the same time, he attacks all forms of Non-realist writing. He says that, in the early parts of the century,

> What was new in poetry were certain experiments in form—including surrealism, sound poetry, automatic writing, the unconventional rearrangement of words on page: Some writers today still imagine that what was startling half a century ago must remain the path to the future. But in our time the new in poetry is to be found rather in content, specifically this content (*Job,* 72).

Wayman ignores the politics and content of Modernist poetry. Both Dada and surrealism blasted out protests against the debacle of European society, which led to the carnage of World War I. French

surrealists made scathing critiques of society, allied themselves first
with the Communist Party in the 1920s and then with the Trotskyites
in the 1930s. They dismissed realism as unable to provoke any real
change in society; they wanted to forge a new language using nonrealistic art forms because "to propose a new language is to propose a
changed life for men and an alternative and revolutionized society"
(Short, 303).

Wayman is blind to the sociopolitical critique of the original surrealism or of Dada, so he is also blind to how this critique has been
continued by at least some of the subsequent generations of Modernist
poets. A small French Trotskyist sect merged with Dada artists in the
1950s to produce the International Situationists, who were the theo-
reticians for the May 1968 French uprising. Their ideas inspired much
Postmodernist art; a small group of northern California Situationists
started *Process World,* an avant-garde San Francisco magazine for
workers in the information-processing industries (Ward). A feminist
Trotskyist group, the Freedom Socialist Party, includes two contemporary Bay Area poets, Nelly Wong and Merle Woo, and the late Karen
Brodine was also a member. A politicized modernism, drawing on
both Marxism and the French avant-garde, has been integral to
twentieth-century poetry from the 1920s up to the 1990s.

Wayman feels that most Nonrealist art is escapist literature that
keeps people confused about their lives in industrial society. He
thinks Nonrealist art promotes the interest of the bourgeois class,
since this class wants people confused and mystified about everyday
reality. Wayman condemns four forms of nonrealistic art: magical
realism, myth, symbolism, and alternate visions. After briefly discussing his criticism of each form, I would like to compare Wayman's
criticism with some poetry by contemporary working-class poets.

Wayman dislikes magical realism, calls Gabriel García Márquez's
magical realism "a bizarre and arbitrary surrealism" that "eases the
reader's flight into fantasy" (16). But other literary scholars think
magical realism is an integral part of Chicano literature about the
working class. At the 1991 Modern Language Association conference,
in a session titled "Relations between U.S. Hispanic and Latin American Literature," Carl Guitterez-Jones discussed "The Magical in Mo-
rales's [novel] *Brick People,*" about Chicano workers in a brick factory.
Chicano poet Jimmy Santiago Baca has many magical figures in
"Meditation on South Valley," including *cuaranderas* (spirit healers)
and *brujas* (witches). *Curanderas* and *brujas* have been part of Chicano
and Mexicano culture for centuries. Wayman does not see how magical
realism is an integral part of Chicano literature.

Wayman dismisses symbolism and myth in literature as a result of social hierarchies in literature. He says critics like symbolism and myth in writing because the ability to understand Greek and Roman myths or to decode obscure symbolism is an accomplishment only of an upper-class minority. He thinks of myths solely as an outdated means that earlier civilizations used to comprehend their world; this knowledge, he feels, has largely disappeared from the general population. Literature relying heavily on myth and symbol, he argues, teaches as a subtext that ordinary, daily life is not important as literature.

Wayman praises feminist, Chicano, and black writing, yet all these literatures have accepted mythical writing and symbolism as relevant to contemporary audiences. Feminists have rewritten many Greek and Roman myths to the delight of women's audiences. Alta rewrote the Orpheus myth from the viewpoint of Eurydice, while Greek actress Melina Mercouri acted in the film *Crime of Passion,* a feminist retelling of Medea. Native American poets—including Simon Ortiz, Wendy Rose, and Leslie Silko—have written poems using their Native American symbolism and mythical characters. Third World cultural nationalisms in the 1960s encouraged Chicanos, blacks, Native Americans, and Asian-American writers to use their religious symbols and mythic past, forging connections between that past and the present.

Wilma McDaniel, who is part Native American and part Euro-American, uses Christian symbolism to such a great extent in *Sister Vadya's Song* that she sounds often like a present-day biblical prophet. In "Kinship" she says:

> the Bible
> has seeped into the marrow
> of our souls
> Old Testament
> and New
> We have both seen the wicked
> in great power.
>   (38)

The characters in this book live in a Bible-saturated world: in "Close Neighbors" Jesus and His mother "live down the Okie Road only a / little piece" (66); in "Psalms" Odie Hicks in his California exile

> might as well been
> sitting by the rivers of
> Babylon

the muddy Kings held him
as tight.

(62)

McDaniel fuses her deep spirituality with politics in *Primer for Buford*. In "Red Is for Martyrs" the priest strangely wears the red vestments honoring Saint Matthew, the patron saint of tax collectors. The poet, believing that the real martyrs are the young men who died in the war, wants her taxes back since the taxes paid for their deaths. McDaniel's deep religious beliefs are typical of many in the working class. E. P. Thompson, in his monumental study *The Making of the English Working Class*, discusses the many religious revivals among the English rural and urban poor in the early nineteenth century. When many of these poor Christians, like McDaniel, became politicized, they expressed their politics using a biblical discourse: revival-style meetings, politicized hymns, and religious slogans (438–39). Both Thompson's and McDaniel's writings show that myth, symbolism, and spirituality are important to European-American working-class writers as well as to Third World authors.

Wayman dismisses literature that imagines alternative possibilities. He does admit that some critics defend visionary literature, as it "provides a vision of other human possibilities, often of an ideal world or situation" (*Job*, 17). But he immediately criticizes visionary literature, if it is in any way disconnected from daily work, as one more escape fantasy. He writes as if no such visionary literature dealing with production exists. But the writings of Marxist critic Christopher Caudwell inspired labor poets such as Tom McGrath to write a visionary literature that was connected with daily work.

A young British Marxist poet and critic, Caudwell wrote *Illusion and Reality* (1937), which had a great impact on leftist intellectuals in England and New York directly after World War II. Caudwell gave a Marxist rationale for the spiritual in art and for alternative visions. Caudwell argued that poetry, the rhythmical language of public emotion, is necessary for the economic well-being of tribal societies. He used the example of a harvest. Before the harvest the tribe will have a public festival in which it uses poetry to call up a fantasy of the harvest:

> As man by the violence of the dance, the screams of the music, and the hypnotic rhythm of the verse is alienated from present reality, which does not contain the unsown harvest, so he is projected into the phantastic world in which these things phantastically exist. That world becomes more real, and even when the music dies away the

ungrown harvest has a greater reality for him, spurring him on to the
labours necessary for its accomplishment. (27)

Poetry gives the alternative visions that help channel human instincts
into economic activities.

Thompson recalls how British and American leftist literary critics
and intellectuals hotly debated Caudwell's theories during the late
1940s. In a long essay on Tom McGrath in Stern's *Revolutionary Poet in
America,* Thompson says that Gertrude R. Levy's book *The Gate of Horn,*
which examines totemism and cave art in Lascaux, vindicated Caudwell's view of tribal art. Cave art and tribal art both had complex
symbolism that embodied the tribe's totems. Thompson discusses how
both Levy and Caudwell helped Marxists understand how the shaman
or artist in tribal society led the religious rituals that promoted the
economic well-being of the tribe. These ideas about the artist as
visionary shaman clearly influenced many 1950s and 1960s poets,
such as the Beats and Tom McGrath.

Both Levy and Caudwell clearly influenced Tom McGrath. McGrath
entitled one novel *The Gates of Ivory, the Gates of Horn* and introduces
part 4 of his epic poem *Letters to an Imaginary Friend* with the Caudwell
quotation about how the tribe uses collective emotion to call up the
fantasy of the harvest. McGrath borrows heavily from Hopi myth,
especially Hopi symbolism of resurrection and renewal. He repeatedly
calls himself "a resurrectionist man" who acts very much like a Native
American shaman. McGrath sees his whole epic poem as a kachina
that will help fulfill Hopi prophecy: ending the present world, the
Hopi Fourth World; and ushering in the Hopis' Fifth World, which he
identifies as the postcapitalist world. Of course, he also has wonderful
descriptions of work throughout his epic poem, from his joining a
farm labor crew in his early teens to his working as a woodcutter
during the Depression. He describes how he "sweated and froze" in
the migrant woodcutting crew and how he

> participated in the solidarity of forlorn men
> Firm on our margin of poverty and cold
> Communitas
> Holy City
> Laughter at forty below
> Round Song
> The chimes of comradeship that comes once maybe
> In the Winter of the Blue Snow.
>   (46)

This round song of the woodcutters is McGrath's utopian vision of labor solidarity, which could constitute a new world of *communitas* in the future. McGrath was part of a small group of poets who throughout the postwar years still retained their utopian visions.

E. P. Thompson argues that Tom McGrath is not an isolated literary figure but, rather, is representative of an important leftist current from the 1940 through the 1980s. Memory of this current has been erased:

> I find, rather often, a curious amnesia within American radical culture as to certain moments in its own past.... Not only some part of the 1930s but a large amount in the 1940s has fallen out of polite discourse.
>
> Orthodox academicism and post-Trotskyist criticism and historiography have obliterated this moment under some general theory of the universal contamination of "Stalinism." (Stern, 113)

Thompson tells how McGrath was part of a British and North American dissident group that used Caudwell and Levy to battle Communist orthodoxy within the Communist Party during the 1950s. When the dissidents lost to the Party bureaucrats, McGrath and many others left the Communist Party. McGrath remained an independent radical whose nonorthodox radicalism permeated his poetry. Thompson thinks that McGrath's trajectory was typical of his generation. Thompson himself as well as many other British and North American leftist intellectuals shared this history from the 1940s through the 1980s. Though these British and American writers split from the Communist Party, they still remained political radicals, and their politics was central to their literary work. Nelson mentions some of the radical writers continuing to publish individual poems as well as complete books in the 1940s and 1950s: "Langston Hughes, Muriel Rukeyser, Kenneth Fearing, Alfred Hayes, Don West, Genevieve Taggard, Norman Rosten, Edwin Rolfe, Thomas McGrath, Aaron Kramer, Ruth Lechlitner, Walter Lowenfels, Melvin Tolson, Olga Cabral and others" (166). Many of these poets continued to publish through the 1990s, their work developing with each decade, largely appearing in tiny press editions and alternative magazines, yet they have been largely ignored.

The North American literary establishment has successfully marginalized these poets as part of a larger effort to "imagine that radical political poetry as a whole came to an end in America in 1939" (Nelson, 164). Unfortunately, many young working-class writers have

never heard of these poets or their history. Nelson argues that ignorance of radical literary history "suggests how successful has been the
process of repression and the construction of a diminished, sanitized
cultural memory" (166).

Wayman criticizes modernism and visionary poetry in this landscape of cultural amnesia described by Thompson. The New Critics
and the myth critics not only buried leftist history but also stripped the
politics out of modernist texts. Wayman seems to be responding to the
landscape that he sees before him: a derivative modernism totally
divorced from any social or political content and a new generation
whose members were beginning to write working-class literature. But
Wayman overstates his case when he dismisses postwar literature
influenced by nonrealistic modernism.

All of working-class poetry from 1820 to the present needs to be
retrieved and studied. Contemporary work poets can no longer hold
onto their cultural amnesia, no longer remain in ignorance of their
history. Perhaps as labor poets, both historical and contemporary,
receive more critical attention, the belief that labor poets need to use
realism will be debated. Cary Nelson uses Poststructuralist theory to
deconstruct twentieth-century literary history, and in the process he
retrieves 1910–40 proletarian poetry for the 1990s. Poststructuralist
theory, if applied to working-class poetry, could also lead to a reexamination of realism, representation, and labor poetry. From the
Wobblies to the Poststructuralists the basic question is: Who represents the working class? With a immensely diverse and complex working class, can a handful of writers "represent" it or give the "realistic"
portrait of it?

Wayman has carried on the tradition of Wobbly dissent, and that
is courageous. I used the Wobbly definition of the working class
rather than the traditional Marxist one. The Wobbly definition included the homeless and the unemployed as well as preindustrial
workers such as farm laborers, fishermen and miners. If work literature includes preindustrial workers, then could it also include
workers in a postindustrial economy now developing in the United
States? The postindustrial working class has its homeless, part-time,
and marginalized workers, many of whom are women. Clearly, the
nature of the postindustrial working class and the beginnings of a
postindustrial work literature in such magazines as *Processed World*
should be studied further. Literary critics of noncanonical working-
class literature need to recover and study all of the past literature as
well as look with open eyes at how this literature is changing in
the present.

REFERENCES

Aaron, Daniel. *Writers on the Left.* New York: Harcourt, Brace and World, 1961.

Baca, Jimmy Santiago. *Black Mesa Poems.* New York: New Directions, 1986.

———. *Immigrants in Our Own Land.* Baton Rouge; Louisiana State University Press, 1979.

———. *Martin and Meditation on the South Valley.* New York: New Directions, 1987.

Bold, Alan. *The Penguin Book of Socialist Verse.* Baltimore: Penguin Books, 1970.

Brodine, Karen. *Illegal Assembly.* Brooklyn: Hanging Loose Press, 1980.

———. *Women Sitting at the Machine, Thinking.* Seattle: Red Letter Press, 1990.

Buhle, Paul, ed. *The Origins of Left Culture in the United States: 1880–1940.* Cultural Correspondence nos. 6–7 and Green Mountain Irregulars no. 6 (Spring 1978).

Caudwell, Christopher. *Illusion and Reality.* New York: International Publishers, 1937.

Clubbe, John, ed. *Selected Poems of Thomas Hood.* Cambridge, Mass.: Harvard University Press, 1970.

Coiner, Constance. " 'Pessimism of the Mind, Optimism of the Will': Literature of Resistance." Ph.D. diss., University of California–Los Angeles, 1987.

Coleman, Mary Jane. *Take One Blood Red Rose.* Minneapolis: West End Press, 1980.

Daniels, Jim. *Places/Everyone.* Madison: University of Wisconsin Press, 1985.

———. *Punching Out.* Detroit: Wayne State University Press, 1990.

Fell, Mary. *The Persistence of Memory.* New York: Random House, 1984.

Giovanitti, Arturo. *Arrows in the Gale.* Riverside, Conn.: Hillacre Brookhouse, 1914.

Grahn, Judy. *The Work of a Common Woman.* New York: St. Martins Press, 1978.

Howe, Irving. *World of Our Fathers.* New York: Harcourt Brace Jovanavich, 1976.

Harris, Marie, and Kathellen Aguero, eds. *A Gift of Tongues: Critical Challenges in Contemporary American Poetry.* Athens: University of Georgia Press, 1987.

Kessler-Harris, Alice, and Paul Lauter. "Introduction," *The Unpossessed,* by Tess Slesinger. Old Westbury, N.Y.: The Feminist Press, 1984.

Kornbluh, Joyce, ed. *Rebel Voices, An I.W.W. Anthology.* Ann Arbor: University of Michigan Press, 1964.

Laska, Peter J. *D.C. images and other poems.* Beckley, W.V.: Mountain Union Books, 1975.

Levine, Philip. *1993.* New York: Atheneum, 1974.

———. *Selected Poems.* New York: Atheneum, 1984.

———. *They Feed They Lion.* New York: Atheneum, 1972.

———. *What Work Is.* New York: Knopf, 1991.

Levy, G. R. *The Gate of Horn.* London: Faber and Faber, 1948.

Llewellyn, Chris. *Fragments from the Fire.* New York: Viking, 1986.

McDaniel, Wilma. *A Primer for Buford.* Brooklyn: Hanging Loose Press, 1990.

McGrath, Thomas. *Letter to an Imaginary Friend: Parts 1 and 2.* Chicago: Swallow Press, 1962.

————. *Selected Poems, 1938–1988.* Port Townsend, Wash.: Copper Canyon Press, 1988.

Nelson, Cary. *Repression and Recovery in Modern American Poetry and the Politics of Cultural Memory, 1910–1945.* Madison: University of Wisconsis Press, 1989.

Oresick, Peter, and Nicholas Coles, eds. *Working Classics, Poems on Industrial Life.* Chicago: University of Illinois Press, 1990.

Patchen, Kenneth. *Before the Brave.* New York: Random House, 1936.

Rideout, Walter B. *The Radical Novel in the United States, 1900–1954.* Cambridge, Mass.: Harvard University Press, 1965.

Robbins, Bruce. *The Servant's Hand.* New York: Columbia University Press, 1986.

Salzman, Jack, ed. *Years of Protest, A Collection of American Writers of the 1930s.* Indianapolis: Bobbs-Merrill Educational Publishing, 1967.

Shelley, P. B. "Song to the Men of England." *The Complete Works of Percy B. Shelley.* New York: Gordian Press, 1965. 31: 288–89.

Short, Robert. "Dada and Surrealism." *Modernism,* 292–308. New York: Penguin Books, 1976.

Stern, Frederick, ed. *The Revolutionary Poet in the United States: The Poetry of Thomas McGrath.* Columbia: University of Missouri Press, 1988.

Tarlin, Carol. "Today." Poem, copy in author's collection, n.d.

Thompson, E. P. *The Making of the English Working Class.* London: Victor Golancz. 1980.

Voss, Fred. *Goodstone.* Long Beach, Calif.: Events Horizen Press, 1991.

————. *Survivor.* Long Beach, Calif.: Guillotine Press, 1989.

Ward, Tom. "The Situationists Reconsidered." *Cultures in Contention,* 144–64. Seattle: Real Comet Press, 1985.

Wayman, Tom. *Going for Coffee. Poetry on the Job.* Madiera Park, B.C.: Harbour Publishing, 1981.

————. *Inside Job: Essays on the New Work Writing.* Madiera, Park, B.C.: Harbour Publishing, 1983.

————. *Introducing Tom Wayman: Selected Poems, 1973–1980.* Princeton: Princeton University Press, 1980.

Wright, James. *The Branch Will Not Break.* Middletown, Conn.: Wesleyan University Press, 1959.

Zandy, Janet, ed. *Calling Home: Working Class Women's Writings.* New Brunswick: Rutgers University Press, 1990.

Julia Stein is a poet and critic. Her books of poetry are Under the Ladder to Heaven *and* Desert Soldiers.

U.S. Working-Class Women's Fiction: Notes Toward an Overview

Constance Coiner

A Partial History of Efforts to Promote Working-Class Women's Writing

We now have in print a discrete body of work that can be identified as writing by or about U.S. working-class women.[1] The Feminist Press, founded in 1970 by Florence Howe and Paul Lauter, has a distinguished history of publishing and reprinting working-class women's writing—including, among numerous other titles, Rebecca Harding Davis's *Life in the Iron Mills,* the first significant portrait in U.S. literature of industrial workers' lives (1861; 1972; a 1985 edition contains additional stories by Harding Davis); Agnes Smedley's *Daughter of Earth* (1929; 1973; 1987); *Women Working: An Anthology of Stories and Poems* (1979), edited by Nancy Hoffman and Florence Howe; Paule Marshall's *Brown Girl, Brownstones* (1959; 1981) and *Reena and Other Stories* (1984); Meridel Le Sueur's *Ripening: Selected Work, 1927–1980,* edited by Elaine Hedges (1982; 1990); Josephine Herbst's *Rope of Gold* (1939; 1984); and *Writing Red: An Anthology of American Women Writers, 1930–1940* (1987), edited by Charlotte Nekola and Paula Rabinowitz.

West End Press, largely through the efforts of John Crawford, has since 1976 published and reprinted literature by working-class women writers, including Meridel Le Sueur, Paula Gunn Allen, Wendy Rose, Cherríe Moraga, and Nellie Wong. Arno Press has reprinted some working-class women's writing, including two of Herbst's novels, *Money for Love* (1929; 1977) and *Nothing Is Sacred* (1928; 1977). The ILR Press (the press of the School of Industrial and Labor Relations at Cornell University) has begun a Literature of American Labor Series that includes Theresa Serber Malkiel's *The Diary of a Shirtwaist Striker* (1910; 1990). A note in texts published in the ILR series explains its purpose: to "bring back into print some of the best literature that has emerged from the labor movement" in the United States and Canada. "We are defining literature broadly," the note continues, to include "novels, biographies, autobiographies, and journalism."

The Politics of Literature: Dissenting Essays on the Teaching of English (1972), edited by Louis Kampf and Lauter, raises issues still relevant for scholars of working-class writing, who are "up against the great tradition," to borrow the title of one of the collection's essays. And, since its inception in 1975, the journal *Radical Teacher* has consistently supported working-class studies, as has the Radical Caucus of the Modern Language Association (MLA). Since 1968 the caucus has organized MLA sessions addressing working-class concerns, including working-class women's writing.

Tillie Olsen's *Tell Me a Riddle* (1961) and *Yonnondio: From the Thirties* (1974) are prominent among working-class texts. Olsen has also worked to restore forgotten, out-of-print women's writing, especially working-class women's writing. Shelley Fisher Fishkin gives us Florence Howe's account of Olsen's role in The Feminist Press:

> In 1970, when Tillie Olsen "gave *Life in the Iron Mills* to the Feminist Press and said she had written a biographical and literary afterword that we could have as well, that changed the whole course of publishing for the Feminist Press." Up to that point the Feminist Press had planned to bring out "short biographical pamphlets about writers and women of distinction in all kinds of work, and ... feminist children's books," observes Howe, "but we had not thought of doing works from the past until [Tillie] handed [us] *Life in the Iron Mills,* and followed that up the following year with *Daughter of Earth.*" A key chapter of publishing history was in the making. At first "the Feminist Press had the reprint field to itself." Then other publishers jumped in—Virago and the Women's Press in the mid '70s, and Beacon, Rutgers, Pandora, Illinois, ILR Press, Oxford, and scores of others in the '80s. (5)

Moreover, Olsen has tirelessly encouraged and promoted working-class women writers—with Linda McCarriston, an Irish-American poet (*Eva-Mary,* 1991), and Fae Myenne Ng, a Chinese-American fiction writer (*Bone,* 1993), providing only two recent examples.

The pioneering work of The Feminist Press, *Radical Teacher,* the Radical Caucus, and others has been furthered by publications such as Janet Zandy's *Calling Home: Working-Class Women's Writings* (1990); Peter Oresick and Nicholas Coles's *Working Classics: Poems of Industrial Life* (1990); Rabinowitz's *Labor and Desire: Women's Revolutionary Fiction in Depression America* (1991); Laura Hapke's *Tales of a Working Girl: Wage-Earning Women in American Literature, 1890–1925* (1992); Jon Christian Suggs's edited volume, *American Proletarian Culture: The Twenties and Thirties* (1993); Coles's "Democratizing Literature: Issues in Teaching

Working-Class Literature" (*College English* [November 1986]); and Pam
Annas's "Pass the Cake: The Politics of Gender, Class, and Text in the
Academic Workplace" (*Working-Class Women in the Academy: Laborers in
the Knowledge Factory*, edited by Michelle Tokarczyk and Elizabeth A.
Fay [1993]). Moreover, biographies of Josephine Herbst (by Elinor
Langer, 1984), Agnes Smedley (by Janice R. and Stephen R. MacKin-
non, 1988), and Mary Heaton Vorse (by Dee Garrison, 1989) have
appeared. And a national conference on working-class studies will be
held at Youngstown State University in northeast Ohio in June 1995.

Such publications and efforts signal that working-class writing may
be emerging as a visible, if not yet "legitimate," category of literary studies. (I agree, however, with Lillian Robinson's assertion—
especially when it is applied to English departments—that "the most
massive and brutal attempts to deny the existence of an analytic
category occur with respect to class" [66]). Theorizing working-class
writing is linked to and extends the efforts of those expanding the
literary canon and examining the aesthetic and political bases on
which it is constructed. Theorizing working-class writing is also linked
to the work of scholars revisioning the 1930s literary Left.[2]

Toward a Definition of Working-Class Writing

Since the 1960s U.S. working-class writing has been variously defined.
In an important essay in *Culture and Crisis in Britain in the '30s* (1979)
Carole Snee uses the term "working-class writing" to denote works
written by a member of the working class, whether or not the writer
has class consciousness. In charting working-class writing in a pioneering essay first appearing in *Radical Teacher* (1979), Lauter deliberately employs "relatively loose definitions" and "broad categories."
He discusses texts "by *and* about working people, written and oral
forms, 'high,' 'popular,' and 'mass' culture." He designates as members of the working class "those who sell their labor for wages; who
create in that labor and have taken from them 'surplus value,' to use
Marx's phrase; who have relatively little control over the nature or
products of their work; and who are not 'professionals' or 'managers.' " Lauter refers "to people who, to improve their lot, must either
move in *solidarity* with their class or leave it (for example, to become
managers)," and he includes not only factory workers but also slaves,
farm laborers, and those who work in the home (110).[3] Of course,
working-class writing often coincides with other literary categories
(e.g., writing by women, radicals, and people of color may also qualify
as that of the working class).[4]

Working-class writing cannot be clearly delineated from bourgeois texts. As Terry Eagleton observes:

> The languages and devices a writer finds to hand are already saturated with certain ideological modes of perception, certain codified ways of interpreting reality; and the extent to which he can modify or remake those languages depends on more than his personal genius. It depends on whether, at that point in history, "ideology" is such that they must and can be changed. (*Marxism and Literary Criticism*, 26–27)

Working-class writing of necessity exists within the dominant cultural formation. But, because ideology is contradictory rather than homogeneous, working-class writing can variously interrogate, emulate, challenge, and appropriate the forms of the dominant culture while straining beyond them.

Mary Jacobus and Rachel Blau DuPlessis, in their work on women writers, help illuminate this fundamental tension within working-class women's writing. As Jacobus argues, women writers, "at once within this culture and outside it," must simultaneously challenge cultural terms and work within them (20). Acknowledging Jacobus's work, DuPlessis notes that women writers experience a "split between alien critic and inheritor." They are "neither wholly 'subcultural' nor, certainly, wholly main-cultural, but negotiate difference and sameness, marginality and inclusion in a constant dialogue" (43). (DuPlessis reminds us that W. E. B. Du Bois first postulated this "double consciousness" for African Americans, who constantly negotiate with the dominant culture.) Such a split occurs with working-class women writers as well.

"To approach working-class culture," Lauter argues, we must lay aside many of our presuppositions about what literature *is* and is *not*": "We must begin by asking in what forms, on what themes, in what circumstances, and to what ends working people spoke and sang to one another. How did they gather, examine, transmit, and renew their experiences? First, we need a broader definition of what we can call 'literature' " (111). In her introduction to her study of working-class British literature, *The Industrial Muse* (1974), Martha Vicinus similarly calls for a broader definition of literature: "What we call literature, and what we teach, is what the middle class—and not the working class—produced. Our definitions of literature and our canons of taste are class bound; we currently exclude street literature, songs, hymns, dialect and oral story telling, but they were the most popular forms used by the working class" (1).

Lillian Robinson's *Sex, Class, and Culture* (1978; reissued in 1986) also unmasks the class-bound nature of what universities consider "literature" and calls for "a radical redefinition" of the term (224). "Working/Women/Writing," one of the dozen essays (all written by Robinson), examines the personal histories—collected in the scrapbook *I Am a Woman Worker*[5]—of rank-and-file female factory workers who studied at the Associated Schools for Workers in the 1920 and 1930s. (Perhaps the best known among these schools was the Bryn Mawr summer institute, the subject of a memorable documentary, *The Women of Summer* [1985], and of recent work by Karyn L. Hollis [see works cited].) About *I Am a Woman Worker* Robinson concludes:

> I wish to suggest that, whatever we have been taught, cliches or sentimentality need not be signals of meretricious prose, and that ultimately it is honest writing for which criticism should be looking. It is essential to recognize literature that can enhance our understanding of the conditions that define women's lives, and, in order to gain insight into what women experience, I do not feel that we have to "relax our standards." Instead, writing like this can force a reevaluation and a reordering of those standards and turn them on their heads. And this sort of process, this sort of reading, tells us something we urgently need to know about both women and literature. (252–53)

Robinson reminds us that working-class women's writing "gives form to the experiences of the *majority* of women" (225; my emphasis). She offers an alternative standard for literature, shocking for its simplicity and for its revolutionary implications: It "should help us learn about the way things are, in as much depth and fullness as possible and by any means necessary" (230).

Lauter notes the importance of comparing African-American and Euro-American working-class cultural materials. "Almost all writing produced by African-Americans is, by any definition, working-class literature," Lauter rightly asserts, observing that "most of the authors have working-class origins, and their subjects and audiences are generally working-class people like themselves" (119). Although African-American and Euro-American working-class cultural forms derive from different traditions, if we examine how these forms were produced and how they functioned within working-class communities, some important similarities emerge. In *Black Culture and Black Consciousness: Afro-American Folk Thought from Slavery to Freedom* (1977), for example—which Lauter considers "required reading" for those interested in working-class cultural forms—Lawrence Levine has collected firsthand descriptions of the creation of spirituals, mainly in post-bellum African-American churches. Levine found that originality and innovative form, both prized by the bourgeois aesthetic, were not primary considerations in creating spirituals. New songs, which varied tunes and lyrics familiar to people's communities, were deliberately constructed from old ones. Moreover, like oral storytelling, the spirituals were often created communally, with an individual's creation often considered less significant than that of a group.

Indeed, as Lauter observes, "Much working-class art is created and experienced in group situations—not in the privacy of a study, but in the church . . . the work site, the meeting hall, the quilting bee, or the picket line. It is thus rooted in the experiences of a particular group of people facing particular problems at a particular time. It is not conceived as timeless and transcendent" (113–14). Similarly, the contributors to *I Am a Woman Worker* violated "a fundamental precept of bourgeois aesthetics that good art . . . celebrates what is unique and even eccentric in human experience or human personality. Individual achievement and subjective isolation are the norm, whether the achievement and the isolation be that of the artist or the character" (226). The contributors to *I Am a Woman Worker,* in contrast, "wrote about their lives in order to develop their potential as part of their class and its struggle—a commitment that they did not separate from self-actualization." Although Robinson does not dismiss the importance of oppressed people's writing as a means of establishing identity, she is "even more impressed by the notion that doing so may be understood as a process that integrates one into one's community and helps to create and unite the community itself, instead of under-scoring the purportedly inherent conflict between the individual and the group" (232).

Toward Theorizing Working-Class Writing

Fiction by working-class women writers that comes immediately to mind includes Harriette Arnow's *The Dollmaker* (1954; 1972); Meredith Tax's *Rivington Street* (1982); Bobbie Ann Mason's *Shiloh and Other Stories* (1982) and *In Country* (1985); Carolyn Chute's *The Beans of Egypt, Maine* (1985), *Letourneau's Used Auto Parts* (1989) and *Merry Men* (1993); Denise Giardina's *Storming Heaven* (1987) and its sequel, *The Unquiet Earth* (1992); Barbara Kingsolver's *The Bean Trees* (1988) and *Animal Dreams* (1990); and Dorothy Allison's *Trash* (1988) and *Bastard Out of Carolina* (1992). And yet there are still relatively few scholars addressing working-class writing. While there are differences among these scholars' approaches to theorizing working-class writing, they share the recognition that canonical views of the nature and status of "literature" have seriously impeded attempts to understand and value working-class discourse. These scholars have variously argued that we must look through something other than "aesthetic" lenses when evaluating working-class writing.

I suggest that all these scholars are looking through various pragmatic lenses: that is, they are looking at connections between discourse and society, asking, among many other questions, how society shapes discourse and how discourse shapes society. Those employing pragmatic lenses are less preoccupied with the undecidability of meaning than with language uses. They think of language, as Eagleton has put it, "as something we *do*" (*Literary* 147).

If extended to working-class writing, an argument Annette Kolodny made in 1980 about women writers partly explains working-class writing's current marginal status in the literary canon. Discussing writers such as Charlotte Perkins Gilman, whose work dropped out of sight until The Feminist Press reissued *The Yellow Wallpaper* in 1973, Kolodny argued that the reason for Gilman's disappearance

> may not be due to any intrinsic lack of merit in the work but, instead, to an incapacity of predominantly male readers—those readers who have traditionally been invested with the authority to record literary history—to interpret competently and appreciate fully women's texts. Such readers may have been as unacquainted with the texts' real-world contexts as with their informing literary contexts. The result was that these readers did not read the texts well; and, blaming the difficulty on *what* was read rather than on *how* it was read, they accorded the text—and not themselves—diminished status. (590)

Change *male readers* to *readers from the professional-managerial class*—the class in which most literary agents, editors, reviewers, taste-making intellectuals, critics, and professors reside—and we begin to see that canon-making aesthetic values arise partly out of class conflict.

Working-class writing offers its readers something rarely found in modern and postmodern art. While modern/postmodern art strives to renew our perception of the world, it seldom accounts for the causes of our perception's "initial numbness" (Jameson 374). In contrast, working-class texts foreground some of the causes—the trappings of an economic system that transforms humans into commodities. Working-class writing unmasks the fact of work and production, which is, as Jameson notes, "the very key to genuine historical think-ing" and "a secret as carefully concealed as anything else in our culture" (407).

To view working-class discourse through other than canonical aes-thetic lenses is, however, not enough. We must also explore other than-canonical ways of reading that discourse. Theorizing working-class writing begins in recognizing that the term *literature* has long implied "aesthetic" (or what I will call "romantic") ways of reading and think-ing about discourse and, second, in recognizing that some working-class writers disrupt those ways of reading and thinking. To avoid the trap of trying to evaluate writings by the very standards those writings challenge, I propose, as have others, that we examine those works and ways of reading them not from an aesthetic or romantic perspective but, rather, from a *pragmatic* one.

Long-standing principles of romantic reading theory aim to guar-antee that individual readers become passive receivers or appreciators of canonical discourses and the cultural values they embody. Prag-matic reading strategies, on the other hand, require close scrutiny of language structures such as figuration—but structures viewed not as *aesthetic* components but, rather, as tools with which writers and readers make texts do various sorts of social or cultural work. By "cultural work" I mean the work any text does, implicitly or explicitly, to support or subvert the dominant culture. (Both supporting and subverting elements are often present in any single given text, even in one clearly intent on subversion.) The working-class discourse with which some of us are concerned disrupts romantic passivity by de-manding that readers become active interrogators of texts and cul-tural values, at times questioners and critics of meanings, at times participants in constructing meaning.

Stylistic experiments to draw readers into collaboration are, of course, as old as the activities of reading and writing; such experi-ments probably date from the writer who first consciously used ellipsis for the purpose of forcing a reader to fill in the gap. Many of those experiments have arisen from a recognition, at least as old as Plato's *Phaedrus* (with its own experiments with disrupting passive reading), that reading tends to be a privatized, individual—rather than com-munal—activity. J. Paul Hunter comments on one genre, the novel, in relation to reading's solitariness. Hunter is concerned with ways in which the reading process and the central subject of the modern novel "seem to have a common meeting ground in their attention to isola-tion. . . . the act of reading a novel is, like the act of contemplating one's own consciousness, an anti-social (or at least asocial) act—very different from the sociality involved in hearing a story or attending the performance of a play" (42). It is certainly the case that many writers, for a variety of political and aesthetic reasons, have exploited the individualistic tendencies of the act of reading, while other writers—again, for a variety of political and aesthetic reasons—have attempted to disrupt this isolation. Most of the scholars theorizing working-class writing, however, are concerned with formal experiments that attempt to subvert traditional notions of bourgeois individualism and promote collective social change.

Bakhtin and Volosinov's theories of discourse provide some useful tools for pragmatic reading strategies. Bakhtin's concept of "heteroglossia"—a "multiplicity of social voices and a wide variety of their links and interrelationships" (*Dialogic* 263)—provides one tool for examining working-class discourse, much of which is heteroglossic. Of course, working-class writers are not the only writers to experiment with heteroglossia. Many others have experimented with versions of the multivocality Bakhtin identifies as characteristic of the novel's form. Those attempting to theorize working-class writing, however, are concerned with the ways in which the formal explorations of some working-class writers derive from their desire to oppose the ideology of individualism and other "naturalized" cultural values.

A second tool we can draw from Bakhtin and Volosinov is their concept of the "dialogic" nature of all discourse. Volosinov finds that all "verbal performance in print" engages in "ideological colloquy of large scale: it responds to something, objects to something, affirms something, anticipates possible responses and objections, seeks support, and so on" (95). Heteroglossia and the dialogic provide critical lenses for viewing the resistance embodied in working-class texts.

Bakhtin and Volosinov's version of pragmatics provides several additional tools. Volosinov suggests "little behavioral *genres*" as subdivisions of heteroglossia and discourse's dialogic structure. Examples of "little behavioral genres" include "the full-fledged question, exclamation, command, request" (*Marxism* 96).[6] Some of these rhetorical genres have been contemplated extensively within British and American speech-act theory, and in my own work I have drawn on a few insights of speech-act analysis to examine structures of commands, urgings, and pleas as those structures contribute to the dialogic character of Tillie Olsen's and Meridel Le Sueur's writing (see, e.g., " 'No One's Private Ground': A Bakhtinian Reading of Tillie Olsen's *Tell Me a Riddle*,"[7] *Feminist Studies* 18 [Summer 1992]: 257–81, which is part of *Better Red: The Writing and Resistance of Tillie Olsen and Meridel Le Sueur*, Oxford University Press, 1995).

Peter Hitchcock, who proceeds from what I am terming a pragmatic approach, believes that "the multiple voicing of working-class fiction represents not only its most salient aesthetic quality, but also its specific internal polemic" (2). About one of his additions to Bakhtinian theory Hitchcock says, "To adequately explain the class purview of working-class fiction Bakhtin's theory of voicing must be tempered by a theory of silence; for to understand the dialogism of the oppressed one must articulate the dialogism of the suppressed, those ideological and institutional relations that have often left working-class and women's utterances unuttered" (44). In my own work I have found Bakhtinian language theory and the issue of silences to be vital to the study of working-class women's discourse.

In calling attention to a pragmatic perspective, I want to emphasize again that those attempting to theorize working-class writing are not interested in the romantic training of readers to "appreciate" the rhetorical tools of working-class writing as aesthetic devices peculiar to an "elevated" literary realm. Rather, we want readers to decipher the cultural work done by working-class texts and the ways in which readers are invited to participate in that cultural work.

Because the methods of historical analysis and those of literary analysis, long viewed as separable disciplines, have not equipped us to read working-class writing, most scholars of working-class writing are also allied with those encouraging people to cross traditional categorical boundaries, including those dividing genres and academic disciplines. Such divisions have long been under scrutiny in feminist theory, but challenging them seems particularly crucial for theorizing working-class writing. In "History as Usual? Feminism and the 'New Historicism,'" Judith Newton suggests for academics an enlarged collectivity: "I can see it now—a materialist feminist literary/historical critic working with a 'New Women Historian' and, in a brave move beyond the dyadic bond, with a cultural materialist too, and perhaps with others as well" (120). Historian Joan Scott has also transgressed traditional boundaries between history and literary theory. Rather than viewing literature as residing in an elevated, transcendent, "universal" realm untainted by history, Scott argues that history and literature are both "forms of knowledge, whether we take them as disciplines or as bodies of cultural information" (8). And in "Literature as Women's History" Nancy Armstrong attacks disciplinary boundaries, outlining "an antidisciplinary notion of culture" that would not sharply delineate between "literary" and "nonliterary" discourse. In arguing that working-class writing often challenges such boundaries, my aim—like that of Newton, Armstrong, and others—is to problematize such boundaries in order "to overcome," as Armstrong has so straightforwardly put it, "the divisions of knowledge that prevent us from understanding who we are and what we do" (367–68).

If, however, we are to challenge traditional boundaries, we must, as I have suggested, carefully examine and rework long-standing cultural assumptions about what it means "to read." Armstrong expresses this concern in a reference to figurational reading of some nonliterary texts by women. She notes that these texts must be "read with all the attention to technical detail that a literary text alone has formerly deserved" (356). Armstrong advocates what I would call a pragmatic approach to reading. As she recognizes, reading methods that reserve complex analysis, such as figurational scrutiny, for literary texts obscure many of the rhetorical and cultural complexities marking much nonliterary discourse.

In "Toward a Feminist Theory of Reading" Patrocinio P. Schweickart has noted a similar problem in what she terms the "utopian" impulses in reading theory, by which she means the attention on the (variously problematized) relationship between text and reader to the exclusion of considering the text's and reader's historical situations. Such bracketing has produced many reading theories that overlook "issues of race, class, and sex, and give no hint of the conflicts, sufferings and passions that attend these realities" (35). Reading theory's movement away from utopian disregard for gender issues, for example, would include consideration of how gender is inscribed in texts and the roles played by the reader's gender in the reading process. Recognizing that "literature acts on the world by acting on its readers," Schweickart calls for reading theory and pedagogy that generate active readers who will scrutinize a text for "the nature of the choices proffered by the text and, equally important, what the text precludes" (39, 50). Schweickart argues that dialogue between feminist theory and reader-response theory provides the best possibilities for replacing utopian theory.

David Bartine's work is also useful to those attempting to theorize working-class writing. Bartine has traced the 250-year history of what he calls "romantic reading theory" in U.S. education and culture and the long-eclipsed "pragmatic" alternatives to romantic theory. Bartine argues that attempts to dismantle cultural myths and canons provide an "incomplete solution to the problem without reconstructing, according to a radically different plan, the reading activity and the reader" (55). Bartine, like Armstrong, argues for employing pragmatic reading methods such as complex figurational analysis in a multiplicity of literary and nonliterary texts, and he believes that the rudiments of such analysis can be introduced to students at an early age and systematically developed throughout their education. Armstrong, Schweickart, and Bartine recognize the need to reteach readers to see what they have been systematically taught to overlook.

Because theorizing working-class women's writing at points coincides with the materialist-feminist approach to culture outlined in Judith Newton and Deborah Rosenfelt's introduction to *Feminist Criticism and Social Change,* I want to call attention to this introduction as a useful starting point for approaching working-class women's writing. Working-class studies, committed as much to historic and economic concerns as to gender relations, often lies within the province of materialist feminism, opposing the flight from history evident in much literary theory, including much feminist criticism. Eagleton rightly identifies "the *extremism*" of much literary theory as "its obstinate, perverse, endlessly resourceful refusal to countenance social and historical realities," even though " 'extremism' is a term more commonly used" to dismiss those who "call attention to literature's role in actual life" (*Literary* 196). Scholars approaching working-class writing have often done so dialectically, embracing contradictions and locating "in the same situation," as Newton and Rosenfelt have put it, both "the forces of oppression and the seeds of resistance" (xxii).

The Obfuscation of Class as a Category of Literary Analysis

New constituencies have emerged in the advanced industrial world during the past two decades—feminists, national minorities, peace and anti-intervention activists, environmentalists, gays and lesbians, AIDS activists, tenants and other neighborhood groups—that have kept radical tendencies alive after the eclipse of the New Left. Whereas Old Leftists considered the working class to be the decisive revolutionary protagonist, many leftists now believe we must confront multiple and overlapping forms of domination (class, patriarchal, racial, bureaucratic, consumer, and media related) without reducing that reality to any one of its elements. The new social movements must build ties to working-class and labor struggles, but the class dimension of domination must be taken into account without minimizing other such dimensions.

Yet, although many Old Left intellectuals mistakenly subordinated all social issues to those of class, at this historical juncture—as is suggested by the relatively few scholars focusing on working-class writing—class is not a fashionable category of analysis among literary critics, including feminists. Canon reformation has legitimized the study of literary texts by women and people of color, but multicultural educational reform will defeat its egalitarian purpose if gender and racial identities are allowed to suppress class identities.

Despite its place in the now familiar list—race, gender, class, ethnicity, sexuality, and disability—class is often the least addressed of these issues. There may be several explanations for this more specific than the nature of U.S. academic liberalism. One may be that few people of working-class origin make it into the ranks of the professoriat, so few people with an "insider's" sensitivity to this issue are undertaking scholarship and shaping curricula.[8] Another explanation may be that many faculty and students have imbibed, at least to a certain degree, the myth of classlessness in the United States, a myth that has been used historically in the United States for social control. Dispelling that myth is complicated by the fact that class origin—like sexual orientation but unlike race, gender, and some forms of ethnicity—is not always apparent, remaining hidden unless it is disclosed. In my experience at the University of California–Los Angeles and at the State University of New York–Binghamton (a medium-sized public institution that draws a majority of its students from the New York City / Long Island area), many university students of color have proudly identified themselves with their particular cultural groups, while few students of working-class origin have announced—or, in some cases, even recognized—themselves as such.

This lack of class identification among working-class students provides a third explanation for the diminished status of class as a category of analysis among literary scholars. While many students rightly exert pressure on literature departments to consider gender, race, and sexual orientation as interpretive categories and to include texts by women, people of color, and gays and lesbians in college courses, few protest exclusions based on class. Indeed, few students seem even to *see* class markers, typically identifying Rita Mae Brown's *Rubyfruit Jungle* (1973), for example, as a lesbian but not also a working-class novel; Sandra Cisneros's *Woman Hollering Creek* (1991) as both Chicana and women's literature but not, additionally, a working-class text; Ann Petry's *The Street* (1946) as both African-American and women's writing but not a working-class novel as well.

The obfuscation of class as a category of analysis has consequences within the academy, forestalling alliances across identities of race, culture, gender, and sexuality among scholars and among our students. I am reminded of classroom experiences in which students who are active in campus groups (e.g., the Asian-American Student Union, the African-American Student Alliance, the Gay and Lesbian Task Force) react with surprise and confusion at their identification with the "wrong" text—the Chinese-American who wonders why Eva in Olsen's "Tell Me a Riddle" "is my grandmother"; the *puertorriqueña* who says she never expected to find her "mother's story" in Olsen's *Yonnondio;* the African American who sounds an alarm when Anzia Yezierska's "Children of Loneliness" (1923) resonates more for her than Zora Neale Hurston's *Their Eyes Were Watching God* (1937).

Progressive literary scholars must expose the common working-class basis of much of the writing now identified solely on the bases of race, ethnicity, gender, and sexuality and must also create a space in cultural studies for work by Euro-American radical and working-class writers that has been ignored even in recent efforts to broaden the parameters of the U.S. literary canon. Again, I am reminded of a classroom experience: a working-class Euro-American, virulently opposed to multicultural education, recognized her miner-grandfather's struggle in Denise Giardina's *Storming Heaven* and announced that, "if including texts like *Storming Heaven* in the curriculum is part of what multiculturalism is all about," she must begin to examine her prejudices. Anthologies such as Cherríe Moraga and Gloria Anzaldúa's *This Bridge Called My Back: Writings by Radical Women of Color* (1983) and Anzaldúa's *Making Face, Making Soul / Haciendo Caras* (1990) help students see the ways race, ethnicity, and sexual orientation *intersect with class* to produce distinctive narratives of working-class women's lives. Moreover, we can point out to our students that Zandy's *Calling Home: Working-Class Women's Writings* (1990) could be as accurately termed "multicultural" as a "working-class" anthology; its contributors include many women of color as well as Euro-American working-class women, lesbians as well as heterosexuals. And, with writings by immigrants such as the Jewish writer Anzia Yezierska, students can learn that ethnic and immigrant writing is often working-class writing as well.

Far too often students who have rejected what Richard Ohmann terms "the fatuous universalism of the right" do so by taking up a politics of identity that, as Ohmann observes, "makes any sort of embracing social movement against capitalist patriarchy hard indeed to imagine." We see on college campuses, Ohmann continues, "a politics of separate issues" with little perception "that these issues are knit together in a whole system of domination" that might be collectively opposed (33). Yet analyzing working-class writing helps in developing such perception and in students' beginning to understand that "the core curriculum is neither Shakespeare nor Alice Walker. It is accounting, computer programming, training for service jobs [for some] or for Wall Street high flying [for others], acceptance of such divisions of labor as natural and unchangeable, the quiet reproduction of inequality, and political hopelessness" (34). One way to subvert this "core curriculum" is to discuss with our students the intersections—and potential alliances—embedded in much multicultural working-class writing. As working-class writing begins to emerge as a legitimate category of literary analysis, I begin to imagine a course in multicultural working-class writing in which students do not get the sense that they have identified with the "wrong" text—a course in which identity politics is scrapped in favor of a political consciousness capable of decoding the middle-class myth and organizing to give ordinary people better life chances.

Much of my own scholarship, thus far, lies at the nexus of two related fronts in the culture wars neglected even by many progressive academics: the efforts I have been discussing to legitimate working-class writing and the struggle to preserve and revision the history of the American Left. One result of anticommunist, pro-capitalist ideology in literary studies has been, as Alan Wald points out,

> the disempowerment of the population of ordinary people who are denied a genuine history of their own cultural activities through access to authors who wrote about strikes, rebellions, mass movements, the work experience, famous political trials, the tribulations of political commitment, as well as about love, sex, the family, nature, and war from a class-conscious, internationalist, socialist-feminist, and antiracist point of view. Instead, the population [of ordinary people] is often exclusively presented with literary role models that inculcate notions of culture that distort visions of possibilities for social transformation. ("Culture," 284–85)

Wald's remarks about the disempowerment of ordinary people remind me, again, of my disempowered "ordinary" students, who can neither hope for nor envision forms of coalition building in an increasingly multicultural United States, partly because they lack knowledge of labor history and progressive movements for social change prior to the civil rights movement and feminism's second wave. My students are astonished—even incredulous—when I tell them, for example, that in 1912 in Lawrence, Massachusetts, textile workers representing about forty-five language groups united in a successful strike against long hours, pay cuts, and speed-up. And professors who in their scholarship and pedagogy are moving away from narrow conceptions of English and American literature to broader notions of

"cultural studies" rarely think, despite their interdisciplinary inclina-
tions, about the place of labor and working-class studies under that
rubric. Roger Kimball's tenured (and untenured) radicals in literature
and cultural studies departments have much to learn from U.S. historians such as those who composed the American Social History Project,
founded by Herbert G. Gutman, and produced the groundbreaking
two-volume *Who Built America? Working People and the Nation's Economy,
Politics, Culture, and Society* (1989; 1992).

"Men make their own history," says Marx, "but not of their own free
will; not under circumstances they themselves have chosen but under
the given and inherited circumstances with which they are directly
confronted." And so it is with women. Working-class women's writing
often exemplifies the "audacity within confinement"—to repeat a
phrase from Thomas Mann that Tillie Olsen is fond of quoting—that
this well-known passage from Marx implicitly advocates. Politically and
culturally, working-class women's writing represents what Raymond
Williams describes as a *"pre-emergence,* active and pressing but not
yet fully articulated, rather than the evident emergence which could
be more confidently named" (*Marxism*, 126). In necessarily "partial,
scrappy, subsidiary, and preparatory" form (Trotsky 163), the most
subversive of working-class women's writing strains toward the postin-
dividual, collective, associative cultural forms of a different social order.

Toward a Bibliography of Working-Class Women's Writing in the United States

Bibliographies that include working-class women's writing can be
found in the following sources:[9] Walter Rideout, *The Radical Novel
in the United States, 1900–1954* (1956; reprint 1992); Jayne Loader,
"Women in the Left, 1906–1941: A Bibliography of Primary Sources,"
University of Michigan Papers in Women's Studies 2 (1975): 9–82 (cata-
logued in libraries under the series title); Paul Lauter, "Working-Class
Women's Literature—An Introduction to Study," *Radical Teacher* 15
(1979) (reprinted in Joan E. Hartman and Ellen Messer-Davidow, eds.,
Women in Print I [1982], and in Robyn R. Warhol and Diane Price
Herndl, eds., *Feminisms: An Anthology of Literary Theory and Criticism*
[1991]); Cherríe Moraga and Gloria Anzaldúa, eds., *This Bridge Called
My Back: Writings by Radical Women of Color,* 2d ed. (1983); Mari Jo
Buhle, *Women and the American Left: A Guide to Sources* (1983); Janet
Zandy, ed., *Calling Home: Working-Class Women's Writing* (1990); Paula
Rabinowitz, *Labor and Desire: Women's Revolutionary Fiction in Depres-
sion America* (1991); Laura Hapke, *Tales of a Working Girl: Wage-Earning*

Women in American Literature, 1890–1925 (1992); Jon Christian Suggs, *American Proletarian Culture: The Twenties and Thirties,* vol. 11 of the Documentary Series of the *Dictionary of Literary Biography* (1993).

NOTES

1. For a useful discussion of the distinctions between the working class and the bourgeoisie, see the conclusion to Williams, *Culture.* Because my scholarship and teaching thus far have focused chiefly on fiction, I should acknowledge from the outset that these "notes toward an overview" will emphasize that genre.

2. Christina L. Baker, James D. Bloom, Barbara Foley, Laura Hapke, Walter Kalaidjian, Barbara Melosh, Cary Nelson, David R. Peck, Paula Rabinowitz, Deborah Rosenfelt, Suzanne Sowinska, Jon Christian Suggs, Harvey Teres, Alan Wald, and Douglas Wixson are among the literary scholars reexamining the 1930s. I also want to alert readers to *Revisioning Thirties' Culture: New Directions in Scholarship,* edited by Sherry Lee Linkon and Bill V. Mullen (1995). But it is important to underscore what Alan Wald has pointed out to scholars of the literary Left: too often radical literature has been viewed within the narrow confines of the 1930s as if that decade were an aberration in U.S. history rather than part of a sustained resistance to capitalism. As Wald argued persuasively in a presentation at the 1993 American Studies Association Convention, the Left cultural practices of the 1930s through 1960s are all linked to the same tradition. Thus, Wald is editing a series, titled "The Radical Novel in the United States Reconsidered," of leftist novels originally published between the 1920s and the early 1960s; the novels will be paperback reprints with new introductions.

3. I have cited a reprint of Lauter's "Working-Class Women's Literature—An Introduction to Study," which appeared in *Women in Print I,* edited by Joan E. Hartman and Ellen Messer-Davidow (1982): 109–25; it is a slightly edited version of the original essay with no substantial changes. The essay was also reprinted in *Feminisms: An Anthology of Literary Theory and Criticism,* edited by Robyn R. Warhol and Diane Price Herndl (1991): 837–50. See two other relevant essays by Lauter, "American Proletarianism," in *The Columbia History of the American Novel,* ed. Emory Elliott et al. (1991): 331–56; and "Race and Gender in the Shaping of the American Literary Canon: A Case Study from the Twenties," *Feminist Studies* 9, no. 3 (Fall 1983): 435–63; "Race and Gender" has been reprinted in Newton and Rosenfelt.

4. The categories of "radical" writing and "working-class" writing often intersect. In *Labor and Desire* (1991) Paula Rabinowitz uses the term "revolutionary" for the more than forty Depression-era novels written by women that she surveys. In "From the Thirties: Tillie Olsen and the Radical Tradition," Deborah S. Rosenfelt uses "socialist feminist" to describe the literary tradition to which Tillie Olsen belongs. I will discuss the overlapping of "women's writing," "working-class women's writing," and writing by women of color at other points in this essay.

5. This scrapbook, like the other collections from the Associated Schools, was a mimeographed volume. *I Am a Woman Worker* has been reissued by Arno Press (1974) in its Women in America series; the reprint is a reduced photocopy of the original.

6. See also Bakhtin, *Speech*, 60–102.

7. An expanded version of this essay appears in Hedges and Fishkin; in *The Critical Response to Tillie Olsen,* ed. Kay Hoyle Nelson and Nancy Huse (1994); and in *Tillie Olsen's Tell Me a Riddle: A Casebook,* ed. Deborah Rosenfelt (1995).

8. I can offer limited evidence of some improvement on this score. Three collections of essays about intellectuals of working-class origin (many of them academics, many of them professors of English) have recently been published. See Zandy, *Liberating Memory;* Tokarczyk and Fay; and Dews and Law.

9. My subject in this essay is working-class women's writing in the United States. But for those interested in British working-class writing, see the bibliographies included in Vicinus and in Hitchcock.

REFERENCES

Armstrong, Nancy. "Introduction: Literature as Women's History." *Genre* 19 (Winter 1986): 347–69.

Bakhtin, M. M. *The Dialogic Imagination.* Ed. Michael Holquist. Trans. Caryl Emerson and Michael Holquist. Austin: University of Texas Press, 1986.

———. *Speech Genres and Other Late Essays.* Ed. Caryl Emerson and Michael Holquist. Trans. Vern W. McGee. Austin: University of Texas Press, 1986.

Bartine, David. *Reading, Criticism, and Culture: Theory and Teaching in the United States and England, 1829–1950.* Columbia: University of South Carolina Press, 1992.

Dews, C. L. Barney, and Carolyn Leste Law, eds. *This Fine Place So Far from Home: Voices of Academics from the Working Class.* Philadelphia: Temple University Press, 1995.

DuPlessis, Rachel Blau. *Writing beyond the Ending: Narrative Strategies of Twentieth Century Women Writers.* Bloomington: Indiana University Press, 1985.

Eagleton, Terry. *Literary Theory.* Minneapolis: University of Minnesota Press, 1983.

———. *Marxism and Literary Criticism.* Berkeley: University of California Press, 1976.

Fishkin, Shelley Fisher. "Reading, Writing and Arithmetic: The Lessons *Silences* Has Taught Us." In *Listening to Silences: New Feminist Essays.* Ed. Elaine Hedges and Shelley Fisher Fishkin, 1–38. New York: Oxford University Press, 1994.

Hedges, Elaine, and Shelley Fisher Fishkin, eds. *Listening to Silences: New Feminist Essays.* New York: Oxford University Press, 1994.

Hitchcock, Peter. *Working-Class Fiction in Theory and Practice: A Reading of Alan Sillitoe.* Ann Arbor: UMI Research Press, 1989.

Hollis, Karyn L. "Liberating Voices: Autobiographical Writing at the Bryn Mawr Summer School for Women Workers, 1921–1938." *College Composition and Communication* 45, no. 1 (1994): 31–60.

———. *Resisting Voices: Writing at the Bryn Mawr Summer School for Women Workers, 1921–1938.* Englewood Cliffs, N.J.: Prentice Hall (forthcoming).

Hunter, J. Paul. *Before Novels: The Cultural Contexts of Eighteenth-Century English Fiction.* New York: W. W. Norton, 1990.

Jacobus, Mary. "The Difference of View." In *Women Writing and Writing about Women.* Ed. Mary Jacobus. London: Croom Helm, 1979.

Jameson, Fredric. *Marxism and Form.* Princeton: University Press, 1971.

Kolodny, Annette. "Reply to Commentaries: Women Writers, Literary Historians, and Martian Readers." *New Literary History* 11 (Spring 1980): 587–92.

Lauter, Paul. "Working-Class Women's Literature: An Introduction to Study." In *Women in Print I.* Ed. Joan E. Hartman and Ellen Messer-Davidow. New York: Modern Language Association of America, 1982. The essay originally appeared in *Radical Teacher* 15 (December 1979): 16–26.

Nekola, Charlotte, and Paula Rabinowitz. *Writing Red: An Anthology of American Women Writers, 1930–1940.* New York: The Feminist Press, 1987.

Newton, Judith. "History as Usual? Feminism and the 'New Historicism.'" *Cultural Critique* 9 (Spring 1988): 87–121.

Newton, Judith, and Deborah Rosenfelt. *Feminist Criticism and Social Change: Sex, Class, and Race in Literature and Culture.* New York: Methuen, 1985.

Ohmann, Richard. "Political Correctness and the Obfuscation of Politics." *Radical Teacher* 42 (1992): 32–34. A longer version of this essay appeared as "On 'PC' and Related Matters." *The Minnesota Review* 39 (Fall/Winter 1992/1993): 55–62. Reprinted in *PC Wars.* Ed. Jeffrey Williams. New York: Routledge, 1995.

Rabinowitz, Paula. *Labor and Desire: Women's Revolutionary Fiction in Depression America.* Chapel Hill: University of North Carolina Press, 1991.

Rideout, Walter. *The Radical Novel in the United States, 1900–1954.* 1956. Reprint. New York: Columbia University Press, 1992.

Robinson, Lillian S. *Sex, Class, and Culture.* 1978. Reprint. New York: Routledge, 1986.

Schweickart, Patrocinio P. "Reading Ourselves: Toward a Feminist Theory of Reading." In *Gender and Reading: Essays on Readers, Texts, and Contexts.* Ed. Elizabeth A. Flynn and Patrocinio P. Schweickart. Baltimore: Johns Hopkins University Press, 1986.

Scott, Joan W. *Gender and the Politics of History.* New York: Columbia University Press, 1988.

Snee, Carole. "Working-Class Literature or Proletarian Writing?" In *Culture and Crisis in Britain in the '30s.* Ed. Jon Clark et al. London: Lawrence and Wishart, 1979.

Tokarczyk, Michelle M., and Elizabeth A. Fay, eds. *Working-Class Women in the Academy: Laborers in the Knowledge Factory.* Amherst: University of Massachusetts Press, 1993.

Trotsky, Leon. *Literature and Revolution*. 1924. Reprint. Ann Arbor: University of Michigan Press, 1960.

Vicinus, Martha. *The Industrial Muse: A Study of Nineteenth Century British Working-Class Literature*. New York: Barnes, 1974.

Volosinov, V. N. *Marxism and the Philosophy of Language*. Trans. Ladislav Matejka and I. R. Titunik. Cambridge: Harvard University Press, 1986.

Wald, Alan. "Culture and Commitment: U.S. Communist Writers Reconsidered." In *New Studies in the Politics and Culture of U.S. Communism*. Ed. Michael E. Brown et al. New York: Monthly Review Press, 1993. Reprinted in *Writing from the Left: New Essays on Radical Culture and Politics*. Verso, 1994.

Williams, Raymond. *Culture and Society: 1780–1950*. 1958. Reprint. New York: Columbia University Press, 1983.

———. *Marxism and Literature*. Oxford: Oxford University Press, 1977.

Zandy, Janet, ed. *Calling Home: Working-Class Women's Writings*. New Brunswick: Rutgers University Press, 1990.

———, ed. *Liberating Memory: Our Work and Our Working-Class Consciousness*. New Brunswick: Rutgers University Press, 1995.

Constance Coiner *is an Assistant Professor of English at SUNY-Binghamton and the author of* Better Red: The Writing and Resistance of Tillie Olsen and Meridel Le Sueur *(Oxford University Press, 1995). She is currently at work on a book about poet Carolyn Forché.*

Newsbriefs

CONFERENCES

The Fate of Feminism: Is There a Next Generation? will be the theme of the Fifth Annual Women's Studies Conference at Southern Connecticut State University, to be held September 30-October 1, 1995. For information, contact Karen Radman or Vara Neverow, Women's Studies, EN 271, Southern Connecticut State University, 501 Crescent St., New Haven, CT 06515; (203) 392-6747.

Praxis/Nexus: Feminist Methodology, Theory, Community, an interdisciplinary conference to be held 18–20 January 1996 at the University of Victoria, will address the relationship between research and activism, the nexus between theory and practice. Questions to be considered include: Which community projects have successfully combined theory and practice? Why have some attempts failed? How do feminists develop the action component in the research process? Can we justify doing research "for" women without doing research "with" women? Submit one-page abstracts or proposals by 25 August 1995 to: PRAXIS/NEXUS, c/o Pamela Moss, Department of Geography, University of Victoria, P.O. Box 3050, Victoria, BC, Canada V8N 3P5; (604) 721-7347; fax (604) 721-6216; E-mail: moss@uvic.uvvm.ca.

NEW PUBLICATION

Challenging the Culture of Silence: Building Alliances to End Reproductive Tract Infections represents the first time that women leaders, activists, health professionals, journalists, and social scientists from around the world have raised their voices on a major public health issue that is the root cause of chronic pain, miscarriage, cervical cancer, and infertility, but that in most cultures is not talked about. Forty-four women from twenty countries met in Barbados under the auspices of the International Women's Health Coalition (IWHC) and the Women and Development Unit (WAND) of the University of West Indies to discuss the impact of reproductive tract infections on women's lives,

how power imbalances in sexual relationships make women especially vulnerable, and how service providers may unintentionally put women at increased
risk or ignore their plight. For more information, or to receive a copy of the
report, contact Joan B. Dunlop, President, IWHC, 24 East 21 Street, New York,
NY 10010; (212) 979-8500.

NEW FILM

"A Litany for Survival: The Life and Work of Audre Lorde" is a 90-minute
documentary portrait that vividly explores the poet's embodiment of three
dynamic social justice movements: the Civil Rights movement, the women's
movement, and the struggle for lesbian and gay rights. For information,
contact Veena Cabreros-Sud, Third World Newsreel, 335 West 38 Street, New
York, NY 10018; (212) 947-9277.

WORKING-CLASS LITERATURE FROM
THE FEMINIST PRESS

BROWN GIRL, BROWNSTONES. By Paule Marshall. Afterword by Mary Helen Washington. $10.95 paper.

CALL HOME THE HEART. By Fielding Burke. Introduction by Alice Kessler-Harris and Paul Lauter. Afterwords by Sylvia J. Cook and Anna W. Shannon. $9.95 paper.

THE CHANGELINGS. A Novel by Jo Sinclair. $8.95 paper.

DADDY WAS A NUMBER RUNNER. By Louise Meriwether. Foreword by James Baldwin. Afterword by Nellie McKay. $10.95 paper.

DAUGHTER OF EARTH. By Agnes Smedley. Foreword by Alice Walker. Afterword by Nancy Hoffman. $11.95 paper.

DAUGHTER OF THE HILLS: A WOMAN'S PART IN THE COAL MINERS' STRUGGLE. By Myra Page. Introduction by Alice Kessler-Harris and Paul Lauter. Afterword by Deborah S. Rosenfelt. $8.95 paper.

FOLLY. By Maureen Brady. Afterword by Bonnie Zimmerman. $12.95 paper, $35.00 cloth.

LIFE IN THE IRON MILLS AND OTHER STORIES. Second Edition. Rebecca Harding Davis. Edited and with a Biographical Interpretation by Tillie Olsen. $10.95 paper.

MARGRET HOWTH: A STORY OF TO-DAY. By Rebecca Harding Davis. Afterword by Jean Fagan Yellin. $11.95 paper, $35.00 cloth.

MY MOTHER GETS MARRIED. By Moa Martinson. Translated and with an afterword by Margaret S. Lacy. $9.95 paper,$35.00 cloth.

THE PARISH AND THE HILL. By Mary Doyle Curran. Afterword by Anne Halley. $12.95 paper.

THE SEASONS: DEATH AND TRANSFIGURATION. A Memoir by Jo Sinclair. $12.95 paper, $35.00 cloth.

THE SILENT PARTNER. Including "The Tenth of January." By Elizabeth Stuart Phelps. Afterword by Mari Jo Buhle and Florence Howe. $12.95 paper.

SONGS MY MOTHER TAUGHT ME: STORIES, PLAYS, AND MEMOIR. By Wakako Yamauchi. Edited and with an introduction by Garrett Hongo. Afterword by Valerie Miner. $14.95 paper, $35.00 cloth.

THIS CHILD'S GONNA LIVE. By Sarah E. Wright. Appreciation by John Oliver Killens.$10.95 paper.

WOMEN AND APPLETREES. By Moa Martinson. Translated and with an afterword by Margaret S. Lacy. $8.95 paper.

WOMEN HAVE ALWAYS WORKED: A HISTORICAL OVERVIEW. By Alice Kessler-Harris. $9.95 paper.

WITH THESE HANDS: WOMEN WORKING ON THE LAND. Edited and with an introduction by Joan M. Jensen. $9.95 cloth.

Prices subject to change. For VISA/MasterCard orders, call (212)360-5794. Individual orders may also be prepaid by check or money order (in U.S. dollars) plus $4.00 postage and handling for one book, $1.00 for each additional, to: The Feminist Press at CUNY, 311 East 94 Street, New York, NY 10128. Bookstore, library, and school orders should be directed to: Consortium Book Sales & Distribution, Inc., 1045 Westgate Drive, St. Paul, MN 55114, (800) 283-3572, Fax (612) 221-0124.

UPCOMING ISSUES OF
WOMEN'S STUDIES QUARTERLY

FALL/WINTER 1995, Volume XXIII, Numbers 3 & 4:
"Rethinking Feminist Teaching on War and Peace."
Coedited by Amy Swerdlow and Linda Forcey.

Coedited by Amy Swerdlow, editor of a 1984 issue of
Women's Studies Quarterly entitled "Teaching about Peace,
War, and Women in the Military," and Linda Forcey of
Binghamton University, this issue will share theories,
research, and pedagogical and curriculum materials from top
scholars in the field of peace studies. The issue will consider
new perspectives on feminist peace studies, gender and the
culture of militarism, and women and World War I. It will
also offer reflections on and resources for teaching peace
studies. Contributors include: Harriet Alonso, Jacklyn Cock,
Frances Early, Margaret Higonnet, Ynestra King, Anne Sisson
Runyan, Elizabeth Salas, Simona Sharoni, Kathryn Kish Sklar,
Anne Tickner, Claire Tylee, Lynne Woehrle, and Susan Zeiger.

Look for future issues on the U.N. Fourth World Conference
on Women (Beijing), women and violence, women and
music, and African women's studies. For more information,
contact the Managing Editor, WSQ, The Feminist Press at
CUNY, 311 East 94 Street, New York, New York 10128.
Phone: (212)360-5791; fax: (212) 348-1241.

BACK ISSUES AVAILABLE

Single copies available for $18 each:

Women's Studies: A World View (94:3-4)

Feminist Teachers (94:1-2—contains the Women's Studies Programs List)

Feminist Pedagogy: An Update (93:3-4)

Spirituality and Religions (93:1-2)

Women's Studies in Europe (92:3-4)

Feminist Psychology (92:1-2)

Single copies available for $13 each:

Literature and History (91:3-4)

Women, Girls, and the Culture of Education (91:1-2)

Women's Studies in Economics (90:3-4)

Curricular and Institutional Change (90:1-2)

Women's Nontraditional Literature (89:3-4)

Women and Aging (89:1-2)

Teaching the New Women's History (88:1-2)

CHINA FOR WOMEN
Travel and Culture

Essays, personal accounts, and fiction by women–some living in China, emigrants, and inveterate travelers–give you inside information not available in standard guide books, painting a rich portrait of the women who "hold up half the sky."

With one-fourth of the world's population, a rich history and culture dating back over centuries, a vast and varied landscape, and bustling cities, China offers travelers a panoply of delights. As *Australia for Women* did for the land down under, *China for Women* makes visible women's social, political, and cultural history, focusing on the effects of a century of tremendous changes as well as the persistence of long-held traditions on the lives of women. This unique guide offers views into the lives of ordinary Chinese women today and the experiences of women travelers in this beautiful country.

Perfect for the tourist or the armchair traveler, *China for Women* brings one of the world's oldest and richest nations to life with writings from a variety of vantage points. The guide focuses both on history and on China today–its people and its cities, land, rivers, and cultural life. In vivid personal essays, a textile worker, a painter, a doctor, a soldier, an architect, a musician, and others tell their stories, and women who lived through the massacre in Tiananmen Square describe the days and weeks in which their hopes for change were dashed. Descriptions of the hidden beauties of modern Beijing, the fragrant woods of Guilin, the paradise of Hangzhou, a train journey through the countryside, and the splendors of Chinese meals, as well as lists of do's and don'ts for the new traveler to China, complete the tour in *China for Women*.

328 pages/39 b&w photos/ISBN 1-55861-112-6/$17.95 paper/May 1995

CHINA
FOR WOMEN
Travel and Culture

Lost Paradises • Rafting on the Yangzi
• Landscapes and Cityscapes . . . and More

STREETS
A Memoir of the Lower East Side

Bella Spewack

Introduction by Ruth Limmer, Afterword by Lois Elias

❖ **The Helen Rose Scheuer Jewish Women's Series**

Born in Transylvania at the turn of the century, Bella Cohen Spewack arrived on the streets of New York's Lower East Side when she was three. At twenty-three, while working as a reporter with her husband in Europe, she wrote this memoir of her early years which she never chose to publish. We have chosen to publish it now because of its literary merit and historical fidelity. For those who loved Kate Simon's *Bronx Primitive*, it is as though we have here a Kate Simon very close to the streets she has just been walking.

The young Bella describes with wit, candor, and a sense of the telling anecdote, the sights, sounds, smells, and especially the appearance of a wide array of people, as her family moves annually to save rent or to find a still cheaper apartment. Her mother works as a live-in domestic, then takes on sewing, and eventually boarders, and a new and unfriendly husband. Bella's world also includes two younger brothers, one of whom is ill enough to need constant nursing.

Streets includes the story of Bella's high school years—her mother was determined to make "a lady" of her daughter and would not allow her to work in a factory—and ends before she meets and marries Sam Spewack. At once street-smart, unsentimental, and sensitive to her poverty, Bella is a sturdy American heroine who overcomes the obstacles of her life in a world that will later welcome her as a celebrated author.

For nearly forty years, **Bella Cohen Spewack** (1899-1990) collaborated with her husband, Sam Spewack, on over thirty-five films and plays, including such popular classics as *Boy Meets Girl, My Favorite Wife, Weekend at the Waldorf,* and *Woman Bites Dog.* In 1948, the Spewacks collaborated with Cole Porter to create the Tony award-winning musical *Kiss Me, Kate.* A reporter, foreign correspondent, and press agent, Bella Spewack also published over forty short stories before the age of twenty–three, including "The Laugh," which was selected for *Best Short Stories of 1925.* Among her many friends and colleagues were George and Ira Gershwin, Fyodorovich Stravinsky, Rebecca West, Thornton Wilder, Mary Martin, Laurence Olivier, Robert Sherwood, and Eleanor Roosevelt. **Ruth Limmer** edited *What the Woman Lived: Selected Letters of Louise Bogan 1920–1970* and Louise Bogan's autobiography, *Journey Around My Room.* She is currently the editor of *Tenement Times.* **Lois Elias** is a media specialist in New York City.

180 pages/10 b&w photos/ISBN 1-55861-115-0/$19.95 hardcover/October 1995

Keep current on the issues to be taken up at the 4th World Conference on Women

(September 1995, Beijing, China),
by reading some of our best sellers.

How does privatization impact on women?

How many world leaders are women?

Why does poverty impact unequally on men and women?

Why does technological change impact disproportionally on men and women?

Available from:

United Nations Publications,
Room DC2-0853, Dept. 272A, New York, N.Y. 10017
Tel. (212) 963-8302, (800) 253-9646 Fax. (212) 963-3489
Visa, MC and AMEX accepted. Please add $3.50 for shipping & handling.

The following recommended publications answer your many questions. They offer essential, up-to-date and comprehensive background information.

The World's Women: Trends and Statistics, 2nd Edition

This new and expanded edition is modelled after the first edition which has been hailed by the Toronto Star as - *"...a promising step in assessing the lives of half the world's population"*. This unique publication presents comprehensive data so vitally needed to influence policy and institute change. It covers such issues as: the welfare of women - her family, household, health, education and the environment. The special focus of this edition is "the empowerment of women".

E.95.XVII.2 2nd Ed. 92-1-161372-8 $15.95
E.90.XVII.3 1st Ed. 92-1-161313-2 $19.95

Women: Challenges to the Year 2000

Paints a discouraging picture as to the status of women. It is without a doubt educational, as it increases the awareness of the obstacles facing women in politics, educational opportunities, health and employment. This is a valuable piece of work that should be read by all.

E.91.I.21 92-1-100458-6 $12.95

Women in A Changing Global Economy: 1994 World Survey on the Role of Women in Development

"Where women have advanced, economic growth has been usually steady; where women have not been allowed to be full participants, there has been stagnation", states this World Survey.

Using a gender perspective, this Survey, which constitutes an important input to the dialogue about development, analyses three central development issues - poverty, productive employment and economic decision-making. The investigative approach and up-to-date statistics make this readable book - unique.

E.95.IV.1 92-1-130163-7 $29.95

Women in Politics and Decision-Making in the Late Twentieth Century

Citing numerous case studies and analysing the similarities and differences between countries, the study examines why there are only a few countries where the influence of women on public policy is comparable with that of men. It also analyses the problem of women not being available for selection or election to public office, and the political, structural, economic and social factors related to participation in decision-making. An extremely readable book.

E.91.IV.3 92-1-130144-0 $30.00

"Before Hugh Hefner, Ted Turner, and Oprah Winfrey there were Cyrus and Louisa Curtis, Edward Bok, and George Horace Lorimer. In this incisive cultural study, Helen Damon-Moore brings vividly alive the world of the great mass magazines that shaped the outlook of generations of Americans. Exploiting primary sources and current theoretical perspectives, Damon-Moore documents the magazines' role in the commercialization of gender and the gendering of commerce. MAGAZINES FOR THE MILLIONS merits the close attention of all students of American popular culture—and anyone looking for a good read." — Paul Boyer, Institute for Research in the Humanities

263 pages • $17.95 paper • ISBN 0-7914-2058-2

State University of New York Press
c/o CUP Services • PO Box 6525
Ithaca, NY 14851 • 1-800-666-2211
Please add $3 shipping/handling. NY State residents, add 8% sales tax.

Please Enter My Subscription to the
Women's Studies Quarterly

	U.S. *1 year*	Outside U.S. *1 year*
Individual	[ ] $25.00	[ ] $35.00
Institution	[ ] $35.00	[ ] $45.00

	3 years	*3 years*
Individual	[ ] $ 70.00	[ ] $100.00
Institution	[ ] $100.00	[ ] $120.00

A charge has been added to foreign subscriptions for surface delivery.

Total enclosed $ _____ .

All orders must be prepaid with checks or money orders payable to The Feminist Press in U.S. dollars drawn on a U.S. bank.

Or charge your VISA/MasterCard *(circle one).*

Acct # _____   Exp. date _____

Signature _____

Name _____

Institution _____

Address _____

_____

Phone ( ) _____

Mail to: *Women's Studies Quarterly,* The Feminist Press at The City University of New York, 311 East 94th Street, New York, NY 10128.
Tel. (212) 360-5790   Fax (212) 348-1241

NOTICE TO PROSPECTIVE CONTRIBUTORS

Women's Studies Quarterly publishes contributions that introduce new feminist scholarship and theory applied to teaching and the curriculum, original sources and resources of direct use in course and program development, and reflective essays and original creative work on various themes of concern to women's studies practitioners. The intersections of race and class with gender are of special concern, as are the perspectives of members of minority groups within the United States and those of the international community.

Contributions should run from nine to twenty manuscript pages, typed double-spaced throughout, including notes, and are expected to be written in language that is accessible to the nonspecialist. Submissions are reviewed by outside readers in the field. Please send three copies and consult *The Chicago Manual of Style* for manuscript form.

Because many of the issues are planned by guest editors and feature collections of material on specific themes, contributors are urged to consult announcements of upcoming issues in the *Quarterly* and communicate with the guest editors.